Sanctuary Denied

FEB 1 7 1994

MAR 8 1994

APR 1 3 1995

FEB 9 1996

JUL 2 8 1996

JUL 2 9 1997

FEB 2 5 1999

FEB 2 7 2003

MAR 2 8 2006

D1599101

Social and Economic Studies No. 48
Institute of Social and Economic Research
Memorial University of Newfoundland

Sanctuary Denied

*Refugees from the Third Reich and
Newfoundland Immigration Policy, 1906–1949*

Gerhard P. Bassler

ISER

**Institute of Social and
Economic Research**

ERINDALE
COLLEGE
LIBRARY

© Gerhard P. Bassler 1992
All rights reserved

Published by the
Institute of Social and Economic Research
Memorial University of Newfoundland
St. John's, Newfoundland, Canada
ISBN 0-919666-75-2

Printed on paper
containing over 50%
recycled paper including
10% post-consumer fibre.

Canadian Cataloguing in Publication Data

Bassler, Gerhard P., 1937–

    Sanctuary denied

    (Social and economic studies, ISSN 0847–0898 ;
no. 48)

    Includes bibliographical references and index.
ISBN 0-919666-75-2

1. Refugees -- Government policy -- Newfoundland --
History -- 20th century. 2. Newfoundland --
Emigration and immigration -- Government policy --
History -- 20th century. I. Memorial University of
Newfoundland. Institute of Social and Economic
Research. II. Title. III. Series: Social and
economic studies (St. John's, Nfld.) ; no. 48.

JV7290.N5B37 1992   325.718'09'04   C92-098636-6

To the refugees for whom Newfoundland held hope . . . .

This book has been published with the help of a grant from Multiculturalism and Citizenship Canada.

Contents

Acknowledgements   ix
Preface   xi

Part I Origins of Refugees from the Third Reich and of Newfoundland's Immigration and Refugee Policy

1 Refugees and Newfoundland History: Introduction and Historiographical Context   1

2 "Rette sich wer kann" (Save yourself while you can): Becoming a Refugee from the Third Reich   19

3 "Leave to land shall not be refused:" The Origins of Newfoundland's Immigration and Refugee Policy   39

4 "Newfoundland—Attractive to Capitalist, Settler and Tourist:" The Quest for Immigration, Exclusion and Deportation, 1919–1934   70

Part II Newfoundland's Response to the Refugee Crisis, 1934–1939

5 "It would have been so beneficial to the country:" Refugee Settlement Projects and Economic Development, 1934–1939   93

6 "We should first look to British Stock:" Public Perceptions and Reactions, 1933–1939   116

7 "There is no prospect of room being found:" Immigration Regulations and the Fate of Individual Refugee Applications, 1934–1939   137

Part III The War and Postwar Aftermath, 1939–1949

8 "Dangerous" Internees Who Never Were: The Victoria Camp and Paterson Schemes, 1940–1943   163

9   "Intern or Deport:" Refugees as Fifth Column   181
       Suspects, 1939–1945

10   "What Price Immigation?" Epilogue 1945–1949,   211
       Synopsis and Conclusions

Notes   233

Bibliography   265

Index   278

ISER Books   286

Tables

Table 1 Intending Settlers in Relation to Returning Residents   47
        Inwards, Emigrating Passengers Outwards, and Total
        Outward Passengers (Transients and Émigrants)
        1903–1913

Table 2 Passengers Inwards by Gender in Relation to Travellers   47
        and Sportsmen/Tourists 1903–1913

Table 3 Passengers Inwards by Place of Birth 1903–1913   48

Table 4 Passengers Outwards by Place of Birth 1903–1913   48

Table 5 Immigration by Place of Birth: Balance of Passengers
        Inwards/Outwards 1903–1913 in Relation to Residents   49
        Reported in 1901 and 1911 Census

Acknowledgements

This book could not have been written without the help of others: the inspiration of colleagues, the willingness of local residents to be interviewed, the assistance of archivists, the help of editors, and the financial support of funding agencies. I deeply appreciate Tonya Kurt Bassler's encouragement and critical questions throughout the various stages and drafts of the project. Harold Troper's work with Irving Abella, *None Is Too Many* (1983), his critique of my first conference paper and article on this topic, and deliberations I had with him, prompted me to determine whether the findings of *None Is Too Many* might also apply to Newfoundland.

In fleshing out the Newfoundland context, Melvin Baker's generosity in sharing his unique knowledge of the sources of twentieth century Newfoundland history has proved invaluable. His scrutiny of the manuscript's first draft piloted my research more than once within the framework of Newfoundland history. An exchange of views with Paul Bartrop provided interesting Australian and Commonwealth perspectives. I thank him for referring me to indispensable British government sources. I have also profited greatly from various discussions with Peter Neary and Lisa Gilad. Thanks go to Paula Draper for kindly offering me her copies of documents from the Canadian Jewish Congress Archives in Montreal relating to Canada's interned refugees and their planned release via Newfoundland.

I am very grateful to local residents Betty and Andreas Barban and Ernst Deutsch for allowing me to interview them about their flight from the Third Reich and permitting me to reproduce parts of those interviews in this book. Among other persons providing valuable personal insights, I would like to thank Cyril Banikhin, William J. Browne, Pat Brownrigg, Margaret Chang, Charlie Daley, George

Earles, Hayford Fong, Peter Furey, Robert S. Furlong, Alan Gilling-
ham, John J. Green, Michael Harrington, Ferd Hayward, the Rev.
E. Clifford Knowles, Jack J. McCormack, Hans Meier, Augusta
Mercer, Gerald Ottenheimer, Gordon F. Pushie, and George
Snelgrove.
    Many archivists helped me with identifying and locating relevant
documents. Special thanks go to Calvin Best, Howard Brown, Ann
Devlin Fischer, and Shelley Smith of the Provincial Archives of
Newfoundland and Labrador for accommodating my frequent requests. At the National Archives of Canada in Ottawa Carolyn Heald
and Bennett McCardle provided indispensable advice and help.
Joan Ritcey of the Centre for Newfoundland Studies went out of her
way to solve special problems for me. The staff of the Zentrales
Staatsarchiv Potsdam (now Bundesarchiv, Abteilungen Potsdam),
especially archivists Zarwel, Ebel, and Gresens, brought me more
than the prescribed daily allotment of *Akten* to enable me to see as
much material as possible within the short duration of my visit. At
the Bundesarchiv Koblenz I benefited from the advice of Dr. Wilhelm
Lenz and the help of Herr Bauer. Harold Pretty's and Jeannie
Howse's diligent screening of old newspapers deserves recognition.
Hayford Fong helped establish the identities of members of the
Chinese community shown on pages 61 and 62.
    While it is a pleasure to acknowledge the information, assis-
tance, and encouragement received from friends, colleagues, and
interviewees, the responsibility for any inadvertent errors or conten-
tious views is of course entirely my own.
    Some of the material in chapters 4, 5, and 6 was first made
available to the public in articles that appeared in *Newfoundland
Studies*, III:1 (1987), and *Simon Wiesenthal Center Annual*, V (1988).
The story of the first part of chapter 8 was originally published in
Newfoundland Studies, V:1 (1989), and the abridged contents of
chapter 9 are included in a forthcoming collection of essays edited
by Paul Bartrop under the title *False Havens of Hope: The British
Dominions and the Refugee Crisis of the 1930s*.
    A grant from the Government of Canada allowed me to start this
project. The research was completed with the support of a Joint
Appointment Fellowship of the Institute of Social and Economic
Research at Memorial University of Newfoundland. Preparation of
the manuscript for publication was a pleasure thanks to Jeanette
Gleeson and Susan Nichol of ISER Books.

Preface

My preoccupation with immigration issues dates back to my arrival in this province more than a quarter century ago. At that time immigrants were officially welcome in conjunction with Premier Joseph R. Smallwood's ambitious strategy of modernization and development for the province. Memorial University, for example, unquestionably one of Smallwood's most ambitious and successful new enterprises, recruited faculty from all over the world to launch and expand academic programs for the benefit of Newfoundland.

As one of thousands of newcomers since Confederation in 1949 and one who has been part of the emergence of a multicultural society in this province, I have always found it puzzling that Newfoundland's record of immigration in the twentieth century has remained unexplored, despite the considerable public and academic interest in Canadian and American immigration. Was immigration considered too insignificant in relation to other aspects of Newfoundland history? Is the connection between immigration and nation-building, which is so obvious in Canada and the United States, not relevant to Newfoundland's pre-confederation experience? Have the manifold personal relationships and dependencies that govern life in Newfoundland's relatively small society encouraged apology rather than criticism of a system that has helped to perpetuate backwardness and poverty?

Because so little is known of the immigrant experience in Newfoundland's history, popular myths have proliferated that have adversely affected certain development policies of successive provincial governments since 1949. One myth is that Newfoundland must not offer any attractions and opportunities to newcomers so long as the native-born are emigrating in large numbers. Instead of providing opportunities for newcomers, the argument usually runs, employment should be created enabling the return of emigrated native-born. A related myth suggests that the out-migration of native-born and in-migration of foreign-born are unnatural, and that patterns of inter-provincial and inter-state geographical mobility that are an entirely normal phenomenon for all of North America do not apply here.

Not surprisingly, therefore, the myth is nourished among some circles that immigrants as "come-from-aways" and "foreigners" are by definition incapable of identifying with their country or province of adoption, and that Newfoundland's well-being depends on the occupation of all influential places in the local economy and society by the native-born. "Luckily," lectures a prominent, well-educated Newfoundlander in the April/May 1991 issue of *Newfoundland Lifestyle*,

> we haven't been swamped by pushy mainlanders and Europeans. Not that we haven't had our fair share of them to endure; but so far we haven't been overrun, that's my point . . . It has always amazed me how quickly members of the immigrant bourgeoisie in Newfoundland assume that they can and should run certain of our institutions, or that they should occupy influential places in local society . . . They appear to think that, given the primitive state of Newfoundland society, their administrative skills and other services are sorely needed. Not only that: in the media they presume to let us all know how people in these parts should think on certain key issues, and even dare to speak out on their behalf . . .

> The origin of this pushiness lies in contempt. Mainlanders and foreigners who come here tend to assume an attitude of superiority over the locals, who are, they think, incapable of running the show. They willingly step in to fill the vacuum.

If members of the community's native-born intellectual elite, whom one would expect to rise above xenophobic tunnel-vision, are straining themselves to propagate such irrational notions about newcomers, how could one criticize the reaction of the man in the street? It is to the credit of ordinary Newfoundlanders that they have maintained untarnished their reputation for hospitality towards visitors and outsiders.

Indiscriminate negative stereotyping of "the foreigner" by persons in privileged positions helps to perpetuate the idea that immigrants are of dubious value, if not harmful. This assumption, whatever validity may have been attached to it, has long been refuted in theory and practice. In a 1991 study entitled *New Faces in the Crowd*, the Economic Council of Canada reviewed the record of Canadian immigration and stressed a number of significant points.

First, immigrants seldom take jobs from natives and rarely have had any effect on the employment rate. Second, immigrants themselves have lower unemployment rates and a smaller proportion of welfare recipients than the native-born. Furthermore, increased immigration reduces rather than increases levels of intolerance and prejudice in society. Based on prevailing demographic patterns, and regardless of Canada's adoption of significantly higher levels of immigration, the study also projected an alarming decline of population for Newfoundland by the year 2015. Irving Abella's appeal to a 1988 *Policy Forum on the Role of Immigration in Canada's Future* (edited by Charles M. Beach and Alan G. Green) may therefore assume acute relevance for Newfoundland: "Open your gates, the country you save may be your own."

This book took shape in the winter of 1989–90 when in the brief period from December 1989 through March 1990, approximately 2,000 relatively skilled East European—mostly Bulgarian—refugee claimants entered Newfoundland through its international airport in Gander. (In all of 1989 not quite 500 persons had asked for refugee status, and in 1988 the number was a mere 200.) The province's immediate reaction was one of impending doom: how was it to support all these people? Three quarters of the arrivals took advantage of the government's offer of assistance to depart for mainland Canada. Only when it was too late did the province's Economic Recovery Commission recognize the potential contribution of these educated, resourceful, and talented people to Newfoundland's economic development. The provincial government, lacking imagination and ignorant of historical precedents, acted in response to public pressure. That, in turn, was shaped, if not made, by the local daily newspaper. At first the paper fuelled anti-foreign sentiment, but it changed its stance and began to view the matter on compassionate terms after most of the refugees had left.

Astonishing about these reactions were not only the parallels to Newfoundland's attitude towards the European refugee crisis of the 1930s, but also that neither the government, nor the media, nor any voice among the public was willing or able to draw on the lessons of this earlier experience in the search for a suitable and responsible approach to the refugee issue. The *Evening Telegram's* many feature articles and editorials on the refugee influx since the 1980s contain no reference to the experience of the 1930s, despite the paper's extensive coverage in the 1930s of refugee-related developments, and despite its tradition of harking back to events it reported fifty years earlier in its daily column "From the Files." For instance, an article of 18 June 1987 featuring the "Dominican Republic as a wartime haven for Jews" made no mention of Newfoundland's closely related situation.

But Newfoundland's response to the refugees of the 1930s and '40s also needs to be remembered, indeed scrutinized, if we want to build the future "on our strengths" (as the report of the 1986 Newfoundland Royal Commission on Employment and Unemployment recommends). No matter how one may interpret the events described in this book, they tell a vivid tale of their own and they raise the question whether some of the woes of this "land of historic misfortune" have not been self-inflicted.

NEWFOUNDLAND IMMIGRATION DEPARTMENT.

Headquarters at ....

....

Date ....

Name of Alien (in full) .... Sex ....

Where detained ....

Age .... Date of Birth .... Nationality ....

Race .... Subject of .... Occupation ....

Place of Birth ....

Nearest large City ....

(City) (Distance and direction from place of birth.)

Date left Native Country ....

Last Address in Country of Citizenship ....

Last Foreign Address ....

Date left last Foreign Address .... Date of Arrival in Nfld. ....

Port of Arrival .... Name of Vessel ....

Married or Single .... Name and Address of Wife or Husband ....

Father's Name and Place of Birth ....

Father's Present Address ....

Mother's Maiden Name and Place of Birth ....

Mother's Present Address ....

Names and Addresses of near Relatives in Nfld. ....

Names and Addresses of Relatives Abroad ....

Names and Locations of Foreign Schools Attended ....

Names and Locations of Foreign Churches Attended ....

Where Baptized? .... Date of Baptism ....

Name and Address of last Employer in Country of Citizenship ....

.... Has Alien Passport? ....

Other Documentary Evidence ....

Charges Against Alien ....

Personal Description: Height .... Weight .... Eyes ....

Hair .... Face .... Nose .... Mouth ....

Distinctive Marks ....

Ordered Deported at Expense of ....

Application for Permit to Land in Newfoundland used in the 1930s.

Form of Application for Admission Into Newfoundland

1. This form must be completed **IN DUPLICATE** by every person who applies to be admitted into Newfoundland.

2. The form (and duplicate copy) should be filled out, if possible, before the applicant arrives and in any event before presenting the form to the Immigration Officer.

3. The form (and duplicate copy) must be signed in the presence of an Immigration Officer at a port of entry.

4. ALL particulars required by the form must be given except in the case of any person permanently resident in Newfoundland returning from a visit abroad, who may be exempted by an Immigration Officer from completing any part of the form not applicable to his case.

5. If the applicant is not a Newfoundland citizen and desires to take up permanent residence in Newfoundland, he should not seek to enter without having obtained prior permission of the Chief Commissioner of Immigration, which, if issued, will be subject to conditions requiring identity to be established.

6. If the applicant is a Newfoundland citizen and is not personally known to an Immigration Officer at the port of entry or readily identifiable there, he is advised to supply himself with proof of nationality and identity.

7. If the applicant is accompanied by any person being under the age of 18 years whom he seeks to have admitted and for whom he is responsible, full particulars must be set out in the form in the space provided. Separate forms must be completed for all persons over the age of 18 years.

---

1. Name ....

2. Sex *Jeannede* .... Race ....*Syrian* ....

3. Date of birth. Day............... .... Month *March* .... Year...............

4. Place of birth ....

5. Married, single, widow, widower or divorced .... *Single* ....

First page of Form of Application for Admission into Newfoundland in the early 1940s.

(c) Any letters intended for delivery to any person in Newfoundland. *No*

....

(d) Any packages intended for delivery to any person in Newfoundland? *No*
Note: If any of the articles in this item are held by the applicant they must be produced.

17. Have you ever been in the armed forces or service of any Government? *No*

If so, state the nature and period of employment ....

....

18. Do you consent to your finger prints and photograph being taken on or after your

admission into Newfoundland, if considered desirable? *yes*

19. State name, age, sex, place of birth and relationship of each member of your

family who is accompanying you to Newfoundland ....

....

....

20. Are the members of your family who accompany you of the same nationality as

yourself, if not, give particulars. ....

....

....

21. If the nationality you hold has been obtained by naturalisation, state

(a) the nationality of your parents and how obtained *Syrian*,

Canadian born

(b) place of birth of your parents *Father in Syria*,

Mother in ....

....
Signature of Applicant.

FOR OFFICIAL USE ONLY

Signature of applicant made in my
presence, or acknowledged by him.

Final page of Form of Application for Admission into Newfoundland.

Part I

*Origins of Refugees from the Third Reich
and of Newfoundland's Immigration and
Refugee Policy*

Refugees and Newfoundland History   1

Introduction and Historiographical Context

Newfoundland's encounter with refugees in the half century prior to confederation with Canada has been an unknown chapter in Canada's and Newfoundland's history. Indeed, little seems to be known about refugees having sought entry throughout the centuries of Newfoundland's history. Even when their existence was acknowledged, as in the case of the refugees of the 1980s, they have been so little noticed that one analyst referred to them and their network of local contacts as an "invisible, concealed society."[1] Immigrants who claimed to have come as refugees, such as the pre-World War I influx of so-called "Syrians" and Russian-Polish Jews, have never been identified in the historical and public consciousness as refugees.

The vast literature on the Jewish Holocaust contains no reference to refugees from the Third Reich seeking entry into or being accommodated in Newfoundland. However, this is no reason to assume that refugees did not consider Newfoundland as a realistic temporary or permanent refuge. At a time when hundreds of thousands were so desperately fleeing Nazi terror, they were grateful to be admitted even to such remote places as Shanghai or the Dominican Republic. In fact, its extraordinarily generous refugee law of 1906, low population density, moderate climate, and economic challenges for immigrants would have made the Dominion of Newfoundland (which also included the territory of Labrador) a more suitable haven for refugees than was Shanghai.

Government records and newspapers document the fact that between 1934 and 1941 some 12,000 refugees from Nazi persecution sought sanctuary in Newfoundland, but only a handful of them managed to enter. Moreover, had it not been for an accident, Britain would have transferred one thousand interned refugees from its internment camps to Newfoundland in 1940. The Newfoundland government even built a detention camp—never occupied—near St. John's for the awaited internees. According to official records, Newfoundland was party to an international agreement to bring another one thousand interned refugees to the island in 1941, this time from Canada. They were to be released in St. John's prior to being resettled in the United States. These refugees never arrived because the agreement was not ratified by all the parties involved. One of the main objectives of this book is to retrieve from historical obscurity the significance of these various encounters which never were.

This book looks at the refugee experience of the 1930s from three interlocking perspectives. First, it examines the experience of the refugees who from 1934 to 1939 vainly looked to Newfoundland as an escape route and a country of asylum. It is the story of who these people were, how they became refugees, and why they would want sanctuary in a poor and obscure country like Newfoundland.

The book is therefore, secondly, about Newfoundland as a potential refugee-receiving country in the 1930s. How did the government, the press, and the people of Newfoundland respond to the humanitarian, social, economic, and cultural challenges of refugee settlement? The appointed Commission of Government, in office from 1934 until 1949, seemed ideally poised to take up some of these challenges. It was equipped with a mandate to carry out reforms that would restore the country's economic well-being and enable the return of democratic government. As early as 1934 one available option was refugee settlement generating industrial activity and employment. Why did the Commission reject this option, and what does this rejection tell us about the politics, the society, and the seemingly insolvable economic problems of the Dominion of Newfoundland whose small native-born population liked to refer to their self-governing country as "the colony?"

An answer to these questions is sought not only from the perspective of the 1930s, but also from the vantage point of Newfoundland's twentieth-century immigration policy. The examination of this pattern from the first immigration legislation in 1906 to confederation with Canada in 1949 forms the book's third theme. Of interest is not only the history of immigration and refugee policy over a fifty-year period, but also the forces shaping it, especially the endurance of vested interests and the impact of public attitudes. The broader inquiry into how and why Newfoundland immigration policy evolved the way it did thus provides the backdrop and frame of reference for the analysis of Newfoundland's experience with refugees in the 1930s and the experience of these refugees with Newfoundland.

Sanctuary Denied traces the evolution of Newfoundland immigration and refugee policy through five stages: 1906–1918, 1919–1933, 1934–1939, 1939–1945, and 1945–1949. This chronological approach has several advantages. It reveals the dynamics of the progressive unfolding of immigration controls from 1906 to 1949. Furthermore, it permits the flight of some of the refugees to be traced from their expulsion in Germany, Austria, Czechoslovakia, or Poland to way stations in England, western Europe, or the Far East (from where requests for admission to Newfoundland were made), and in some cases, to ultimate resettlement. Finally, it helps to establish and relate the historical contexts for such different aspects of the refugee experience as the economics of refugee group settlement, the impact of the media, individual petitions for asylum, arrangements for internment, and the enemy alien trauma.

The book is divided into three parts. Part I (chapters 1 to 4) establishes the setting in Central Europe and Newfoundland. Chapter 1 introduces the topic and its problems, defines terms, raises issues to be addressed, reviews the literature, and refers to historical models of economically beneficial refugee settlement. Chapter 2 examines the process: how was a growing segment of the population of the Third Reich turned into refugees, and what were their escape routes? Particular attention is paid to the circumstances under which those who sought sanctuary in Newfoundland became refugees. Chapter 3 explores Newfoundland's immigration and refugee legislation of 1906 and the circumstances of its introduction. It also inquires into the island population's pre-World War I migrations and encounters with refugee settlement. Chapter 4 traces the tightening of immigration controls and the recourse to deportations from 1919 to 1933 under the impact of Canadian and American entry restrictions and deteriorating economic conditions.

Part II (chapters 5 to 7) deals with Newfoundland's response to the refugee crisis of the 1930s. Chapter 5 draws attention to the various proposals for sponsored refugee group settlement in Newfoundland and Labrador in the 1930s, the prospects for economic development associated with them, and the reasons for their failure. Chapter 6 examines the extent to which the Newfoundland newspaper readers were made aware of the fate of persecuted minorities in the Third Reich, and attitudes toward refugee settlement in Newfoundland and Labrador. Chapter 7 looks at the theory and practice of the Commission of Government's immigration policy and reviews the handling of a number of well-documented cases of individual refugees' petitions for asylum.

Part III (chapters 8 to 10) is devoted to an examination of war-related and post-World War II policies and practices. Chapter 8 describes the construction of an internment camp for one thousand refugees near St. John's in 1940 and delves into the reasons for its abandonment before use. This chapter also brings to light the role assigned to Newfoundland in a British-Canadian-American project to facilitate the release of hastily interned refugees from Canadian camps to freedom in America. Chapter 9 looks at the impact of the war on Newfoundland's treatment of individuals and groups seeking a haven. Particular attention is paid to six refugee physicians that the government of Newfoundland specifically recruited in London to work as nurses and medical practitioners. The focus is on the escalation of their adjustment problems as they found themselves cast in the role of enemy aliens. The book concludes with a glance at Newfoundland's refugee and immigration policy from 1945 until confederation with Canada in 1949.

The evidence presented in this book is derived primarily from archival materials, interviews, and contemporary newspapers. The archival sources consist of the records of the Newfoundland, British, Canadian, and German governments deposited in St. John's, London, Ottawa, Koblenz, and Potsdam and of documentation in the Canadian Jewish Congress Archives in Montreal.

DEFINITIONS AND QUESTIONS

A meaningful inquiry into the refugee experience requires a definition of such terms as refugee, asylum, migrant, economic migrant, emigrant, immigrant, and multicultural. It also touches on a wide range of historical issues centering on refugee migration and settlement, as well as the society and politics of pre-confederation twentieth-century Newfoundland. Some of these issues are controversial and some hitherto barely explored, and hence they provoke a host of questions. Unfortunately, many of these cannot be pursued in detail within the scope of this study, but some can be raised in this chapter.

Refugees may be defined as forced international migrants, i.e., persons compelled to flee their home countries in fear for their lives by forces beyond their control. Persons do not become refugees until they have abandoned their place of abode and they do not become immigrants until they have been granted permanent asylum. Flight or expulsion from their home countries frequently entails a desperate search for temporary asylum or a secure place of resettlement.

Although in a broad sense a refugee would include anyone uprooted from his home by *force majeure*, for the purposes of this study the term refugee will be confined to those compelled to abandon their home countries, whether due to war, revolution or persecution, or for political, religious, ethnic or racial reasons.[2] The definition by John Hope Simpson, the foremost authority on the refugee question in the interwar period, comprises the generally accepted characteristics of refugee status in the late 1930s:

> A refugee is one who has left his country of regular residence of which he may or may not be a national, as a result of political events in that country which render his continued residence impossible or intolerable, and has taken residence in another country or if already absent from his homeland, is unwilling or unable to return without danger to life or liberty as a direct result of political conditions existing there.[3]

The protection from the laws and practices of another state which a government may grant to refugees on its territory is a status known as asylum. The definition of asylum includes the principle that refugees may not be surrendered to countries where their life or liberty may be endangered.[4]

The term migrant applies to anyone who moves for whatever reasons from one place to another, including a refugee. It encompasses both the definition of an emigrant (i.e., a person departing from a country to settle elsewhere) and that of an immigrant (i.e., a person who comes to a country to take up permanent residence). Refugees are often contrasted with economic migrants. While the refugee flees because he fears for his life, the economic migrant seeks personal satisfaction, material improvement, or upward social mobility, or a combination of these. Economic migrants tend to follow the pull of an immigrant-receiving country's lure and of opportunities, while refugees are usually pushed to emigrate without the privilege of being able to consider the most desirable destinations. In contrast to refugees, economic migrants usually have the choice to return to their home countries, either permanently or for visits.

To the countries granting asylum, refugees usually represent what may be called a multicultural immigration. That is, with regard to their ethnic and cultural background, refugees differ from the host society, and frequently also from each other. In the context of this book the term multicultural simply denotes ethnic or cultural heterogeneity, and not (as is implied in the official policy of Canadian multiculturalism) any specific government policy or ideal of equality or mutual respect among ethnic or cultural groups.[5]

Questions arise in connection with the process by which Europeans became refugees from Nazi persecution, the timing of their flight, their countries or territories of origin, the difficulties of finding temporary asylum, and their immigration and adjustment problems in connection with permanent resettlement. Of particular interest is the impact these questions have on Newfoundland. For example, did refugees approach Newfoundland as a haven in the early or late 1930s, did they come predominantly from Germany or other countries occupied or influenced by the Third Reich, were they able to take any of their assets with them, did they represent particular types of refugees, and did they have experiences with Newfoundland that were in any way unique?

At what stage in their flight did refugees from the Third Reich think of Newfoundland and Labrador as a potential place of temporary or permanent asylum? Was Newfoundland discovered as a haven in the process of the refugees' search for information about possible escape routes or from a place of temporary asylum in Britain or elsewhere? What kind of a pull, if any, did Newfoundland's relatively small pre-World War I Jewish influx from Russia and the 1906 law welcoming refugees from political and religious persecution exert? Was locally initiated sponsorship a factor? To what extent did international refugee organizations suggest Newfoundland as a sanctuary, offer funds for settlement, and work out proposals for industrial activities?

Since Newfoundland was understandably apprehensive about increasing welfare costs, of importance is whether the refugees of the 1930s could have been expected to have resourceful characteristics that (to quote Lisa Gilad's portrayal of Newfoundland's refugees of the 1980s) would "make them good immigrants, and propel them towards self-sufficiency?"[6] Or were they migrants who, as victims of persecution, expected to be granted asylum solely on humanitarian grounds? Was their suitability as settlers questionable—were they anxious to return as soon as conditions in their home country changed or did they exhibit crushed psyches and dependent behavior on account of the persecution or fear of persecution that precipitated their flight? Did their social backgrounds, education, and skills prepare them to make economic or other contributions? Did they have the connections or capability to generate industrial activity, jobs, and revenue for Newfoundland?

Another set of questions concerns the assimilability of refugees as immigrants whose culture and mores were largely foreign to Newfoundland. As natives of Germany, Austria, Czechoslovakia, Poland, Hungary, and Romania, their language, cultural baggage, attitudes and views, and urban lifestyles deviated considerably from those of Newfoundlanders. In addition, they were involuntarily abandoning their homes. The majority of the refugees were Jewish by faith or descent. But there were also non-Jewish refugee applicants, including a group of Hutterites. They were looking for sanctuary in a society that was a composite of one third Irish Roman Catholics and the remainder English Protestants, and that had a Jewish community of only some twenty families. In terms of their socio-economic structure and ethnocultural identities, could the refugees be expected to adjust to Newfoundland's quite dissimilar socio-cultural landscape?

Today we are used to considering refugee issues as legal-political-humanitarian matters *per se*. We tend to treat the economic aspect of immigration as an issue separate from the duty to adjudicate asylum seekers' requests for protection in accordance with enacted legislation. How widely accepted was the right to asylum in the 1930s? It is well to remember that—although until the early nineteenth century emigration from continental Europe was often restricted[7]—until the beginning of the twentieth century asylum seldom needed to be claimed since most states had come to regard migration as a basic and inalienable right and immigration was virtually unrestricted. The post-World War I erection of high barriers to immigration everywhere, however, has entailed the frequent denial of the rights of refugees to seek asylum. In 1933 the League of Nations passed the first Convention relating to the International Status of Refugees. It was signed by eight states.[8] Not until 1948 was the concept of the right to seek territorial asylum universally recognized in the United Nations Declaration of Human Rights,[9] and confirmed in the 1951 United Nations Convention on Refugees.[10] For the pre-World War II period, legislation offering asylum to those eligible upon landing was thus quite unusual.

Considering that until the post-World War II era refugee issues were widely treated as immigration concerns, might not the patterns of Newfoundland's refugee policy be viewed as unexceptional? The history of refugee immigration in the twentieth century shows that the governments and the public of resettlement countries have in some instances welcomed refugees, and at other times rejected their

appeals. Among the factors determining government refugee policy,
humanitarian motivations have seldom been decisive. Instead, *bona
fide* refugees have usually been subjected to similar admissions'
criteria as regular immigrants. As a recent study of American refugee
policy found,

> humanitarian considerations are not easily translated into govern-
> ment policy. Official indifference to suffering in faraway lands and
> unwillingness to take responsibility for persons whose care might
> require tax dollars is still with us in the 1980s.[11]

The refugee policy of a country like Canada, too, reputed for its many
instances of admitting refugees and its current generous refugee
settlement program, is known to have reflected primarily the "opportunism" of domestic economic and political requirements.[12]

It is a truism that refugees seldom seek entry at the right time.
All too often, therefore, they tend to be perceived as undesirable
intruders, economic opportunists, and immigration queue jumpers.
This was as true in the 1930s as it is today. It took the United States
seventeen and Canada eighteen years to accede to the 1951 U.N.
Convention on the Status of Refugees, and as civilized and highly
developed countries to agree to accept their full humanitarian
obligations to the international community. Canada's history of
twentieth century refugee immigration is known to abound with
episodes where entrenched anti-foreign sentiment superseded both
humanitarian considerations and economic interest.[13]

Although Newfoundland was not a traditional refugee receiving
country, the nagging question remains whether the island dominion
could not have been expected to take some refugees, if for no other
reason than economic self-interest? The refugees did not come with
empty hands and all of the other dominions and even Latin American
countries no richer than Newfoundland opened their doors to some
refugees. Indeed, it is difficult to comprehend how, in Newfoundland, opposition to refugees appealing for a haven could override
humanitarian concerns, the much vaunted traditional hospitality
extended to strangers, a twenty year-old law guaranteeing asylum
to people persecuted on religious or political grounds, as well the
desperate need for industrial activity and for the skills conducive to
it.

The search for an answer to that question leads to an inquiry
into the reception Newfoundland accorded to refugees and immigrants before 1933 and after 1945. Among Newfoundland's
known pre-World War I groups of foreign immigrants were small
communities of Syrians, Russian-Polish Jews, and Chinese. Did
their admission and adjustment indicate a pattern that might help

us understand the treatment accorded to refugees from the Third Reich? A study of refugee experiences in Newfoundland in the 1980s found Newfoundlanders' attitudes to immigrants and refugees "typically not positive."

> In Newfoundland xenophobia prevails even with respect to mainland Canadians; any newcomer to the province is considered a Come-From-Away (CFA) and will never be considered to be "from Newfoundland." The implications of this discrimination for social relations are varied and difficult to document. Nor are they straightforward. . . . .Suspicion is probably a more common response to newcomers than curiosity and it is expressed in ways directly related to the reception of refugees in this province.[14]

Bearing in mind that nativism[15] was deeply rooted in American culture and that America's, Canada's and Australia's white Anglo-Saxon Protestant ruling elites treated their own racial and religious minorities with suspicion, how significant was anti-foreign sentiment in Newfoundland? Which sectors of society and public opinion encouraged such sentiment, and did it serve any identifiable purpose? Did suspicion and apprehension of the newcomer emanate from Newfoundland's isolation, both geographic and cultural? Were negative attitudes towards immigrants and foreigners conditioned by unemployment and limited economic opportunities, were they fostered to shield vested interests, or did they help guard a small ruling elite against the feared loss of entrenched social and economic control? Was xenophobia[16] a consequence or a cause of the island's poverty and backwardness?

Could perceptions of or interactions with Newfoundland's twentieth-century immigrant community help to explain local xenophobic attitudes? Both the Newfoundland census and Newfoundlanders distinguish between residents and immigrants of British origin on the one hand, and those categorized as "foreign-born" on the other. Those classified as of British origin included persons born in other parts of the British Empire, while "foreign-born" was the standard designation for residents and immigrants of non-British origin. In contrast to their numbers and importance in Canada and the United States, the "foreign-born" in Newfoundland —termed "foreigners" in Newfoundland English—constituted a tiny minority of the ethno-culturally homogeneous resident population. The census reports from 1884 to 1945 suggest an almost total lack of immigration and ethno-cultural diversity: 0.6 percent or fewer were "foreign-born," (i.e., neither native-born nor of British origin), while no less than 96 percent of the population were born in Newfoundland.

Regardless of local nativist attitudes, why did the appointed Commission of Government not seize upon the foreign-funded development opportunities offered by the European refugee crisis? Considering the few options of rehabilitation available to Newfoundland at a time of severe economic depression and mass unemployment, one would tend to assume that any such opportunity was bound to be welcome. Would it have meant taking too great a leap into uncharted socio-economic territory? In one of its first and most ambitious reforms aimed at resettling the unemployed local population on the land, the Commission demonstrated that it was not afraid of risks. Or was the Commission restrained by the Dominions Office which, because it appointed the members of the Commission, had to assume responsibility for the latter's policies?

In the ongoing search for new answers to the prospects for Newfoundland's economic plight and development, the exploration of its immigrant experience in the twentieth century can make us acutely aware of aborted options in the past.

RELATED RESEARCH AND PUBLICATIONS

Apart from Lisa Gilad's recently published monograph and my own articles,[17] there is no literature on refugees in twentieth-century Newfoundland or on Newfoundland's immigration policy. Gerald E. Dirks provides valuable insights into Canada's refugee immigration in general,[18] while Simon Belkin, Irving Abella and Harold Troper focus on the exclusion of Canada's pre-World War II Jewish refugees in particular.[19] The odyssey of Britain's and Canada's refugee internees has been portrayed by Eric Koch, Paula Draper, Fred Jones, Peter and Leni Gillman, Miriam Kochan, and Bernard Wasserstein.[20] The trials and tribulations of German Jewish refugees deported from Britain to Australia have been documented by Paul Bartrop.[21] None of these studies, except for Belkin's, contain any significant references to Newfoundland.

To some, our ignorance of Newfoundland's encounter with refugees in the 1930s is justified by this episode's seeming insignificance. Isn't it after all, as two interviewees wondered, only the story of cursory contacts which resulted in few concrete encounters, and of plans and policies never implemented? The profound impact which the Great Depression and the Second World War have had on the lives of contemporaries and the minds of historians has preempted local interest in the history of the 1930s and early 1940s. The vain pleas of refugees for sanctuary between 1934 and 1941 may not easily be reconcilable with the harsh record of deprivations which many Newfoundlanders suffered bravely during the Depression, nor with the cherished memory of Newfoundlanders' heroic sacrifices in World War II.[22]

Newfoundland guide books proudly extol the island population's traditional hospitality toward strangers.[23] Yet, apart from marginal observations by a few folklorists,[24] Newfoundlanders' perceptions of outsiders, i.e. attitudes toward visitors and tourists as well as toward immigrants and settlers, have never been systematically examined. Except for Alison Kahn's interviews of the local Jewish community,[25] the non-British ethnic experience in Newfoundland is a *tabula rasa*. Historical research has documented the pervasiveness of anti-alien sentiment in Canada,[26] especially between the wars, and has established the record of America's and Canada's deportations of undesirable aliens.[27] Recent scholarship has also brought to light the existence of a widespread hostility towards Jews in the United States,[28] Canada,[29] and Australia[30] as a reason for restricting the admission of refugees from the Third Reich. In these countries the exposition of anti-foreign and anti-Semitic sentiment up to and through the Second World War had a cathartic effect. More importantly, the realization of the pervasiveness of prewar anti-Semitism in the western world outside the Third Reich heightened sensitivities toward the legacy of the Holocaust and hastened the introduction of a less discriminatory and more generous refugee settlement policy in these traditional immigrant-receiving countries.

Migration studies on Atlantic Canada have focused exclusively on the extent and impact of out-migration from the region as a consequence or cause of economic failure, and have ignored the question of the benefits of immigration altogether.[31] To be sure, recent social scientific migration research has also tended to view contemporary (i.e. primarily Third World) refugee migrations largely in terms of their cost to the receiving country.[32] But some new social scientific findings confirm older hypotheses that migrants in general, and refugees in particular—regardless of social class and severity of persecution—are "more resourceful than average, more highly motivated, more willing to run risks,"[33] because they are the product of a process of selection and because they are forced to develop strategies for survival and the ability to engage in information-seeking behavior.

To the ongoing debate about the underlying reasons for Newfoundland's underdevelopment and dependence, the failure to take up the challenge of refugee settlement may add a new twist. Newfoundland, so the standard arguments go, had its development stunted "by British malevolence and neglect, Canadian machinations, and wily international corporations."[34] Historian David

Alexander and his school, rejecting this oversimplified approach, have postulated that the Newfoundland ruling elite were swayed by mainland models to concentrate on the development of land-based, foreign-owned, primary industries at the expense of the fishing industry.[35] William R. Reeves countered that in the fishery as in land-based industry the maneuvering space was not sufficient for significant initiatives and development options, despite American involvement.[36] The debate now comes full circle with the revelation that by excluding the refugees of the 1930s, Newfoundland chose for no compelling reasons to reject opportunities for social and economic development.

The findings of historical research have suggested some hypotheses for Newfoundland's apparent defiance of economic self-interest with regard to refugee-related options in the 1930s. Was Whitehall afraid to back the Commission in conflicts with the local elite, as Peter Neary argued?[37] Were Newfoundland's fortunes at the mercy of a small merchant elite who, in the words of Ian McDonald, looked upon their country merely as a "projection of their balance sheets?"[38] Or did Newfoundland, as David Alexander wondered, "fail to maximize its potential through incompetence?"[39]

With the recent critical study of American refugee policy of the 1933–1945 period by Richard Breitman and Alan M. Kraut this investigation shares "the complex interaction of precedent, process and individual personalities" as a focal point.[40] Like the monograph by Breitman and Kraut, *Sanctuary Denied* views Newfoundland's denial of asylum as the product of several major variables: preexisting immigration legislation and policy patterns, an entrenched bureaucracy committed to the protection of the interests of the ruling elite, opposition to foreign immigration generated by influential opinion-making sectors of the public, and, ultimately, the reluctance of Newfoundland's British commissioners to defy the local elite and its representatives in government.

The relative importance of these variables changed in the course of the refugee crisis from 1934 to 1941 and at no point did the outcome appear a foregone conclusion. Some commissioners advocated refugee settlement on rather generous terms while others were dead set against it. Throughout the 1930s the Newfoundland government wrestled with the problem and debated whether, what kind of, how many, and in what ways refugees might be settled. The final outcome is comprehensible only in the light of the colony's traditional approaches to foreign immigration and the role of vested interests. The pervasiveness of these interests has been critically analyzed by S.J.R. Noel, Ian D.H. McDonald, David Alexander, and Peter Neary.[41]

MODELS OF ECONOMICALLY BENEFICIAL REFUGEE SETTLEMENT

In a country where economic hardship is endemic and each newcomer tends to be viewed as a competitor for scarce employment and business opportunities, the question whether there is any economic gain to be derived from refugee immigration becomes a crucial issue. History offers numerous well-documented cases attesting to the beneficial impact of refugee settlement on ravaged or underdeveloped countries, from the sixteenth century migrations of the Scots to the absorption of post-World War II refugees in Western Europe and North America.

For instance, the impact on various receiving countries of the 200,000 Huguenots who fled France after Louis XIV's revocation of the Edict of Nantes in 1685 has been widely recognized as beneficial. In the state of Brandenburg-Prussia, whose rulers received them with open arms, an estimated 19,000 to 25,000 French refugees formed a cultured and innovative new urban "Ersatz-bourgeoisie"[42] among the one million largely German-speaking and rural native population. Owing to the unusually high proportion of merchants, professionals, and craftsmen, these refugees introduced numerous new industries, stimulated commerce and trade, and increased revenue in a country devastated by the Thirty Years' War and situated in the most barren and backward region of Germany. Berlin alone, the capital of Brandenburg-Prussia, offered sanctuary to 10,000 French refugees. Without them, it has been argued, that city might not have become an intellectual and economic metropolis. The refugees' positive economic, social, and cultural impact facilitated Prussia's rise to a great European power in the eighteenth century.[43] British North America's 14,000 Huguenot immigrants settled in nearly every colony where they were reputed to have achieved an extraordinary degree of political and commercial prominence by the time of the American Revolution.[44]

It may be relevant to look at the impact of the 150,000 refugees from the Third Reich who settled in the United States from 1933 to 1941, despite the considerable differences in socio-economic and cultural conditions in the United States and Newfoundland. The newcomers were a highly educated group of professionals and businessmen. Although they became more famous for their cultural achievements than for their economic contributions, a 1941 study refuted charges that the refugees were a burden to the American economy. According to this study, the refugees had established 239 businesses in 82 cities and had created jobs for others.[45] Within a few years, "while their English was still threadbare," the emigres had achieved a remarkable success, as Anthony Heilbut put it:

> The artists and radicals among them saw themselves as vanguardists, anticipating a future that would transcend the cultural and political limits of the present, while the more typical members of the bourgeoisie were quite content to perform the functional roles of doctor and lawyer, merchant and scholar, that were required by society as currently constituted. . . .Knowing so much already—no matter how partial or artificial the knowledge—they became in short order professional interpreters of the American temperament. . . .By maintaining rigorous standards, they introduced new forms and levels of professionalism.

Heilbut went so far as applying the attribute "staggering" to the range of their accomplishments. "From the arts to the social and natural sciences, from the chairs we sit on to the movies we see, to the nuclear weapons that trouble our nights—results of their work are all around us."[46]

Equally impressively documented are the unanticipated benefits of the influx into post-World War II West Germany of over twelve million destitute refugees from the East—ethnic German minorities from eastern Europe, German nationals expelled from the German territories annexed by Soviet Russia and Poland, as well as Germans from the Soviet zone and East Europeans fleeing the tightening of communist controls. Although at first a serious destabilizing factor and burden for the war-ravaged West German society and economy, they not only were fully integrated by the 1960s, but also became "one of the most potent stimuli for economic development."[47] As a Frankfurt banker characterized them:

> The refugees were pacemakers for all of us. Because they had lost everything they possessed, they were willing to take any jobs, to accept low pay, if necessary, to work long hours, just to make a new start. In a sense they took the places of millions of able-bodied workers who were killed in the war. We should never have come so far in economic build-up without them.[48]

Wherever these refugees appeared they stimulated competition. Yale economist Henry C. Wallich noted that "well-established but perhaps somewhat staid local firms found themselves faced with aggressive upstarts who brought new techniques and new ideas. Fixed habits and attitudes had to be modified where they came into contact with those of the refugees." A number of industries lost in the East were entirely rebuilt in West Germany by refugees who brought their know-how and reputations. Some of these industries were highly export-intensive, while others economized imports. The millions of refugees, furthermore, created a high and expanding level of demand. Their backlog of needs per capita had been greater than that of the resident population. All these positive factors outweighed several undeniably negative effects so that on balance the refugees' indigence is credited with having underwritten an escalating level of national prosperity.[49]

As early as 1916 the renowned economic historian Werner Sombart advanced the intriguing thesis of the historical significance of various European refugee movements as the initiators of capitalist industrial activity in modern Europe.[50] His focus was on the migrations of persecuted Christians, especially Protestants, since the Reformation. Besides the migrations of the Huguenots, Sombart reviewed the large movements of Protestant refugees from Scotland, from the Palatinate and the Netherlands into various regions of economically backward Europe. For instance, colonies of Scottish refugees were credited with having been the leading commercial and business elements in Silesian, East Prussian, and Polish towns. The city of Posen (Poznan), for example, owed its wealth and importance as a center of trade in the seventeenth century to its Scottish emigres. To refugees of the Mennonite and Reformed faiths from the Lower Rhine is attributed the origin of Crefeld's silk industry in 1688. Dutch refugees were identified as founders of furniture manufactories, iron and steel industries, and banking houses in seventeenth-century western Germany. According to Sombart, foreign emigres contributed essentially to the beginnings of England's "capitalist" development in the sixteen and seventeenth centuries. He pointed to the arrival of masses of refugees from Flanders: 10,000 in 1560, and 30,000 in 1563, in addition to 80,000 French refugees in the seventeenth century. Contemporary sources are quoted as attesting to the pioneering role of these refugees in launching England's industrial development. Sombart considered it an indisputable fact that the economic development of Russia was essentially the work of foreign immigrants and refugees.

Drawing on a wide range of documented cases, Sombart concluded that the introduction of capitalist economic activity was largely the work of foreigners. He postulated that foreign immigrants formed the subjects (entrepreneurs) as well as the objects (workers) of this new form of economic development, because those who emigrate from their home countries have usually gone through a process of selection: they are the most determined, most energetic, most courageous, most rational, and least sentimental types, regardless of whether they decide to migrate for economic reasons, or because of religious or political persecution.

> Especially oppression at home is the best preparation for capitalist education. Emigration selects from among the oppressed those who refuse to stay alive through adaptation and submission. That even refugees represent a selection of the most competent may be gleaned from the fact that a large number of those persecuted for religious or political reasons decide not to emigrate but rather to adjust at home: most of the Huguenots (four-fifths) stayed in France. Also, many East European Jews waited for years before they began to migrate.

Sombart argued that those who have emigrated—refugees as well as colonists—know no past, only a future. The alien newcomer is not held back by personal considerations in realizing his aspirations. In their business contacts, aliens meet only people that are alien to them, which is the best situation for profitable business deals. There are also no non-personal barriers restraining the aliens' business aspirations in a foreign land—no traditions and no old business distract them. Everything has to be created new. Last but not least, the alien—whether colonist or refugee—is compelled to choose, with no traditions in his way, the most rational economic and technical approach. Refugees have thus become, according to Sombart, the promoters of commercial and industrial progress in Europe.

A systematic analysis of the post-1947 resettlement in India of five million Hindu-Sikh refugees from West Pakistan inspired an unorthodox and highly perceptive model of economic development based on the aggressive economic behavior frequently observed among refugee settlers. Political scientist Stephen L. Keller found that the previously underdeveloped areas of East Punjab where the refugees had settled had experienced phenomenal economic growth within a mere twenty years and by 1975 had become the fastest developing region in India. Ostensibly more promising regions, by contrast, had developed slowly and in some cases even stagnated. Keller concluded that the economic aggressiveness of the refugees accounted for the rapid progress.

> The difference between the refugees and non-refugees was in the way they approached situations in which risk was involved. Probably because of the sense of invulnerability. . .the refugees are more willing to do new things or do old things in new ways. They are more geographically mobile, and more likely to adopt innovations sooner than non-refugees.[51]

Aggressiveness and invulnerability are traits which, as Keller hypothesizes, refugees acquire as a result of having undergone several stages of extreme trauma in their flight—from grief-stricken semi-paralysis to guilt and wonderment for having survived and ultimately to an aggressive willingness to take chances to get ahead in life. Refugees are perceived as typically engaging in innovative behavior that others see as risky. The refugees themselves "either minimize the risk or feel that even if they lose all, it doesn't matter since they have started from scratch before and succeeded." The ensuing success and wealth beget a so-called "synergistic" outlook, i.e., a socially shared world view that sees competition as legitimate and in which each person working for his or her own good helps expand the economy. A synergistic outlook is usually not dominant in an environment where economic scarcity prevails, but once acquired will be transmitted from refugees to non-refugees and to future generations. Refugees thus become a reference group with regard to innovation. The hosts have "seen the refugees achieve success through unorthodox behaviour and this has led them to discount the risks involved and to try some of the changes, the fruits of which are now seen as desirable."[52]

Sketching a specter of potential initial social conflict between the host society and the refugees, Keller argues that

> many refugees do not see competition in economic life as necessarily leading to [social] conflict. The non-refugees, however, do. As a result, the refugees' actions are misunderstood by many non-refugees who see these non-aggressive yet competitive actions as aggressive and aimed at them and they, naturally respond to them aggressively.[53]

Keller's social scientific construct offers a perceptive hypothesis suggesting that the fear of aggressive economic competition by refugee settlers might not make their admission welcome by the vested interests of some receiving countries. Despite some obvious limitations, Keller's findings provide a heuristically useful approach to assessing the problems and prospects of economic development under refugee auspices.

The above mentioned historical examples and models of economically beneficial refugee settlement place Newfoundland's experience into a comparative historical context. They provide a framework of reference for meaningful inquiry into opportunities for development that were rejected and suggest alternatives to the path that Newfoundland had chosen. In Newfoundland's ongoing quest to build a better future, such an inquiry may be a useful starting point. As will be argued in this book, Newfoundland's encounter with refugees in the 1930s was pregnant with the promise of self-reliant industrial development, the growth of the middle classes, and an open—albeit multicultural—society.

"Rette sich wer kann"   **2**
(Save yourself while you can)

Becoming a Refugee from the Third Reich

REFUGEE-GENERATING PATTERNS AND TYPES OF REFUGEES

Becoming a refugee is a process characterized by common features and sequences of stages regardless of when and where the process occurs. The triggering factors involve a threatened loss of life, freedom, or livelihood and prompt the decision to flee. The escape—often lengthy—from such a threat turns a person into a refugee. Frequently the first refuge is only a temporary one, followed by other places of temporary asylum. Eventually the refugee journey terminates in repatriation or immigration to a country of permanent resettlement. The escape process usually necessitates to a greater or lesser degree some survival foresight because often not only information must be collected very quickly, but also plans made for coordinating routes, connections and possible destinations. Where available, refugee agencies enter the picture. Their *raison d'etre* is threefold: facilitate the escape, support the refugee in transit, and arrange for permanent resettlement. In introducing the type of refugee who sought sanctuary in Newfoundland, this chapter focuses on the commonalities of the refugee process within the specific historic context of the 1930s.

Between the two world wars, individuals fleeing European fascism comprised the most common type of refugee. Fascism was a revolutionary movement promising a radical regeneration of the nation through a dictatorship of elites and parties. In Italy, Portugal, and Spain, as well as in Poland, Hungary, and Romania, the establishment of fascist or pseudo-fascist regimes meant the per-

secution of groups and personalities opposed to fascist dictatorship
or ideologically designated to be outside the redefined national
community. Most of the refugees from these regimes initially considered themselves to be temporary political exiles, waiting for an
opportune moment to return.

After the Nazi takeover in Germany in January 1933 the refugee
problem assumed the dimensions of an increasingly insoluble crisis
as the number of refugees unsettled in Europe began to exceed
50,000.[1] From the outset the Nazi regime moved on several fronts,
at home and abroad. At home it ruthlessly purged society of real or
alleged opponents. It moved against political, intellectual, and
spiritual enemies of Nazism, those who resisted *Gleichschaltung* (i.e.,
institutional and organizational integration into the Nazi movement), and those defined by Nazi ideology and legislation as spoilers
of the racially purified society the regime set out to create. Although
the third category included such different groups as gypsies, Slavs,
and the mentally and physically disabled, Jews were the special
target. The Nazi regime managed to export its racial policy to
countries where German influence predominated, such as Italy,
Slovakia, and Vichy France. On the eve of the Second World War a
refugee from the Third Reich meant one who, because of racial,
religious or political persecution was permanently banished from or
had no legal status in his European homeland.

The expanding Third Reich's war against what it defined as Jews
became the single most important cause of a refugee crisis of
unprecedented international proportions. A Jew, according to the
Law for the Restoration of the Professional Civil Service of 7 April
1933, was not necessarily an adherent of the Jewish religion.
Anyone descended from even one grandparent who had belonged to
the Jewish religion was encompassed by this sweeping new definition. Such persons were classified by Nazi racial ideology as
"non-Aryans." This definition, although it involved only about one
percent of the population in 1933, made Germany's 600,000 non-
Aryans (525,000 of whom adhered to the Jewish faith) the largest
minority of Germans declared to be racially undesirable.[2] Nazi
party-organized and government-decreed measures against Jews
escalated from economic and professional discrimination in 1933,
to their disenfranchisement in 1935, expropriation in 1938, and
ultimate physical destruction in 1941. Nazi propaganda depicted
the misfortunes of recent German history and the "evils" of
liberalism, capitalism, and communism as the work of an alleged
world Jewish conspiracy. Jews were systematically dehumanized
until even Germany's official law journal in 1938 defined the Jew as

"not a human being. He is the product of corruption, like fungus creeping into rotten wood."[3]

Official anti-Semitic policies were designed not only to rid Germany of "non-Aryans" regardless of their qualifications and their services to the nation but also, as astute contemporaries noted, to poison international public opinion against the refugees in order to make their reception elsewhere more difficult.[4] To trigger a mass exodus, the Gestapo (*Geheime Staatspolizei*, i.e., Secret Police) pursued a dual approach of cooperating with established German emigration agencies and Zionist organizations, as well as harassing Jews with random roundups and detentions. On the whole, flight remained an individual decision and never became a communal one. As native Germans embracing German culture, many found it inconceivable that their legal right to survive could ever be renounced.[5] Indeed, German Jews fought back with what an American observer in 1939 characterized as their only weapon, namely "their ability . . . to hang on, to hold out, or refuse to be exterminated."[6] The Jewish people had stoically weathered many pogroms, so the possibility of a long-term, expensive, relentless extermination policy did not seem credible to German Jews. Half of Germany's Jewish community thus delayed the decision to escape until it was virtually too late, and those who got out in time encountered a free world that had been brainwashed to view them as undesirable.

Explaining the pattern of Jewish emigration in the 1930s from the perspective of December 1945, deputy director of the *Reichsstelle für das Auswanderungswesen* (Reich Emigration Office, established in 1918) Hermann von Freeden delineated three phases of this emigration. In the first phase from 1931 to 1934, emigration was the result of a more or less spontaneous decision made by far-sighted individuals who had no illusions about coming developments. The second phase which lasted until 1937 was triggered by the progressive exclusion of Jews from public and economic life. Many were forced to look for a new existence abroad, although they felt deeply rooted in Germany and were reluctant to emigrate. However, they still had the time and the freedom to plan their emigration carefully. Only in the third phase from 1938 to the beginning of the war, did the Jewish exodus resemble a frantic mass flight characterized by despair.[7]

Many, perhaps most refugees, however, still perceived their exodus as "always only flight, never emigration."[8] This is illustrated by the experience of a community of Hutterites whose Swiss-born leader Hans Meier approached Newfoundland for sanctuary in 1940.

Hans Meier, 1989. Credit: Gerhard P. Bassler.

Their *Bruderhof* (communal farm) had been started in 1920 in the southwest German Rhön hills of Hesse. It was one of the fruits of the postwar Youth Movement that searched for the realization of a true and just community because of its disillusionment with bourgeois values and lifestyles in the wake of total war and revolution. Its members came from diverse backgrounds—multinational, socialist, Christian, anarchist, naturalist and *völkisch*. Inspired by their founder Eberhard Arnold, they decided to apply the Sermon on the Mount to daily life and to embrace as their guiding principles nonresistance, marital fidelity, love for all men, social justice, and common ownership of material goods. In 1930 they were incorporated into the body of the Hutterite Church in North America since their beliefs and lifestyle were so similar.[9]

After the Nazi takeover they harbored strong reservations against the mandatory public greeting of "Heil Hitler" and the public sanctioning of Hitler's racial politics, which the new regime demanded in a plebiscite held on 12 November 1933. The Hutterites found these demands irreconcilable with their faith and lifestyle based on the principles of Christian communism. Four days after the plebiscite 140 SA (*Sturmabteilung*, i.e., Storm Troopers, or "Brownshirts"), SS (*Schutzstaffel*, i.e., Protection Squad, or Himmler's black-shirted corps) and Gestapo men raided their communal farm searching in vain for traces of subversive activity. Nonetheless, Arnold continued to denounce worship of the state and the Aryan race and the vanishing freedoms of thought, speech and education. His group was then ordered to close their school or accept pro-Nazi teachers, welcome no visitors and not proselytize. In January 1934 they decided to send their school-age children to Switzerland. However, because the Swiss government would not guarantee their children's safety, they were sent to Liechtenstein instead.[10] This marked the first step in their enforced emigration.

The second step was touched off by the announcement of Germany's remilitarization. In March 1935 the impending draft of the traditionally pacifist Hutterites precipitated the relocation to Liechtenstein of all those who were German citizens and of military age. They had no future there since the German government pressed for their extradition, but their search for a new refuge in Switzerland and Czechoslovakia proved futile. In June 1936 the government closed their publishing house in Germany and forbade them to sell books. A letter from the chief of the district police warned them that they were under close surveillance by the Gestapo for being communists espousing a *Weltanschauung* in complete opposition to the National Socialist State. An inquiry at Gestapo headquarters in

Berlin confirmed their fear that the closure of the Rhön Bruderhof was only a matter of time. Searching for allies in the impending spiritual confrontation with the "dark powers" of Nazism, Hutterite leaders appealed to leading representatives of the German Mennonites (Benjamin Unruh) and the Protestant Confessional Church (Martin Niemoeller) for a declaration of solidarity with the Hutterite stand against Nazism. Hans Meier has survived to tell posterity that their appeals fell on deaf ears. Both Unruh and Niemoeller distanced themselves from the Hutterites and from the Hutterite refusal to serve and obey the "God-appointed" government.[11]

The transformation of the Hutterites into refugees was completed in April 1937 when the Gestapo confiscated the Rhön Bruderhof on the basis of the "Law for the protection of the German people and State and its defence against violent communistic attacks." Hans Meier and two fellow members were taken into "protective custody" and the remaining families fled to the protection of Mennonites in Holland. Hans relates that they were released from prison contrary to Gestapo orders. A judge who was not a Nazi at heart used a ruse to inform the Gestapo office only after they were out of reach. Luckily, a safe refuge became available shortly before the Gestapo action. The generosity of English donors had enabled fellow brethren to lease a farm for the refugees near Ashton Keynes in Wiltshire, England, which they called Cotswold Bruderhof.[12] Their adjustment in England and further migration from there will be examined in chapter 9.

CAUSES AND PHASES OF THE JEWISH EXODUS IN THE 1930S

For German Jews, the first phase of flight from the Third Reich was brought on by the institutionalization of anti-Semitic discrimination. The shock of Hitler's appointment as chancellor was deepened by the Nazi party's declaration on 1 April 1933 of a temporary boycott of Jewish business firms, Jewish merchandise, Jewish physicians and Jewish lawyers. The Law for the Restoration of the Professional Civil Service six days later led to the mandatory retirement of non-Aryan civil servants from the public service and the exclusion of non-Aryan professionals from semi-public and private sectors. These events triggered the flight of 38,000 German Jews in 1933 and of 22,000 in 1934. Some were reported to have returned the following year assuming, especially after the leadership of the terrorist SA had been crushed, that the anti-Semitic measures of spring 1933 were a temporary aberration. It took more traumatic experiences to erode their faith in the viability of the German *Rechtsstaat* (rule of law) tradition.[13]

Two events in 1935 inaugurated the second phase of the exodus. In January of that year a plebiscite returned the Saar province to Germany. About 5,000 to 6,000 anti-Nazi refugees, 40 percent of them Jews, fled the Saar after the plebiscite.[14] In September the Nuremberg Laws deprived "non-Aryans" of the full rights of German citizenship and prohibited their intimate contact with "Aryans." Jewish departure figures from Germany remained steady for three years—20,000 in 1935, 24,000 in 1936, and 23,000 in 1937. Although Nazi policies exerted increasing pressures on Jews to emigrate, a rabbi like Max Katz who left Germany in April 1937 and ended up in Newfoundland five months later, could declare upon his arrival that "I was not actually forced to leave Germany but I saw the possibility of war and being an ex-soldier I figured I would be one of the first to be called to fight for my enemy."[15] Instead of emigrating en masse, German Jews tended to move from smaller towns and rural districts to cities where they hoped urban anonymity would protect them from anti-Semitic violence and they would be near relief organizations and foreign consulates, if the need arose.

There were other reasons why the bulk of those classified as non-Aryans were not yet prepared to cut their ties with Germany. Despite the increased difficulty of earning a living, Jews continued to cling to the belief that their fate could not get any worse. Ironically, the new state of law and the soft-pedalling of official anti-Semitism in connection with the 1936 Olympic Games in Berlin confirmed a still widespread myth among Jews that the legal redefinition of their special status by the Nuremberg Laws would mean the end of random harassment. Forcible deportation or even destruction was still inconceivable. And, it took determination to leave. Legal discrimination and a high emigration tax ensured that Jewish emigrants would have to leave most of their property behind.[16] Many were unable to obtain a visa from one of the few countries receiving refugees, others were simply too poor or too old. According to German statistics, nearly 70 percent of Jewish emigrants in 1937 were under 40 years of age but the proportion of the older age groups among the emigrants was steadily increasing.[17]

A major hindrance to a larger emigration of German Jews was their occupational and professional structure because many refugee receiving countries, e.g. Palestine and Argentina, required primarily pioneer skills to cultivate virgin lands. Germany's Jews were a highly urbanized and well established middle class community. In 1933, 61 percent of all Jews in the German labor force were engaged in business and commerce, 25 percent in industry and manual trades,

12 percent in public service and the professions (primarily law and medicine), but only 2 percent in agriculture. Nearly half of the gainfully occupied Jews were self-employed, in contrast with only 16 percent of the total German work force. One third lived in Berlin and 40 percent more in other big cities where they furnished 16 percent of all independent lawyers and 11 percent of all practising physicians. In general, Jews were more highly educated than non-Jews. Because of their high levels of scholarship and entrepreneurial skill, Jews were overrepresented among the leading and middle positions in commerce, banking, corporations, the civil service, and the independent professions.[18] The typical German Jewish refugee, then, may be defined as a native-born, urban businessman or professional with a more passionate attachment to Germany than to Jewishness.[19]

The final act in the European refugee drama, which opened with the abrupt extension of Nazi rule to Austria in March 1938 and to the Sudetenland of Czechoslovakia in September 1938, came therefore as a rude shock. In the annexed parts of the Reich, a violent persecution of Jews from the beginning unleashed new tides of refugees. In the enlarged Third Reich the last illusions of those who had stayed were crushed by the now infamous bloody *Kristallnacht* pogrom of 9–10 November 1938, ordered by Propaganda Minister Joseph Goebbels and staged by the Nazi storm troopers (SA). It brought not only unprovoked destruction and ruthless persecution but also provided the pretext for the complete exclusion of Jews from economic life, their expropriation and disenfranchisement.[20] Even in the League of Nations-administered Free City of Danzig the resident Jewish community of 7,500, half of whom were recent refugees from Poland, suffered violent assaults by local Nazis and the application of Germany's anti-Jewish legislation. By January 1939 most of the German Jews had left Danzig although 3,000 Polish Jews were still there.[21]

Jews from countries like Poland, Slovakia, Romania and Hungary added their desperate pleas for a haven. In Poland, where nearly one million Jews lived on the brink of starvation, anti-Semitism was such a widespread, potent sentiment that every government had to pay lip service to it.[22] Germans, remembered a Polish Holocaust survivor, hated Jews "from the law" while the Poles hated them "from their hearts."[23] Of Poland's 3.3 million Jews (i.e., nearly 10 percent of the population) on the eve of World War II, three quarters lived in towns and cities, 40 percent were occupied in industry and crafts, more than a third in trade and commerce, and about 6 percent in the professions. In Poland the rise of Nazism in Germany encouraged a "torrent of anti-Semitic legislation, brutal pogroms, and an official government policy of 'evacuating' the Jews." From 1935 to 1939 Polish Jews experienced official discrimination in the form of economic boycotts, segregation among university students, and exclusion from certain professions. A law withdrawing Polish citizenship from Jews residing abroad was enacted in 1938. In neighboring Slovakia, which in April 1939 became an independent state allied to Germany, 130,000 Jews (3 percent of the population) were subjected to sudden restrictions and exclusions from various professions and occupations along with arbitrary violence on the part of Slovakia's fascist movement, the Hlinka Guard.[24]

The situation was not much different in Romania and Hungary where pro-German regimes held power. The urban bias and occupational profile of Romania's 750,000 Jews (i.e., about 4 percent of the population) as well as the virulence of popular and official anti-Semitism were similar to those of Poland. In 1938 a decree withdrew Romanian citizenship from a large number of Romanian Jews. King Carol believed that Jews should be eliminated but agreed to let 50,000 emigrate annually. In 1940 Carol's government expelled Jews from cultural, economic, and military life and from government service. Hungary's 445,000 Jews formed 5 percent of the population. Half lived in Budapest, were highly acculturated and had a middle-class profile closer to Germany's than to Poland's. In May 1938 the number of Jews employed in private firms was restricted to 20 percent of total employees, and a year later Jews were barred from the media, trades, and professions. Jews were no longer able to acquire Hungarian citizenship by naturalization, marriage or adoption, and Jewish real estate was expropriated, although with compensation. The voting rights of Jews were cancelled, but could be reinstated if they could prove their ancestors had been permanent residents before 1868.[25]

From the perspective of a refugee receiving-country, the plight of the East European refugees was indistinguishable from that of the German refugees. Their occupational qualifications were similar, and like the latter, the former, too, were victims of an escalating anti-Semitic terror. Refugee applicants from Slovakia approached Newfoundland with skills as electricians, engine fitters, and dental technicians, from Poland as skilled workers, and from Hungary as physicians, engineers, merchants, farmers, and experts in the fishing and timber trades. "I suppose it needs no special explanations under the present conditions in Central Europe why I desire to emigrate from this country," pleaded a 32-year-old Hungarian Jew to the Newfoundland authorities in June 1939. He claimed a perfect knowledge of English and four other languages.[26]

ESCAPE ROUTES

In the enlarged Third Reich the events of 1938 were tantamount to an official expulsion campaign and triggered an unprecedented mass flight. From Germany alone 120,000 panic-stricken people fled during the year preceding June 1939.[27] An officially estimated exodus of 135,000 Jews fled from Vienna by September 1939 after the *Anschluss* of Austria added 192,000 Jews to those of Germany.[28] Czechoslovakia counted 186,000 and Prague 130,000 refugees in the spring of 1939.[29] Everywhere a mood of *"rette sich wer kann"* (save yourself while you can) prevailed.[30] When in the wake of *Kristallnacht* the SA arrested some 26,000 men and detained 10,000 of them in concentration camps, the authorities permitted their release only if they agreed to emigrate immediately. As a result of the increasing mortal fear experienced by the Jews, foreign consulates were overwhelmed by lineups at their offices, travel agencies and Jewish relief organizations were unable to cope, and all orderly emigration collapsed. The trapped Jews' desperate search for a refuge resembled, as one Holocaust survivor remembered, a game of geography where one's fingers restlessly crisscross the map searching for remote, little-known sanctuaries like Paraguay, New Zealand, or Panama.[31]

The urge of panic-stricken Jews to flee Germany meant business for steamship companies, travel agencies and the SS. The German Jews' demand for "excursions" to South America and Shanghai was so strong that they were prepared to pay return fares. Steamship companies like the HAPAG (Hamburg-America Line) made special cruise-line ships available to transport refugees to far-away destinations. One HAPAG luxury liner, the *St. Louis*, set sail from Hamburg on 15 May with 907 Jewish refugees aboard attempting to reach Cuba ahead of two other refugee ships for fear the Cuban authorities might become alarmed and revoke immigration visas.[32] The sad fate of these 907 refugees is told in chapter 6. To accelerate the departure of the Jews, the SS founded in 1938 a *Zentralstelle für jüdische Auswanderung* (Central Office for Jewish Emigration) with branches in Vienna and Prague, and in January 1939 the *Reichszentrale für die jüdische Auswanderung* (Reich Central Office for Jewish Emigration) in Berlin.[33] SS and Gestapo used all available channels and contacts—private, official, German Jewish, and Zionist—to expedite the exodus.

In March 1939 the government of Newfoundland was approached by the Vienna office of the *Hanseatisches Reisebüro* (Hanseatic Travel Agency) inquiring "whether you could see your way to concede to our clients the permission to enter temporarily Newfoundland." Its clients were on the United States quota list and could not immigrate until the fall of 1939, "whilst the German authorities constrained them to leave the country promptly." It was very difficult, the agent claimed, to "shelter Jewish immigrants who are to abandon Germany." Guaranteeing the moral and political integrity of the refugees, the German travel agency gave assurances that the refugees would bring enough money to spend which "we suppose . . . should be in favour of your island." What doomed this approach—and probably many similar ones with other countries—from the outset was the negative stance of the British Passport Control Officer in Vienna in an attached note. He intimated that this travel agency was "believed to work in close touch with certain Gestapo officials and is known to have no scruples in exploiting German Jewish refugees."[34]

In Frankfurt am Main the physicist father of 15-year-old Ernst Deutsch (a distinguished geophysicist on the faculty of Memorial University of Newfoundland from 1963 until his retirement in 1990) scrambled to save his family. As Austrian citizens of "non-Aryan" background, they had neither travel documents nor a place offering asylum at the time of *Kristallnacht*. In his despair, Ernst's father took the New York City telephone directory and wrote identical letters to twenty persons listed under the name of "Deutsch," suggesting they were related and asking for sponsorship. Of the twenty, one high-ranking addressee replied positively. Meanwhile, Ernst's family had been denied passports because his father was alleged to be of war-related value to the large engineering firm he worked for in Germany. Consequently the only travel documents his father could obtain in early 1939 were fake passports. In return for hefty bribes, these were available on the black market with the help of the Gestapo. Next he had to join the waiting line for American visa recipients since the American quota for immigrants from the Third Reich was heavily overbooked. Ernst's father applied to emigrate under the Czech quota since Troppau, his Austrian birthplace, had become a part of Czechoslovakia after World War I. However, before the American immigration papers were processed, he managed to find a temporary haven for himself and his family in England with the help of an organization of British scientists who helped German colleagues flee in 1939.[35]

Dr. Ernst Deutsch, 1991. Credit: Ernst Deutsch.

"Like a wall" (to use the metaphor coined by a refugee)[36] did the growing tide of expelled Jews approach potential refugee-receiving countries. There the argument gained ground that admitting the expellees might encourage a cycle of more persecutions and more expulsions, not only from the Third Reich, but also from allies of Nazi Germany and from countries eager to emulate Nazi anti-Semitic policies. Canada's delegate to the League of Nations and chief immigration officer in Europe, Hume Wrong, put it this way: "The trouble is that the more that is done for them the more there will be. Help abroad will result in greater German militancy at home. So nothing will be done by Canada."[37] Thus, when the need was greatest, the few existing escape hatches snapped shut. Countries bordering on Germany to the West, such as France, Belgium, the Netherlands, Italy, and Britain, were in a state of near war and began to arrest and intern foreign refugees as soon as hostilities broke out.[38] The only western country which increased its refugee intake after *Kristallnacht* and did not deport its German refugee internees to Germany in 1940 was Britain. Of Britain's total number of some 70,000 Central European Jews who had managed to flee from 1933 to 1942, an estimated 40,000 arrived in the year preceding September 1939.[39] From there, many hoped to gain access to North American and Commonwealth countries.

The flight of Andreas and Betty Barban, who immigrated to Newfoundland in 1947, epitomizes the ordeal of German and Austrian Jews. In 1938 Andreas was a 24-year-old student of music at the Leipzig Conservatory and single. He had intended to study law but was deterred by the anti-Semitic restrictions on his lawyer father. The parents of Andreas' mother had converted from Judaism to Christianity but Andreas' parents had preserved the ancestral faith. Andreas remembers that in Germany his family used to celebrate Christmas with a decorated tree and gifts, and that they identified as Germans. Andreas' father was a lawyer who was excluded from the bar in 1933 on racial grounds but would not abandon his faith in the German *Rechtsstaat*. Although forced to live off the meager rent from their real estate, the Barbans had refused to consider leaving Germany until 1939.

In the wake of *Kristallnacht* Andreas was arrested without warning, like so many other "non-Aryans," and he and his father were put into the nearby Sachsenhausen concentration camp for a "recreational leave" (*Erholungsurlaub*), as the Gestapo officer euphemistically put it. There, without adequate winter clothing and having a straw-covered floor for his bed, he was forced to carry out such heavy outdoor manual chores that he suffered severe frostbite

Andreas and Betty Barban on the Italian passenger liner *Conte Biancamano* travelling to Shanghai, 1939. Credit: Andreas and Betty Barban.

on his hands and contracted diphtheria. He witnessed some inmates renouncing their German mother tongue and culture. Nevertheless, he remained convinced that the invaluable culture of Goethe and Beethoven was as much victimized by Germany's Nazi usurpers of power as Germany's Jews were. The purchase of a ticket from Genoa to Shanghai with a pledge of Andreas' speedy departure enabled Andreas' father (who on account of his age had been released from the concentration camp after ten days) to obtain his son's release six weeks after the arrest. Hoping to immigrate to the United States, Andreas had, in late 1938, applied for an American visa and received No. 52,002 on the waiting list.

In the Genoa steamship office Andreas used his knowledge of Latin to communicate with the Italian clerks. While there he made the acquaintance of a person who was destined to become his wife. She had just fled Vienna with her parents after a year of undescribable ordeals under Nazi rule: since they were Jewish their photography business had been confiscated, they had to move five times in that year, and they had such a hard time making ends meet that her father a few times seriously contemplated opening the gas tap. In Vienna she had managed to obtain precious tickets to Shanghai for herself and her parents only after numerous almost insurmountable obstacles. For example, the shipping company had required her to purchase expensive return tickets, and somehow she had had to scrape together the funds to pay for them. Although German Nazi agents were everywhere in Genoa, she trusted this young German (Andreas) because his shorn head proved to her that he had recently been in a concentration camp.

Betty and Andreas Barban were married after their arrival in Shanghai. In 1939 Shanghai was the only place in the world without any immigration restrictions. Anyone could go to Shanghai and stay, with or without a passport. However, because of the immense distance and difference in life there, European Jews did not frivolously uproot themselves to flee there. It could be reached either via the Trans-Siberian Railway to Vladivostok, or by ship from Genoa. The overwhelming hurdle was the exit permit—its procurement and payment. Once safely out of Germany and the annexed Austria, money for living expenses was another problem because only four dollars per person could be taken out of those countries when fleeing. In Shanghai the Barbans lived in a community of 25,000 Central European—mostly German—Jews and supported themselves with piano lessons and professional photography.

Shortly before Italy entered the war, a series of extremely fortuitous events enabled Andreas to rescue his parents from Germany on the last ship that sailed from Genoa to Shanghai. In April 1939 an aunt of his died in Denmark and left him an inheritance. He was legally able to collect it because he had left Germany—otherwise it would have been confiscated. The day before Germany invaded Denmark in May 1940 the money was transferred from there to an American bank and on to Shanghai. If the transfer had been delayed by one day, he would not have received it. With this money he bought ship tickets from Genoa to Shanghai for his parents and cabled them that they were to leave 9 May. When they replied that they could not get their affairs in order until June, Andreas insisted that this was the only time that they *must* obey him. They did. It was the last ship that left Genoa for Shanghai before Italy declared war. In Shanghai the Barbans needed all their energy to survive from day to day and support their parents until, in 1947, they were allowed to leave for Newfoundland.[40]

RELIEF AND RESETTLEMENT AGENCIES

Persons become refugees once they are outside the country of their nationality and unable to return to it by reason of a well founded fear of persecution. As a rule, most of those fortunate few given sanctuary in countries like the United States, Canada, Australia, or Palestine had a brief journey and became immigrants. However, those who sought refuge in Shanghai, and many of those admitted to the United Kingdom, had started on a journey whose final goal they did not know. They became dependent on Jewish charity while their ultimate destiny was in the hands of a network of mostly Jewish international resettlement agencies. These groups combed every possible receiving country, including Newfoundland, in their efforts to identify suitable permanent havens. German, British, American, and Zionist organizations were involved in resettling refugees from the Third Reich in North America.

The *Reichsstelle für das Auswanderungswesen* (Reich Emigration Office), according to the high-ranking official mentioned earlier, used the expertise it acquired before 1933 to cooperate with Jewish and Christian agencies, such as the *Reichsvereinigung der Juden in Deutschland* (RVE), the Jewish Colonisation Association (ICA), and the *St. Raphaelsverein* in Hamburg, in efforts to facilitate organized emigration and resettlement of Germans of Jewish religion and descent. This cooperation lasted—with the permission of the Gestapo—until 1939, though with decreasing success. The *Reichsstelle* was particularly impressed by the carefully and responsibly planned resettlement projects of the ICA (which in 1934 made a major approach to the Newfoundland government). The ICA selected its prospective settlers carefully, prepared them with the help of the *Reichsvereinigung* and the *Reichsstelle* for the challenges ahead and awaited their success before allowing more settlers to join them. As late as April 1939 representatives of the *Reichsstelle* conferred in London with Britain and the United States about the suitability of British Guyana and other territories for a possible mass resettlement of German Jews.[41]

Of particular importance in rescuing Jewish refugees and facilitating their migration to North America was a network of internationally connected Jewish aid organizations. In Germany there were the *Hilfsverein der deutschen Juden*, founded in 1901, and the *Zentralausschuss für Hilfe und Aufbau* (ZA), created in 1933. HICEM was a coalition of HIAS, ICA and EMIGDIRECT (acronym for the Berlin-based United Committee for Jewish Emigration), formed in 1927. It coordinated its international relief efforts from Paris. ICA (founded in 1891 by Baron de Hirsch to resettle Jewish refugees from Russia) and ANGLO-HICEM (German Jewish Emigration Council, formed in 1933) operated from Paris and London and the JDC (American Jewish Joint Distribution Committee, founded in 1914) and HIAS (Hebrew Sheltering and Immigrant Aid Society of America, founded in 1888) from New York.

The German *Hilfsverein* and the ZA operated as the welfare branch of the *Reichsvertretung der deutschen Juden*, the political representative of German Jewry, and they owed their effectiveness largely to the infusion of massive American Jewish subsidies. The *Hilfsverein* disseminated information in Germany about receiving countries, advised about 90,000 Jews considering emigration and financially supported 31,000 emigrants. Prior to 1939, the ICA was able to finance the resettlement of 20,000 to 30,000 refugees in Argentina. HICEM looked after every aspect of refugee migration to the Americas, and subsistence while in transit. HICEM also offered guarantees to receiving countries that its settlers would not become public charges. During 1933-1939, HICEM spent $2.7 million of ICA, American Jewish, and British Jewish funds on organizing migrations, with 32,000 refugees receiving financial support. The London-based ANGLO-HICEM was in charge of refugee settlement in the British Empire.[42]

The most important support for Jewish refugees from the Third Reich came from the JDC or "Joint." Although in the fall of 1940 the United States counted 37 American agencies dealing with refugee problems, nine of them identifiable as Jewish,[43] throughout the lifespan of the Third Reich the JDC remained the sole representative of American Jewry's desire to aid its refugee brethren in Europe, the

Western Hemisphere, North Africa, and the Far East. In 1931–1935, for instance, it helped European (mostly German) Jews with $4.3 million, and with $8.5 million from 1936 to 1938, and again with $8.5 million in 1939 alone. From 1939 to 1945 the JDC funded the escape and survival of refugees from the Third Reich to the tune of $50 million of American Jewish donations. The JDC underwrote the maintenance of displaced Jews in transit—whether in Shanghai, Spain, or Cuba, their education and retraining for resettlement, their integration into the host society, and their economic self-reliance in their eventual country of adoption. JDC representatives negotiated with foreign governments, purchased land, and provided starting capital for refugee industries.[44] Members of the JDC executive also attempted, unsuccessfully, to place refugees in Newfoundland.

Least effective were the international agencies from which comprehensive remedies were expected—the League of Nations' High Commission for Refugees, established in 1933, and the Inter-Governmental Committee on Refugees (IGCR), created by the Evian Conference in July 1938. Their assignments were essentially diplomatic. The League Commissioner tried in vain to sort out the refugee chaos by intervening with the German Government in favor of an orderly refugee exodus and by seeking to extract adequate settlement opportunities from western refugee-receiving countries. The High Commissioner's office experienced a high rate of attrition and awaited its third office holder in 1938. An obvious candidate to head the body was Sir John Hope Simpson, who had retired in 1936 as the senior member of Newfoundland's Commission of Government. His career and publications had established his reputation as the foremost expert on the refugee situation at the time. However, the choice fell on veteran British civil servant Sir Herbert Emerson, who was considered less critical of British refugee policy.[45] Emerson was also appointed Director of the IGCR in January 1939. Throughout 1939 this body was engaged in futile protracted negotiations with German government representatives who were looking for a profitable way to rid Germany of its remaining Jews. At the same time the IGCR investigated, with the help of American and British government agencies, various schemes for financing large-scale settlement in underdeveloped areas of Central America, Africa, and the Far East. By the outbreak of the war, the IGCR had produced no concrete results.[46]

In November 1940, an American expert on the refugee scene painted a grim picture of the refugee population outside China. He estimated it to be twenty million, and, of these, "the German refugees, both Nordic and Jewish, are the most terribly compromised exiles in Europe today." While camps in southern France originally created for refugees from the Spanish Civil War were overflowing with German Jews rounded up by Vichy French authorities and awaiting deportation to Germany, the refugees in other countries occupied by Germany had already been delivered to their Nazi persecutors. Even in neutral countries like Sweden and Switzerland, and in the Balkans, there was "only safety for the day and none for the morrow."[47] In the Western Hemisphere, the economically backward Dominican Republic was the sole country to open its gates; it offered to take 100,000 European refugees.

Ironically, the economic arguments advanced for the refugees' exclusion from America were largely refuted by the evidence which analysts observed. In fact, it was found that enterprises launched by refugees did not compete on the labor market. Rather, the refugee enterprises established in America introduced products, processes, and patents formerly imported from abroad.[48] It was noted that many of the refugees were "qualified to make their own rehabilitation a means of paving the way also for the solution of the larger problem of rehabilitation."[49]

In 1940 the case of some 200 refugee industries with $500 million to invest attracted as much attention in Newfoundland as in the United States. Barred from the United States by rigid immigration restrictions, these industries relocated to Canada instead. The entrepreneurs, and the specialized workers many of them brought with them, were reported by the *New York Times* (3 March 1940) to include Christians as well as Jews. They had escaped not only from Germany, Austria, Czechoslovakia, and Poland while there was still time to salvage some of their capital, but also from Belgium, the Netherlands, Denmark, and Switzerland where they feared for the future. One of these entrepreneurs attempted to launch an industry in Newfoundland in the spring of 1940 but, as related in chapter 9, was expelled. Among his confiscated papers Newfoundland officials found the *New York Times* article.

The article described the diverse products turned out by these refugee industries. They ran the gamut from beet sugar (produced in Manitoba) to fine Bohemian glassware (produced in Ottawa) and included such items as tennis racquets, animal foods, furniture, paper for cigarette tips, kid gloves, plywood, cable, etc. Parts of two Czech plants relocated shortly before the German invasion even helped Canada's war effort against Germany. A munitions plant built at Sorel, Quebec, was actually part of the transferred Skoda gun plant, and the Bata Shoe Company at Frankfort, Ontario,

employing 600 workers by March 1940, claimed to have work for
1,800 when it introduced the production of precision gauges in
armaments. The article referred to "thousands of European refugees
and millions of fugitive dollars rescued by them from the wreck of
their enterprises abroad . . . finding a safe haven in Canada in the
greatest industrial immigration this Dominion has ever known."

Thousands fleeing for their lives from a relentless, government-
sponsored anti-Semitism that had spread from the expanding Third
Reich to adjoining countries were, thus, already giving proof of their
resourcefulness. To contemporaries not blinded by anti-Semitism
and xenophobia it was clear that these refugees would likely be an
asset to any country letting them in. The refugees were
predominantly middle-class and offered a unique range of qualifications: they were generally more highly educated than their
non-persecuted fellow nationals, with occupational emphasis on
entrepreneurship, the professions of medicine, law, and teaching,
and the white-collar as well as the skilled trades. Following reports
in the American and Canadian press, Newfoundland's most widely
read daily newspaper, the St. John's *Evening Telegram* (17 January
1939), identified Germany's Jewish minority as being "composed of
the most highly educated, cultured section of Germany's population." The paper also pointed to well-known historic antecedents
when it referred to the "periods of industrial progress and trade
expansion which have attended every migration from the days of the
French Huguenots to the Empire Loyalists." The 18 January 1939
editorial drew attention to the

> benefits resulting to Britain as a result of the influx of French
> Huguenots with their crafts and industries; the effect upon Pales-
> tine of the return of the Jews; the fact that the refugees admitted
> into England had removed the centre of the fur industry from
> Leipsig to London, and the further fact that 11,000 Jews permitted
> provisionally since 1933 to settle in England have not only
> managed to establish themselves in new industries but are already
> employing 15,000 Englishmen.

"Leave to land shall not be refused"   **3**

The Origins of Newfoundland's Immigration and Refugee Policy

NEWFOUNDLAND, A COUNTRY OF EMIGRATION

In the opinion of the Montreal branch of the Paris-based Jewish Colonization Association (ICA), Newfoundland, because of its reputedly "very liberal" immigration laws, was an obvious choice for settling refugees from the Third Reich in 1934. Since 1906 the island-dominion had explicitly defined itself as a country giving special consideration to the admission of refugees. Clause 1(d) of the 1906 Aliens Act provided that

> In the case of an immigrant who proves that he is seeking admission to this Colony solely to avoid persecution or punishment on religious or political grounds, or for an offence of a political character, or persecution, involving danger of imprisonment or danger to life or limb, on account of religious belief, leave to land shall not be refused on the ground merely of want of means or the probability of his becoming a charge on the public funds.

In the non-European world, Newfoundland was unique for having enacted such a generous welcome to refugees. In light of the legal and moral commitments that this provision entailed, the circumstances of its adoption are of some interest to Newfoundland's refugee policy of the 1930s.

Unlike the United States and Canada, Newfoundland had not been able to attract immigrants since its last major influx of English and Irish settlers in the early nineteenth century.[1] The pull of the American frontier may have been as responsible for this failure as the island's unique fishery-oriented economic life. The virtual absence of immigration throughout the nineteenth century, however, had consequences that further reduced Newfoundland's appeal to prospective European settlers in the early twentieth century. For one, it deprived Newfoundland of the type of people, who as producers and consumers in mainland North America, formed the mainspring of industrial diversification and economic growth. The immigrants' quest for assimilation, upward social mobility, and prosperity provided a constant impulse for social and economic change. In contrast with the open, dynamic, and multicultural societies of the United States and Canada, Newfoundland society was closed, rural, and culturally homogeneous. Social stratification remained characterized by the absence of a sizable middle class; its absence widened the gulf between the upper and lower classes and intensified polarization between them.

It has been maintained that nowhere else in North America were social classes more sharply polarized than in Newfoundland.[2] A ruling elite had acquired a monopoly of virtually unlimited power over the outports and the masses of poor fishermen. It consisted of a few wealthy St. John's merchants — some fifteen firms are said to have controlled the fish export and consumer-oriented trades around 1900 — in association with a small urban middle class. The latter included entrepreneurs, new businessmen, professional people, and church leaders.[3] This elite exercised its hold on the population through the cash-free economy of merchant credits, the pervasive influence of the Protestant and Roman Catholic churches, and the political power structure. Under the prevailing system of credit trading, the merchant himself determined the value of the goods he procured for the fishermen, as well as the value of the fish he took from them in payment of their debt. The merchants owned or controlled most of the local factories producing consumer goods. High tariffs, in turn, protected these from outside competition. Education was entrusted entirely to the churches, and the two houses of the legislature were controlled by the merchant and professional classes.[4]

The power and prestige of the "fishocracy" of "Water Street" were proverbial and became synonymous with exploitation and with the patronage that permeated the churches, the legislature, the political parties, and almost every other aspect of life in Newfoundland. Contemporary portrayals of the merchants' regime leave little to the imagination. Newfoundland's leaders, according to the local-born Rev. Patrick W. Browne, were

> opposed to all progress and development other than their own, often engaged in serious feuds among themselves, their sole ambi-

St. John's harbor from the Narrows, about 1906. Credit: PANL.

tion was centred in the accumulation of wealth—honestly, if con-
venient, but, if needs be, otherwise. . .To realize to the fullest extent
the serfdom and misery of the fishermen under the régime of the
'merchant' of the ancient type, one must live among the fishermen
as I did for many years. The brand of servitude is even visible in
the physique and character of the fishermen of certain localities in
the 'Old Colony.' . .Caste is not seemingly a peculiarity of Brah-
minism; it is found amongst fishing people.[5]

The merchants regarded Newfoundland as "a private trading reserve
to be governed in their own interests" and, in the words of an astute
analyst, "pined for a reversion to Crown colony status."[6] Defending
their privileges against challenges from above and from below, they
opposed confederation with Canada, as well as the democratization
of government at home.

In Newfoundland the paths to power were "so notoriously narrow," that the political arena may be aptly characterized as "a closed
society with limited membership."[7] Elections to the House of Assembly gave people a choice "between merchants and lawyers and
lawyers and merchants."[8] Merchant patronage gave the governing
elite of businessmen, lawyers, educators, and journalists economic
security, kept the elite confined to a small stratum of society, and
secluded it socially from the masses of the people. The Rev. Philip
Tocque's observation of 1877 still held true in the early twentieth
century that "there is no colony belonging to the British Empire
where influence and name tend so much to form caste in society,
and where it is more regarded than in St. John's."[9]

The merchant class "did not fraternize with the people generally
but maintained a class reserve," observed Nova-Scotia-born lawyer
and Newfoundland veteran politician A.B. Morine. He charged that
the merchants "should have had the 'guts' to fight for the colony's
good, however unpleasant the fighting was."[10] Closely inter-con-
nected by ethnic, religious, commercial, and family ties, and
retaining an "abiding loyalty to the mother country," the leading
merchants preferred to live for extended periods in England, have
their children educated abroad, and invest profits outside the island-dominion. The "much neglected" condition of the capital city
of St. John's was attributed by a contemporary editorial to the
"regrettable circumstance that, in spite of all the great fortunes made
in this Colony. . .by those who have developed its principal industries. . ., there has never been any substantial philanthropic
offering on their behalf."[11] Pre-World War I Newfoundland had one
public hospital and no public library, and only 52 percent of the

population could write as well as read.[12] "No improvements could be expected from a merchant class notorious for its lack of philanthropy and of any interest in the community, save the operation of the fisheries along self-interested lines," summed up one perceptive scholar.[13]

By the turn of the century, the stagnation of the island's fishery-centered economy had become painfully obvious. The population proliferated by natural increase from 202,000 in 1891 to 243,000 in 1911 and growing numbers of unemployed fishermen became increasingly preoccupied with emigration to the United States and Canada as a significant alternative to the lack of local opportunities. But the reduced absorptive capacity of the traditional economy appears to have been only one, and frequently not even the most important, among the factors triggering emigration. Once the exodus to New England had started in the depressed 1860s, the "Boston fever" continued for all kinds of reasons, touched all classes of society, and came from all over the island. One analyst identified push factors such as general fluctuations common to a fisheries economy, labor conflicts, marital problems, and the stopover of emigrant ships bound to Canada and the United States, as well as a host of increasingly stronger pull forces generated by the gradual westward movement of the Atlantic economy with its vast network of North American labor markets.[14]

The high rate of return migration in the decade preceding World War I (see Table 1 below) indicated the transient nature of the migration and the frequent superficiality of triggering factors. At that time railway branchline construction, lumbering operations along the railway lines, the development of the Grand Falls paper industry, and the mining of iron ore on Bell Island created seasonal demands for jobs that local labor was not always able or willing to fill,[15] while improved communications encouraged geographical mobility and the search for greener pastures on the mainland of North America. It appears that the combined impact of railways, steamship connections, telecommunications, and increased personal links and contacts with the mainland enabled pull forces from outside rather than push factors at home to determine the levels and source areas of out-migration.[16]

Between 1901 and 1921 migrants to Cape Breton alone accounted for over 50 percent of Canada's Newfoundland-born. Overwhelmingly male and unskilled, they were actively recruited by the Canadian government and the steel and coal companies of Cape Breton for jobs native-born workers were unwilling to fill.[17] Low educational levels impeded internal mobility in Newfoundland, it

was noted, whereas on the mainland greater occupational opportunities were available "even to the most unskilled."[18] The exodus
was welcomed by those seeking political and economic stability. It
kept levels of unemployment down, removed the causes and
proponents of discontent, and subsidized the local economy through
the remittances sent home by successful emigrants.[19] By the 1930s,
out-migration of a seasonal and permanent nature had been a
prominent feature of Newfoundland life for so long that census data
showed 15 per cent of the Newfoundland-born living on the mainland of North America.[20] In its historic experience and popular
mythology, twentieth-century Newfoundland came to see itself as a
country of emigration and the incompatibility of this notion with
immigration came to be taken for granted.

Little consideration has been given to the brain drain that the
small island community could ill afford with its meager supply of
educated people. David Alexander's speculation that a dispropor-
tionate number of the better educated left the country between 1874
and 1901 echoed a 1904 address to visiting expatriates in which
Member of the House of Assembly and future Prime Minister Edward
Morris referred to the "well known fact that it is the man with the
most grit and courage who emigrates."[21] From the perspective of
1935, Newfoundland Commissioner Thomas Lodge characterized
the long-term effect of what he called the "steady progress of negative
selection:"

> Local opportunities for brains and energies above the average have
> been so limited that right up to the crisis in the United States of
> 1929 there has been a steady exodus to the American continent of
> the best individuals of all classes. . .That their departure lowered
> the general standard of both ability and character in the people
> seems to me incontrovertible. What Maine and the Maritime provin-
> ces of Canada gained, Newfoundland lost, and the loss is manifest
> in the post-War political life of the island.[22]

IMMIGRATION AND SETTLEMENT, 1890–1914

A drain of population does not in itself preclude immigration.
Immigration may actually be desirable as a cause or a consequence
of what one scholar termed a "quality exchange of migrants,"[23] i.e.,
skilled, wealthier, and educated in-migrants replacing unskilled,
poor, and less educated out-migrants, or vice versa, as the history
of Canada and other countries shows.[24]

To Newfoundland's leaders, at any rate, the departure of native
sons did not refute their conviction that the country was underpopulated. Instead of alarming the ruling elite, the exodus reinforced their

belief that Newfoundland needed an influx of skilled and productive settlers. The need for a larger population had been a recurring theme in Newfoundland public affairs. It was based on the widely shared view that progress and economic growth meant filling the country's open spaces with people. "We have a country, capable of holding and maintaining an immense population," declared former Liberal newspaper editor and Speaker of the House of Assembly Ambrose Shea in 1882.[25] On 10 August 1899 the editor of the St. John's *Evening Herald* reiterated the view of Governor Sir John Glover (1876–1886) that

> the great disadvantage under which this country suffered was that it was so entirely undermanned. A country one sixth larger than Ireland with a population of 210,000 has a good deal of spare room. We want our solitudes filled up and our resources developed. There is ample space here for a population of five million and that number would be able to find a comfortable subsistence.

Various settlement and development plans were associated with the ongoing construction of the Newfoundland Railway. In 1907, for instance, the Robert Bond government hoped for mass immigration, settlement, and industrial development as a spinoff from the so-called transatlantic or short-line scheme. The stillborn scheme envisaged a fast line of transatlantic passages from the west coast of Ireland to Green Bay, Newfoundland, with connecting trains and ferries to Gaspé and Sydney. This was supposed to save 32 hours over the standard transatlantic crossing to Quebec and Chicago.[26] Inspired by the breathtaking colonization of western Canada, Newfoundland's rulers clung to the dream that it would be possible to develop Newfoundland's resources with the help of independent British or northwest European settlers. Despite the opening up of new districts for settlement and development in the 1890s, however, attempts to attract British settlers, Finnish farmers, and Swedish lumbermen failed, and hopes in 1909–10 to recruit both a Salvation Army farming colony to the interior near Grand Falls, and "boys" from England "of classes suitable for our main pursuits" were dashed.[27]

The data available on "intending settlers" among the inward passengers recorded by the Newfoundland government for the period 1903–1913 suggest an annual influx of between 600 and 800. Whether these represented permanent settlers is questionable. Their origins or destinations are not known. Also not known are how the data were collected and their accuracy. It is unlikely that the traffic to and from outports on small vessels was recorded. The "intending settlers" category included, according to the Deputy

Minister of Customs Henry W. LeMessurier, "a number" of clerks and skilled laborers recruited by local mines, paper mills, and other industries, and "few" agricultural settlers. Table 1 shows that the ups and downs of this immigration over the period of ten years roughly parallels the ups and downs of returning residents, indicating predominantly North American source areas.[28]

Whether the "emigrating passengers" represented actual emigrants is equally questionable in light of the high rate of returning residents who not only matched the number of emigrants but in 1904 and 1908 even surpassed it. A comparison of these statistics suggests that a high proportion of the emigrating passengers were transient migrants and the number of those actually leaving Newfoundland for good comprised a lower percentage of the total outflow.

Tables 1 to 4 suggest the main migratory flows to be in the transient category. Three-quarters of the in-migrants were males, and returning Newfoundlanders comprise on average two-thirds, whereas foreign sportsmen, tourists, and travellers form the rest of the inward passenger traffic from 1903 to 1913. The latter category appears to have consisted largely of Canadians and Americans and the increase in the volume of the passenger traffic after 1910 is proportionate to the increase in American-born arrivals. Throughout the ten-year period, arrivals from "other countries" amounted to from one-third to one-half the number of intending settlers. In 1906 "other countries" seem to account almost entirely for the surge of intending settlers. However, after 1908 the number of intending settlers dropped below their eleven-year average, while inward passengers from "other countries" in 1910 and 1913 rose above their eleven-year average number.

Table 5 balances the passenger inflows and outflows and indicates the net gains or losses by country of birth for the period 1903–1913. These figures suggest that a large number of departing American visitors and a smaller number of arrivals from foreign countries went unrecorded. Other than that, there seems to be little correlation between the calculated surplus of non-Newfoundland-born arrivals over departures, and the 1901 and 1911 Census data on foreign-born. Judged by the 1911 Census, which listed only 3,475 not born in Newfoundland (as against 4,869 in 1901)—and taking into account that 1,129 of these were classified as the wives and children of nonnative-born arrivals, and 401 as clergy, teachers, consuls, doctors and government officials—there was virtually no net immigration.[29]

Table 1

Intending Settlers in Relation to Returning Residents Inwards, Emigrating Passengers Outwards, and Total Outward Passengers (Transients and Emigrants) 1903–1913

Year	Intending Settlers	Returning Residents	Emigrating Passengers	Total Outwards
1903	643	8,535	9,554	12,707
1904	824	6,796	6,288	9,766
1905	884	6,220	6,885	10,618
1906	1,447	7,117	7,460	12,653
1907	851	6,160	7,029	11,197
1908	885	5,498	4,857	9,346
1909	536	4,810	7,540	11,576
1910	707	8,399	9,096	12,899
1911	653	7,612	7,711	13,026
1912	697	7,444	8,724	13,744
1913	785	7,967	8,445	14,255

Table 2

Passengers Inwards by Gender in Relation to Travellers and Sportsmen/Tourists 1903–1913

Year	Total Inward	Male	Female	Travellers	Sportsmen/ Tourists
1903	11,958	9,581	2,377	1,734	1,046
1904	10,292	7,583	2,709	1,643	1,029
1905	9,983	7,278	2,705	1,268	1,611
1906	11,420	8,479	2,941	994	1,862
1907	9,796	7,235	2,561	981	1,804
1908	9,674	6,777	2,897	1,205	2,086
1909	9,643	6,863	2,780	1,885	2,412
1910	12,346	9,040	3,326	887	2,373
1911	13,057	9,214	3,843	893	3,899
1912	12,754	9,129	3,625	936	3,677
1913	13,588	9,665	4,123	964	4,072

Table 3

Passengers Inwards by Place of Birth 1903–1913

Year	Nfld.	Brit.	Can.	USA	China	Other
1903	8,955	571	1,238	979	-	215
1904	7,455	581	1,140	908	-	208
1905	6,497	704	1,111	1,424	-	247
1906	7,269	686	1,185	1,374	168	738
1907	6,439	707	955	1,290	14	391
1908	6,216	676	1,073	1,487	4	218
1909	5,883	670	1,168	1,692	2	228
1910	8,121	753	1,334	1,764	-	394
1911	7,933	866	1,461	2,504	10	283
1912	8,060	893	1,407	2,082	12	300
1913	8,533	780	1,681	2,381	15	378

Table 4

Passengers Outwards by Place of Birth 1903–1913

Year	Nfld.	Brit.	Can.	USA	China	Other
1903	10,089	536	1,199	579	-	304
1904	7,077	563	1,245	595	-	286
1905	7,722	648	1,073	754	-	421
1906	8,758	656	1,299	1,110	42	788
1907	8,137	645	1,075	853	40	447
1908	6,431	684	1,100	813	7	311
1909	8,809	595	1,144	814	1	213
1910	9,773	751	1,170	866	-	339
1911	9,005	746	1,368	1,634	8	262
1912	9,596	803	1,336	1,666	6	337
1913	9,593	849	1,529	1,846	8	430

Source for Tables 1–4: Evidence of Mr. Henry W. LeMessurier, J.P. Deputy Minister of Customs, in Great Britain, Dominions Royal Commission, *Royal Commission on the Natural Resources, Trade and Legislation of Certain Portions of His Majesty's Dominions, Minutes of Evidence Taken in Newfoundland in 1914* (London, 1915), 1–2.

Table 5

Immigration by Place of Birth: Balance of Passengers Inwards/Outwards 1903–1913 in Relation to Residents Reported in 1901 and 1911 Census

Place of Birth	Balance of Passengers	Residents 1901 Census	Residents 1911 Census
Newfoundland	-13,609	214,738	239,144
Britain	411	1,951	1,540
Canada	215	1,309	--
United States	6,355	--	378
China	113	--	26
British Colonies	--	793	1,204**
Other Countries	-538	816*	327

*includes American-born.

**includes Canadian-born.

Sources: Evidence of Arthur Mews, Deputy Colonial Secretary, in Great Britain, Dominions Royal Commission, *Royal Commission on the Natural Resources, Trade and Legislation of Certain Portions of His Majesty's Dominions, Minutes of Evidence Taken in Newfoundland in 1914* (London, 1915), 3. *Report on the Census of Newfoundland 1911* (St. John's, 1914), XXI.

That there had been no net immigration for a long time was confirmed by the three government officials responsible for immigration and settlement in evidence they gave to a Dominions Royal Commission in July 1914. It was because of the greater inducements of Canada and the United States, complained Colonial Secretary Arthur Mews, that desirable settlers "after a few years drifted off again." Both Mews and LeMessurier testified in 1914 that the need for settlers was "most apparent." Despite chronic and seasonal shortages of labor in the timber industries, the pulp mills, the mines and even in the fishery, and openings for wage-earning people, managers and farmers, they lamented that "we get very few immigrants." Newfoundland's only new blood came from "expert men specially brought from abroad." Mews identified as highly desirable "those who will take up new work, who will break new ground, who will develop resources that are not developed yet."

In his 1914 evidence Joseph H. Downey, Member of the Agricultural Board and the House of Assembly, reiterated the point that local agriculture was severely hampered by the lack of farmers and farm labor. Some two million acres of excellent land were available at the nominal price of 30 cents per acre and yet there was no one to cultivate it. In the vicinity of St. John's even cleared land was unutilized. If Newfoundland could produce two thirds of its meats and half its foodstuff—a short while before nearly all was imported—there was no reason why the colony should continue importing any of it. Owing to scarcity of labor, a farmer in Newfoundland had to remain a small farmer because he was doing all his work by himself. The farm labor problem was aggravated by the attraction of the fishery. Fishermen could not be expected to take up farming voluntarily since farming was more arduous and the returns not so speedy, Downey explained. Rather, imported farm labor would tend to drift into the fishery where the returns were quicker and larger. From whatever angle he looked at it, there was no doubt in Downey's mind that the future of agricultural development depended on immigration.[30]

"In the face of there being a demand," what was the government doing to supply it, the Dominions Royal Commission wanted to know? Mews replied that the government had no system of encouraging immigration. There were no laws to facilitate immigration, no local promotional associations, no offers of free land, no inducements other than the duty-free importation of settlers' effects. "We make no effort of any importance to get people. We issue a little literature, but not in any quantity. The slim chances of success, in view of the greater attractions elsewhere, have probably limited activity in this direction." He went on to point out that "we have, however, enactments against undesirable immigrants, enabling us to deport those suffering from disease or likely to become a charge upon the public revenue." Was immigration not being pushed from "fear of interfering with existing interests," one of the commissioners wondered? Mews admitted that the fishermen would be dissatisfied with competition, but Newfoundland preferred people "who introduce capital and new methods; not the fisherman labourer." Still, he insisted that a population of working class immigrants "50 percent over what we have" could make "quite" a good living out of this land. For a member of the Commission it all boiled down to the question, "if you have vacant lands which afford opportunities, and you want population, somebody ought to get a hustle on?" "Yes, that is about it," Mews meekly agreed.[31]

In the future, Mews reasoned, "the scenic attractions of the island will assist in promoting immigration or in developing new industries, which in consequence will bring substantial additions to the population." Newfoundland envisioned itself as the "Norway of the New World" with its "healthful climate" and beautiful scenery.

Tourists, vacationers, hunters, and sports fishermen from America and Canada would be attracted in increasingly larger numbers to come on annual visits and "not improbably hereafter, as in some instances already, some of these people will settle here."[32] The 1911 edition of the officially authorized *Newfoundland Guide Book* promoted, apart from fishing and hunting opportunities, an abundance of "really good agricultural land" and "every inducement for cattle raising."[33]

In the series of popular and internationally distributed travellers' handbooks on all the countries of the world, launched by the German publisher Karl Baedeker and available in the main European languages, the volume on Newfoundland appeared first in 1894 and was reissued unrevised in 1900, 1907 and 1922. In it the Rev. Dr. Moses Harvey compared the grandeur of the coastal scenery to "the best that Norway has to show" and praised the "salubrious" climate—"evidenced by the robust healthy appearance of the people"—as preferable to the intense summer heats and fiercely cold winters of the United States and Canada. Although the area "presently" under culture did not exceed 60,000 acres, Harvey advertised "nearly 3,000,000 acres fit for settlement and capable of sustaining a large population."[34]

NEWFOUNDLAND'S FIRST REFUGEES

Instead of the desired British, northwest European, or North American immigration, however, the island found itself the destination of an unexpected and unwanted alien influx from eastern Europe, the Middle East, and the Far East: Russian-Polish Jews, so-called Syrians (or "Assyrians" as they called themselves sometimes) from the Ottoman Empire (i.e., Turkish nationals of primarily Maronite, Christian Syrian, and Druze, but also of Palestinian and Armenian background), and Chinese. The aliens entered Newfoundland from the 1890s on as settlers as well as onward migrants headed for the North American mainland. The number of those who stayed in Newfoundland was small and consisted at the peak of pre-World War I immigration of an estimated 200–300 Syrians, about 150 Chinese, and a smaller number of Yiddish-speaking Jews.[35] No reliable statistics are available.[36] The Syrians identified themselves as refugees from Turkish ethnic, economic, and political repression, and the Jews from Russian anti-Semitism. The unanticipated influx indicated that the colony did offer opportunities to settlers despite the exodus of native-born.

The coming of these "peculiar people," as one local journalist characterized Russian Jews,[37] was a highly visible event. Despite their small numbers and Newfoundland's quest for immigrants, "these foreign colonies" were soon perceived as "growing abnormally large."[38] From 1905 on, press comments exhibited a growing exasperation that there were already "too many" undesirable settlers here and that they were "driving our people out of the colony." This was obviously not the kind of "quality exchange" the colony's rulers had in mind and it was from this perspective that they became anxious to control immigration in the decade preceding the First World War. "A new country such as ours which is passing through a period of settlement," Minister of Justice Edward Morris announced in 1906, "should have laws which will encourage settlers of the [right] kind to build up our island." There was a growing consensus that Newfoundland needed a dichotomous immigration policy, one that held out inducements to the desirable kind of settlers while excluding or restricting those perceived as a "menace in the national upbuilding of the country."[39]

In the Newfoundland legislature some members openly articulated their reluctance to view the Maronite immigrants as a credit to society. In the debate over the Chinese exclusion bill, the value of the Chinese as well as of the Middle Eastern immigrants' contributions as productive settlers was questioned. Legislative Council Members James Angel (owner of Newfoundland's largest iron foundry) and John Anderson (a wholesale merchant) openly characterized the Syrians' and Maronites' habits and lifestyles as objectionable to the point of requiring restrictive legislation,[40] and provoked spokesmen of these immigrant groups to protest indignantly against such undeserved negative stereotyping. The Syrians defended themselves by drawing attention to their refugee origins and their contributions to Newfoundland.

Simon Tooton, representing a family of St. John's business pioneers, reminded the public in May 1906 that the Maronites came as Christian refugees:

> A number of us immigrated to this country, not for the purpose of trade or to earn a livelihood, but to enjoy the freedom and blessings of English institutions. In our own country we have suffered gross indignities at the hands of "the unspeakable Turk," laws are made which curtail our liberty of action and make us not the equal of the Mohammedans. Hence so many people immigrating. Not being skilled and workmen and lacking the advantages of an industrial and technical education, which is our misfortune and not our fault, we have engaged in an avocation which our mental capacities best fit us for. We have been in this country for some 17 or 18 years and during that time we have paid every man one hundred cents in the dollar, conformed to the laws of the country and through our

industry and perseverance we to-day neither ask nor want assistance from anyone save what our labor brings us.

In defense of the local Syrian community, wholesale merchant Kalleem Noah pointed out that

> We have stores in all the larger centres and besides many of our citizens are engaged in industries and have invested money in mines, sawmills and other channels which tend to develop the country and find employment for its people. . .there is not a month of the year in which my payments to the revenue do not run up into thousands. . .At all times and in all things I think I am worthy of citizenship in this colony. There are many others like me. We do not deserve the remarks of Mr. Angel.[41]

An indignant Thomas N. Sphyres wondered whether the prejudice against the Syrians might be attributable to certain parties who "lacked the industry and hard working capacity of the Syrian inhabitants, and so think they have a mission to denounce us." He reminded the public that he himself was the kind of productive settler the government tried to recruit and was entitled to the status of a Newfoundlander:

> I have been, Sir, seven years in Newfoundland and during the last five of these I have carried on an extensive business at Glenwood, dealing in general merchandise. I have been married and have two children—born Newfoundlanders—and I am a naturalized citizen. I have purchased land, cultivated it, erected buildings thereon and am the owner of cattle. I contribute a considerable sum towards the revenue of this colony, and have invested capital in its industries. Having done all this I think it is pretty hard to be made the subject of attack and abuse.

The bottom line, Ed Boulos maintained, was that the population of Assyrian Maronite background came to this country "in search of liberty of conscience and trade, and to escape the oppression of a hard and unjust ruler and that. . .we have freedom from oppression, justice and toleration in this, Britain's oldest colony."[42]

What seemed to particularly alarm the public was that, in conjunction with the arrival of alien settlers, the island found itself playing host to a transient class of alien sojourners who by default or design were seen as making Newfoundland a "halfway-house" for reaching the United States or Canada. Their alleged aim was to circumvent these countries' restrictions against diseased and impoverished immigrants. Many of these people, a local critic complained

> are suffering from such diseases and infirmities as would debar them from landing in the ordinary way from the Atlantic liners.

Most have very little money. Another feature of the transaction is, that those people are victimized by certain local agents who charge them an exorbitant rate for their tickets whilst pretending to render them assistance.[43]

He urged the enactment of regulations to prevent the landing of any diseased immigrant who would not pass the medical examination in American ports and who would become a charge on the state.[44] While the media exposed two cases of victimized migrants who were temporarily stranded on the island during the peak period of the prewar "alien" immigration (1905–1907),[45] the actual number of such incidents, judged by the news reports, seems to have been negligible. As far as the landing of diseased immigrants was concerned, the St. John's daily newspapers during the same period, despite their acute interest in undesirable aliens, were able to uncover only four passengers who had passed through Newfoundland and were found upon landing in Canada to be suffering from trachoma.[46] Even those diseased migrants who had been refused entry in Canadian ports were known to have no intention of staying in Newfoundland, as the Halifax Immigration Agent complained to St. John's in November 1906.[47]

The available evidence thus does not bear out allegations that aliens using Newfoundland as a way station constituted an economic or a medical danger. Such fears may have been inspired in part by press reports about negative experiences with the "new immigration" elsewhere, in part by Canadian denunciations of the alleged smuggling of undesirables from Newfoundland.[48] The depiction of this danger seems to have been as exaggerated as that about the "abnormally large" colonies of foreign settlers mentioned above. In fact, the benefits derived from the alien sojourners may well have outweighed their costs. The occasional stopover of emigrant ships on their way to Canada put money in the pockets of local baggage handlers, travel agents, boarding houses, eating establishments, retailers, taxis, railways, and coastal boats.

THE 1906 LEGISLATION

To the colonial elite, the contentious alien question raised the specter of unanticipated and uncontrollable social changes in the direction of an open, pluralistic, and multicultural society. Fearing an erosion of its foundations of power, the elite urgently sought to maintain the status quo. To this end, in the name of protecting the self-reliance and traditional homogeneity of the resident population, the government passed in 1906 Newfoundland's first two modern immigration acts: "An Act to regulate the Law with regard to Aliens" (the Aliens Act), and "An Act respecting the Immigration of Chinese Persons" (the Chinese Immigration Act). Both acts were designed to terminate the existing open-door policy and restrict entry. Prior to 1906, only the disembarkation of paupers and sick, old, and infirm persons was an indictable offence under an act which had been on the statute books since 1872.[49] But that law, useful as it had been, did not allow the deportation of immigrants who became paupers after they had become residents, the Minister of Justice complained in 1906.

The Aliens Act was intended not only to prevent the landing of non-Chinese aliens defined as "undesirable," but also to expel them if as residents they were found to be not fulfilling the requirements of the law. To achieve this end, the Aliens Act introduced formal immigration and deportation procedures, as well as restrictions to be administered by the Collector of Customs and a medical inspector. The Act declared—at a time of unique prosperity—persons without the means of "decently" supporting themselves and their dependents, as well as lunatics, idiots, and criminals, to be undesirable and subject to expulsion. Up to the time of the introduction of this act in April 1906, the Minister of Justice revealed, "he knew only one or two cases before in which that class of people were found in the colony" and the legislation would be of value only when any case would arise.[50]

As quoted at the beginning of this chapter, the 1906 Aliens Act entrenched the principle that refugees from political or religious persecution were entitled to asylum even if they arrived in poverty or subsequently became impoverished. The Act thus excluded what was presumed to be a small number of settlers from the general category of undesirables. The origins of this bold refugee policy, it may be significant to note, were unrelated to the fact that most of Newfoundland's new Middle Eastern and Jewish immigrants were refugees. In defending the proposed legislation in the House, the Minister of Justice did not elaborate on the meaning of the provision concerning refugees but admitted that the entire bill was a verbatim copy of an act introduced in Britain in 1905 and known as the Aliens Act. He considered it a "very perfect measure."[51] The British lawmakers intended their Aliens Act to serve as a filter for a new influx of unwanted immigrants, especially eastern European Jews, while at the same time preserving Britain's reputation as a bastion of freedom. Because refugees were still seen as individual activists rather than as impoverished masses fleeing persecution, it has been argued, the provision's inherent contradiction was not apparent at the time.[52] In legally entrenching a refugee's right to asylum, the

United Kingdom and Newfoundland—as far as could be ascertained the only countries legalizing this right—were half a century ahead of its universal acknowledgement by the United Nations.

Despite its apparent generosity towards refugees, the Aliens Act required that from then on, at least in theory, refugee claimants had to prove their case as refugees in order to qualify for admission without sufficient financial means. This was a departure from the traditional absence of any restrictions and a harbinger of more restrictions to come. In practice, refugees in Britain rarely had to prove their case before 1914, and Newfoundland's Colonial Secretary in 1911 confirmed in his reply to an inquiry from Whitehall about the deportation of undesirable aliens that "the amount of immigration here is very small, and the machinery provided under the Statute has been found to be quite effective. So far as Newfoundland is concerned there is practically no deportation of undesirables to the United Kingdom."[53]

The Chinese Immigration Act, even more than the Aliens Act, was a product of exaggerated perceptions. These were inspired by the negative stereotyping of Chinese by the media, the societies, and governments of western immigrant-receiving countries rather than of any negative effects Chinese immigration had on the resident population's economic self-reliance. Typically, a draft bill to restrict Chinese and Japanese immigration was first introduced in 1904 when Newfoundland had no more than a dozen Chinese and no Japanese newcomers. Modelled on Canada's Chinese Immigration Act of 1903,[54] it passed all three readings in the House of Assembly but was defeated in the Legislative Council. Newfoundland's 1906 legislation subjected Chinese immigrants to a head tax of $300 per person and inaugurated the practice—though no authorization existed for this in the act—to limit the local Chinese community to fewer than 200 members and to exclude Chinese women altogether.

Arguing the case in favor of Chinese exclusion, the Minister of Justice stressed four contradictory points: the possibility that the Chinese might increase greatly in number and become a factor in the labor market; their inferiority as laborers (competing only with washerwomen and servant girls) and, hence, utter unsuitability as colony builders; their menace to the health of society; and their alleged transient nature.[55] While associating every Chinese arrival with the specter of an impending "big Mongolian" invasion,[56] the media exploited the *Frolic* incident (41 Chinese being taken on the yacht *Frolic* to the United States) to create the impression that Newfoundland was a major base for smuggling Chinese to the mainland.[57] Chinese community spokesman Kim Lee charged that local authorities overstated the number of Chinese arriving and that they decried their conditions in order to substantiate an unfounded negative image.[58]

In the media the Chinese were portrayed as "heathen," importing leprosy, opium, and criminality, forming "the cruellest and most devilish secret societies," and living in filthy and subhuman squalor. Unfortunately, the abuse of these newcomers was not limited to the level of rhetoric. In their 1905 and 1906 coverage the daily press recorded that from the moment Chinese got off the train in St. John's they were usually surrounded by a crowd who jeered and followed them until they found refuge in one of the city's Chinese laundries. According to newspaper descriptions, teenage boys pelted Chinese regularly in the streets with rocks, sods, and offal, and, when the victims attempted to defend themselves, threatening crowds surrounded them and adults attacked them. Newspapers reported that local Chinese had their premises broken into, their windows and electric lights smashed, and filth thrown through their open doors. In June 1906, one Chinese man was stabbed and another beaten unconscious by two non-Chinese adults. The extraordinary degree of anti-Chinese violence in a community taking pride in its low crime rate shocked even newspaper editors into calling occasionally for better legal protection of the "inoffensive" Chinese, if for no other reason than the reputation of the city.[59]

Although the protection of the native-born worker against cheap Chinese labor was advertised as one of the main reasons for the anti-Chinese legislation of 1906, it may be questioned on several grounds whether the Act was, in fact, motivated by such a concern. For one, there were too few Chinese to constitute a threat to local labor. Also, these were prosperous times and there was a declared shortage of labor. Furthermore, borrowed negative stereotyping of Chinese was found to have permeated Newfoundland society.[60] The local elite ignored the inoffensive nature of the local Chinese and, instead, insisted that there were lessons to be learned from non-local experiences, namely, that the Chinese depressed the labor market wherever they went.

The evidence published in the three local daily papers refutes the assumption that Newfoundland's few Chinese immigrants constituted an economic threat. They established laundries, worked as servants and gardeners, launched a "new industry" of making brushes from seal whiskers, and responded to a seasonal shortage of labor in the Bell Island mines. They did not compete in any trade with local labor and actually appear to have served a largely beneficial economic role. The threats to local labor arose, essentially, from

Chinese arrivals guarded by police, Corner Brook, Newfoundland, 1940. Policeman left: Dolph Nash; policeman right: Stan Martin; woman fifth from right: Mary Murphy, housekeeper at police station. Credit: Margaret Chang.

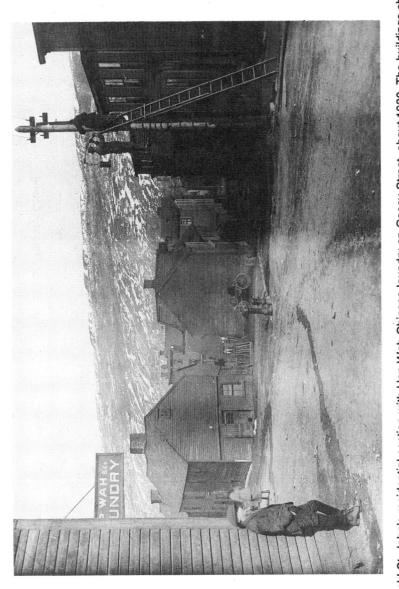

View of old St. John's residential section with Hop Wah Chinese laundry on Casey Street, about 1930. The buildings shown in this picture no longer exist. Credit: PANL.

Jim Lee's Chinese laundry on Casey Street, St. John's, 1930s. Credit: Margaret Chang.

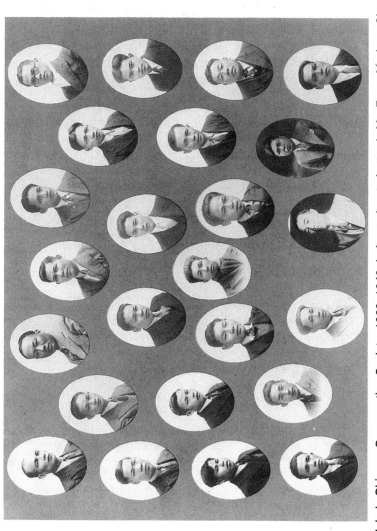

Members of St. John's Chinese Co-operative Society, 1939–1940. Left row (top to bottom): Mr. Fong, Mr. Lee, Chan Fong, Harry Tom; 2nd row from left (top to bottom): William Fong, Mr. Seto, Wing Fong; 3rd row from left:Davey Fong, Mr. Ing (nephew of Peter Ing), Hayford Fong, Lee Pong; 4th row: Peter Ing, George Chong; 5th row: Harvey Fong, Mr. Chan, Victor Inglouen; right row: William Ping, Mr. Ing, Mr ? (owner of West End Laundry), Charlie Chong. Credit: Margaret Chang.

Representatives of Newfoundland Chinese community with visiting Dr. Chao-Ying Shih, Consul-General for China in Canada, 20 October 1940. He spoke to every member of the Chinese community, called on every Chinese establishment, and attended meetings of the local Chinese War Relief Association, the Tai Mei Society, the Hong Hang Society, and the Chinese Co-operative Society. The absence of Chinese females reflects the rigorously enforced immigration policy of excluding Chinese women from Newfoundland. Bottom row center with hat: Chinese Consul; to his left: Charlie Au, Kim Lee, unknown, Charlie Foo; to the Consul's right: Gordon Higgins, Davey Fong and Tim Lee: Hayford Fong; right row 2nd up: Mr. Chan, 4th up: Frank Wong; between George Higgins and Davey Fong: George Hong. Credit: William Ping.

unconfirmed rumors—for example, that "500 Chinese coolies" were about to be employed in the Bell Island mines[61]—and from the imagination. The lawmakers' appeal to standard economic arguments appears to have served the purpose of concealing and buttressing largely different motives.

It is noteworthy that pressures for the restriction of foreign immigration did not appear to originate with those strata that experienced a heavy drain of emigrants, i.e., the rural population, or with the urban labor movement. (The St. John's Longshoremen's Protective Union endorsed the 1906 Chinese Immigration Bill only after it had been introduced by the government.) Rather, entry restrictions were initiated by the class whose equivalent in Canada and the United States had promoted the admission of cheap foreign labor.

MANIFESTATIONS OF ANTI-FOREIGN SENTIMENT

The public debate about the expediency of restricting "alien" immigration to Newfoundland brought to light an apparently ingrained anti-foreign sentiment. The pervasiveness of the stigma attached to the Chinese is indicated by the media's generous employment of a wide spectrum of pejorative ethnic tags. These ranged from "Chinee" and "Celestials" to "pigtails" and "Chinks." In the Legislative Council the conviction was voiced that Chinese were "really an inferior type, lower on the scale of humanity," and aliens like them "could never be expected to become what might be termed 'Newfoundlanders'."[62] Such sentiments seemed quite out of proportion to the very small number of visiting and resident foreigners and the actual or potential economic problems attributable to them.[63] While some of the ethnic slurs were borrowed clichés that mirrored the racism underlying contemporary Western perceptions of China and the Chinese, others were homemade labels reflecting ignorance and suspicion of foreign cultures and their local representatives. Typically, non-resident ethnic groups like the Japanese were also subjected to negative stereotyping and even native-born Newfoundlanders of French descent were not spared.[64]

Dislike and fear of foreigners is endemic to human society and has various roots and causes. As a socio-cultural phenomenon it is espoused by different social strata for a variety of historic, economic, social, political, and cultural reasons. In Canada and the United States, for instance, xenophobia and nativism[65] have largely been exhibited as reactions to a substantial influx of foreign immigrants,[66] while in Newfoundland an influx of minute numbers of foreigners, or even the anticipation of their impending arrival, has sufficed to evoke such attitudes. Suspicion towards outsiders is deeply rooted in Newfoundland's historic experience of geographic and cultural isolation and was reinforced by the lack of any significant immigration since the early nineteenth century.

Newfoundland's European settlers populated hundreds (1,200–1,300 in 1908) of tiny fishing communities (known as "outports") located in remote harbors as near to the fishing grounds as possible. In the absence of immigration this "necklace" of coastal communities experienced isolation from the world and from each other as a stark fact of life. Opportunities for education and cross-cultural contacts were scarce or non-existent and the church was often the only available source of spiritual nourishment and enlightenment. It was possible for community life to remain undisturbed for generations by outside influences.

Historically isolated from the rest of the New World, Newfoundland's cultural landscape is considered unique with its rich repository of Old-World folkways. Anthropologists and folklorists have attributed the abiding popularity of the ancient folk custom of Christmas mumming in Newfoundland to the close-knit outport communities' negative fascination with strangers. In these small coastal communities where everyone knows everyone, the role of strangers is determined by pervasive intimacy in social relations and scarcity of outsiders. Disguising themselves as mummers allows people who live in intimate social contact to appear to each other in the exciting role of the mysterious, unpredictable, potentially malevolent, and frequently dreaded role of persons who have no place in society.[67] It comes, therefore, as no surprise that, as folklore researchers personally experienced during their fieldwork in different parts of Newfoundland,

> people may feel some degree of apprehension about the representatives of different racial, linguistic and even religious groups within their community, and such "strangers" may become the target of suspicion, gossip and legend. It is a relatively easy transition from this to their use as threatening figures. They are, as it were, aliens within the community, and the fear of them, as Firestone observes, is "a means by which adults can displace generally acquired hostility."[68]

In cultural terms Newfoundland has been aptly referred to as an "island-arrested society," although its "outward-looking" English-bourgeois merchant class was admittedly "very distant from the folk culture of the outports."[69] The geographically conditioned distrust of the outsider and his ways was reinforced by ethnocultural isolation. This was, in part, a function of the remarkable ethnic homogeneity of Newfoundland's founding peoples of English, Irish, and Scottish extraction. Most of them had immigrated from southwest England and southeast Ireland in the eighteenth and early nineteenth centuries when the fishery was prospering in Newfoundland. Cultural geographers have noted that nowhere else in North America did such a large proportion of the resident population come from such localized places of origin over so long a period.[70] In the mid-1930s Joseph R. Smallwood observed that an Englishman visiting St. John's "would be deeply impressed by the English bias of the people and of the town." He would probably consider the city "more English than England, more loyal than any part of the Empire." Smallwood pinpointed the educated St. John's business elite as the element that had best preserved the English tradition "in modes of living, accent, manner of speech, dress and general outlook."[71]

Teacher and *Evening Telegram* news reporter in the pre-World War I era, P.K. Devine, conveyed a different reason that suspicion of outsiders was a natural and justifiable instinct. The tenor of his invectives indicates an historically acquired inferiority complex, a sense of having always been unfairly treated by fate. Urging Newfoundlanders to uphold their traditions against "those who come amongst us to get an easy living, and take from us the best fruits of our heritage, by imposing their inane insincere manners and customs upon us," he summed up his prewar perceptions in the following harangue:

> There is no reason why we should defer and apologize to strangers and accord them a merit which may not exist, but which we think they can impose on us because they are strangers. . .Let a well-dressed, glib-tongued stranger come among us from East or West, and he will get our good will and our money, with an ease that will surprise himself. . .Let it be mining shares or bogland, breakfast food, rheumatism cure or spectacles, the stranger will reap a golden harvest and no questions asked. Let a local man, whom we all know, try to do, in a sincere bona fide and honest way, what the foreign Cogliostro [sic] does in a slick, smiling, fraudulent way, and he will thank the stars if he is not kicked out of the office.[72]

The pervasiveness of this engrained sentiment was noted by two engineers from the Montreal Engineering Company. In 1922 they came to St. John's to evaluate the requirements for taking over and upgrading of the Reid-owned Light and Power Company. Posing the question to what extent the cultivation of anti-foreignism was impeding industrial diversification and economic growth, they observed that

while everyone, who has come into contact with him, has a high
regard for the Newfoundlander, it should be remembered that his
insular life has made him suspicious of outsiders. It was this and
the impression that the country was being exploited that hampered
the Reids in their efforts to develop the resources of Newfoundland.
In any operations conducted there, great care must be taken to
avoid offending the susceptibilities of the Newfoundlander. The
Company must retain its local character. Our function must be to
offer advice. . .and to work through the local management rather
than to take any active part in the conduct of affairs.[73]

The susceptibilities of Newfoundlanders towards outsiders have
become evident in various situations and in different ways. In the
rural districts in-migrants (including Newfoundlanders from other
areas) into an established outport community tended to be viewed
and treated as "strangers." There the non-British alien was just
another outsider. In the capital city of St. John's, however, non-
Anglo-Saxon immigrants tended to be classified as "foreigners,"[74]
often into their second and third generations.[75] The depth of this
sentiment surfaced as late as 1989, when a local media debate
instructed the public that the term "Newfoundlander" should be
confined to the native-born and did not include immigrants and
"mainlanders."[76]

Puzzling to any student of inter-cultural and inter-ethnic relations is the entrenched spectrum of classifications by which various
types of non-native residents have been categorized in Newfoundland. The label "Come from Aways" has, for instance, since its first
documented appearance in 1940, been found attached to North
Americans coming to live in Newfoundland.[77] Immigrants from the
British Isles, it has been maintained, have become accepted as
Newfoundlanders within their lifetimes while native-born residents
of French descent whose ancestors settled on Newfoundland's West
Coast centuries ago have been stigmatized as "Jackatars."[78] A local
resident of Middle Eastern descent or any person with swarthy
complexion and foreign features was frequently tagged a "tally man"
or "tally."[79]

The subtleties of local xenophobia have not escaped such
veteran politicians as Alfred B. Morine (1857–1944), a member of
the Newfoundland elite, although born in neighboring Nova Scotia.
To him the "superiority complex" of Newfoundland's native-born
residents and their self-identification as "the salt of the earth" was
an integral feature of life in the colony. During his long public career,
Morine claims to have witnessed more "narrow prejudice" against
"aliens" in St. John's than in the outports, perhaps because, he
believed, aliens were more numerous and competitive in the city.

Englishmen were not so much disliked as Canadians, Morine noticed, and "an 'alien' (as all are called who are not native born). . . may sometimes feel 'out in the cold.'" Morine explains this complex as "a form of loyalty to home and country not uncommon in small communities," a kind of "instinctive protection against dreaded insolence of outsiders, and. . .a great protection against doubt when times are hard and skies are clouded."[80]

The First World War exacerbated xenophobia in two ways. First, it generated hate propaganda and anti-enemy alien sentiments. In the conduct of total war, psychological warfare was employed without restraints. The aim was to brainwash the public into embracing a view of the enemy as a subhuman barbarian who deserved to be despised and, hence, fought to the finish. The propaganda war succeeded in transforming positive prewar images of Germans into negative ones for some time to come. Second, World War I legitimized and encouraged the exhibition of anti-foreign attitudes against an amorphous category of official suspects labelled enemy aliens. For the Newfoundland Patriotic Association (which was responsible for the administration of the war effort) the desirability of restricting the movement of Newfoundland's small community of aliens remained an "uncontroversial" issue from the outset.[81] The only local politician known to have taken up the defence of the rights of resident aliens was A.B. Morine. Wartime suspects included not only all residents of German-speaking or Austro-Hungarian background, but also Yiddish-speaking Jewish immigrants from Russia.[82] Escalating wartime xenophobia resulted in the social ostracism, internment, deportation of enemy aliens. Although the apprehensions in World War I of enemy attacks and sabotage proved as unfounded as the widespread allegations of spying, those residents stigmatized and penalized as enemy aliens were left with the stigma attached to them. In fact, the legend of Germans acting as spies and saboteurs has survived in Newfoundland to this day.[83]

The outbreak of World War II revived what one published letter termed "malicious" and "highly unjustifiable" accusations of disloyalty against residents of foreign descent by certain fellow citizens of St. John's. On 18 April 1940 spokesperson for Syrian Newfoundlanders Hadet-El-Joubbe protested in the *Evening Telegram* that

> there are people who have the bare-faced audacity to look down on the Syrian people here and regard them as "Foreigners" and "Slackers." To them I will say, such an ignorant attitude is highly discreditable and the very epitome of all that is low and mean.
>
> The Syrian-Newfoundlander, as well as the Syrian in general, has

proven his worth, and will continue to do so, despite all who look down from their haughty and despicable perch, and chose to regard them as the very dirt under their feet.

Should they reflect for a moment, they would realize that the Syrian-Newfoundlander is every inch a citizen as much as they are and as such, is just as anxious and concerned, if not more so, for the welfare and prosperity of Newfoundland and the British Empire.

The article reminded newspaper readers that residents of Syrian descent were proud to be an asset to their adopted country. Not only were they descendants of the ancient Mediterranean civilization of the Phoenicians who gave the world the alphabet, they also strove for financial success and were far more conspicuous as donors than as people seeking charity. "Proud and highly appreciative of their British citizenship," the article stated, residents of Syrian descent gave their lives to their adopted country in the Great War of 1914 and were again coming forward. In proportion to their numbers in Newfoundland they were deserving of commendation, the article stated. It also referred to one Syrian from Bell Island who made three vain attempts to enlist before he was finally accepted.

Hadet-El-Joubbe also wanted to correct what he termed "a false impression quite prevalent locally," namely, that "the Syrian people here are not 'Tallies' or 'Italians' and being quite a distinct race, are not associated with the people of Italy in any manner whatever." His protest draws attention to the stereotypical image, persisting long after their immigration, of Syrian Newfoundlanders as "shady," profit-conscious "peddlar[s] from Syria or Lebanon or some such place from the Middle East."[84]

To be sure, the point is not to suggest that Newfoundland had a monopoly on xenophobia in the world. But it would be equally fallacious to assume that such sentiment was non-existent. The Newfoundland government's approach to immigration and ethnic relations fostered nativist attitudes by propagating borrowed perceptions of alleged threats to the economic self-reliance and tranquillity of its closed, ethnically homogeneous society. No doubt, Newfoundland's 1906 immigration legislation was influenced by the tightening of American and Canadian entry controls. On the other hand, Newfoundland officials also realized that their country was in a radically different situation from that of the United States and Canada. These two countries faced such large tides of immigrants that they could afford to restrict access to desirable categories at a time when Newfoundland lamented its striking inability to attract newcomers.

Newfoundland's professed quest for settlers is not easy to square with its policy of deterring, restricting, and excluding the only types of immigrants eager to come and settle. Not even the statutory promise of asylum appeared designed to facilitate the admission of refugees or to procure settlers otherwise unavailable. Legalizing the entrenchment of the elite's manipulative privileges over society emerges as the only comprehensible objective of the 1906 legislation. If Newfoundland had truly wanted settlers, it would have had to adopt a more liberal and active approach to immigration and to counter or neutralize xenophobia, as the Canadian government did in its efforts to draw to the prairies such culturally diverse colonists as Mennonites, Doukhobors, and East European Jews.

"Newfoundland—Attractive to 4 Capitalist, Settler and Tourist"

The Quest for Immigration, Exclusion and Deportation, 1919–1934

THE QUEST FOR IMMIGRANTS AND SETTLERS, 1919–1926

The established pattern of Newfoundland's pre-World War I immigration policy persisted after the First World War. Partly because there was virtually no immigration despite severe Canadian and American entry restrictions (and the coveted British settlers remained as elusive as ever), for a number of years there was no new immigration legislation. From 1924 on, however, external and internal factors conspired to precipitate an expansion of immigration controls that virtually closed Newfoundland's gates to foreign immigration.

The first postwar restrictions were motivated by war-related sentiment. In 1919 the government refused to allow the return of a family of Moravian missionaries deported from Labrador in 1916 for alleged disloyalty.[1] In 1920, an "Act Concerning Former Enemy Aliens" prohibited the landing of any former enemy alien for a period of three years.[2] These measures were of little consequence, and, apart from them, Newfoundland appeared not in a hurry to adopt Canadian- or American-type immigration controls. Canada in 1919 and 1920 excluded immigrants on account of their customs, culture, and perceived unassimilability and indiscriminately deported non-British immigrants on account of their political beliefs. The United States introduced progressively restrictive quota controls which reduced admission in 1921 to 3 percent of each foreign-born group resident in 1910, and in 1924 to 2 percent of the foreign-born groups resident in 1890. In both countries the function of immigration legislation had shifted from one allowing free entry, except for certain prohibited classes, before the war to one of prohibited entry, except for certain permitted classes, after the war.

The war had brought a brief interlude of exceptional prosperity to Newfoundland and on 6 March 1919 Newfoundland's High Commissioner in London Edgar R. Bowring was convinced that "there will be a considerable emigration [from Britain] in the near future." He expressed the aspirations of a joint meeting of the High Commissioners and Agents General with the [British] Government Emigration Committee, held at the Colonial Office in London on 5 March 1919. At this meeting a recommendation by the Government Emigration Committee was discussed that considered "an even and well organised flow of population from this country to other parts of the Empire" to be desirable and a distinction "between settlement overseas within the Empire as opposed to emigration to foreign countries" to be essential. Emigration was to be encouraged by providing increased facilities for transport within the Empire and special treatment to women (of whom there was a surplus in Britain and a deficiency in the Dominions), to ex-servicemen and to widows and orphans. While assisted passage schemes for general emigration were left to the various governments of the Empire, ex-servicemen were to be offered allowances and advances in connection with opportunities for land settlement, educational and agricultural training, etc., in any part of the Empire which they might choose, provided they were *bona fide* intending to settle on the land or had received definite offers of employment.[3]

Newfoundland's Minister of Agriculture and Mines W.W. Halfyard confirmed in April 1919 that there were "very frequent applications from parties in England and other places, who are desirous of emigrating to this country." Both Halfyard and Bowring agreed that emigrants ended up preferring other dominions because Newfoundland offered no incentives of any kind, such as assistance with the passage and starting expenses on the land. Unlike in Canada, no grant was given of 100 acres of free land, and the land available to settlers was mostly covered with forest—a tedious and expensive chore to clear. Newfoundland had no adequate staff of surveyors, no surveyed localities for settlement, no roads and communications for marketing the produce, and no general policy with regard to these questions. Almost all the prerequisites for soliciting settlers, including promotional literature, were missing.[4] An official British guide for prospective female settlers in the Oversea Dominions, published in 1919, contained no information about

Newfoundland except the claim that "the climate is healthy. It is milder than that of Canada."[5]

What prompted the government to take concrete steps in the direction of encouraging immigration was a request from E.R. Bowring in London "that ex-soldiers should be granted a free passage to any Dominion they cared to go to and possibly a grant to help them settle on the land and tide over the unproductive period." The request was endorsed by the Civil Re-Establishment Committee in St. John's. In March 1920 the Executive Council appointed a sub-committee to consider the matter. It developed a policy of "land settlement for ex-service men" which provided for loans on easy terms of repayment for anyone who had already worked for two summers on an approved farm and passed certain courses at an agricultural college. Of 68 requests for application forms 40 actually applied, and 3 out of 4 interviewees were judged suitable candidates. Five men eventually fulfilled the conditions for a loan and in October 1920 were accepted by the Land Settlement Board to be trained at Newfoundland government expense in Truro, Nova Scotia.[6]

A simultaneous initiative undertaken by the government was promotional. In 1920 no advertising literature was available for distribution to prospective settlers because D.W. Prowse's officially distributed *Newfoundland Guide Book* (London, 1905; reprinted in 1911) ran out of print. The government now wanted a book that would devote less space to sports and more "to the various industries of the Dominion, and the possibilities here for the investment of capital and the development of the Island generally." It was therefore decided to commission 2,000 revised copies of a handbook by Dr. H.M. Mosdell, editor of the *Daily Star*. This book appeared in 1920 under the title *Newfoundland: Its Manifold Attractions for the Capitalist, the Settler and the Tourist*. The General Passenger Agent of the Reid Newfoundland Company, F.E. Pittman, expressed his intention to order "perhaps 1,000" copies for distribution to different tourist agencies in Canada, the United States, and "the Old Country." A blurb in the local press (12 April 1922) read as follows: "NEWFOUNDLAND—Attractive to capitalist, settler and tourist. Published by direction of the Nfld Government. Illustrated. Send a copy to your friends abroad."[7]

Mosdell's book featured Newfoundland in unrestrained superlatives as "a country of infinite possibility and manifold attractions." Its people, depicted to be "hospitable to the highest degree and [to] welcome the stranger with open arms," enjoyed "one of the most salubrious climates in the world." Their conditions were enviable indeed, Mosdell submitted, "compared to the pale factory workers, the toilers in the great cities of Europe and America who breathe an impure atmosphere in crowded tenements, often amidst conditions that depress health and spirits and shorten life." Because for centuries the interior was neglected in favor of the fisheries, Newfoundland now had 4.5 million acres of agricultural land available for settlement which were capable of "sustaining in comfort a very large additional population." Lumbering and mineral resources, too, were capable of great development and of "providing employment for many more thousands of workmen than at present." Mosdell maintained, that

> these are not the mere random assertions of over-enthusiastic optimists; they are sustained by solid facts which cannot be brushed aside. The evidence in support of these conclusions is derived mainly from reports of the Geological Survey of the Government of Newfoundland. . .as well as from the accounts given by residents, by intelligent and observant travellers and others who have visited and are well acquainted with the various sections of the country. All these when combined constitute a mass of reliable evidence that utterly disproves the idea so commonly held regarding the barrenness of the soil of Newfoundland and must revolutionise the ideas of settlers and capitalists regarding a much-misrepresented and much-neglected country.[8]

In concluding Mosdell quoted Canadian agricultural expert Andrew MacPhail who, on a visit to Newfoundland to advise on potato-culture, was reported to have recommended that if he were to embark in farming as a business, he would not go to Prince Edward Island, or to Quebec, or to Saskatchewan (in each of which he owned a farm), nor would he be attracted by the much-boasted opportunities of the Canadian northwest, "but I would come right here to St. John's where, under the beneficial influence of a 40 per cent tariff, I would make a comfortable living at the expense of the rest of the community."[9]

In London meanwhile, ex-Newfoundland Prime Minister Morris pulled out all the stops to solicit British immigrants. What he had in mind was a more desirable kind than had hitherto arrived. In February 1922 he was reported to have stated that "what looked like the vanguard of an immigration had come in the shape of 3 or 4 not too reputable Jews upon the *Sachem* and they certainly were not at all desirable immigrants for Newfoundland."[10] Morris' unequivocal appeals alerted Government House in St. John's to the likelihood that "many young people might try to come out from England without any proper prospect in front of them." In April 1922 Governor C. Alexander Harris decided to draft a note to Secretary of State for the Colonies Winston Churchill which couched Newfoundland's attractions in more cautious terms. Newfoundland had much unemployment, Harris conceded, but

> As a home for the settler Newfoundland seems to me to offer good prospects within limits which need to be carefully understood. It has a hard climate with a long winter—exceedingly healthy for those who can stand roughing it. It's [sic] capacity for production is circumscribed by its climate. But once a man gets a start on a small farm relying on grazing, with potatoes as his main crop and only occasionally ripening oats, he can make a good but hard livelihood. If a man has a farm near the sea he can also do some fishing. This is the ideal combination for Nfland. And in the present difficulties of the world this should appeal to some men and women.[11]

A semi-official British publication on Empire settlement emphasized as late as 1927 that Newfoundland's forest and mineral resources and her trade were so significant that the island "sorely needs more capital, more labour, and more enterprise." But in the absence of settlers it was comforting to learn that "the island is year by year attracting more and more tourists, whose encouraging reports may induce to permanent settlement."[12]

To visitors and prospective immigrants the Newfoundland government promoted the impression that its admission policy was liberal. An official guide to Newfoundland's salmon rivers published in 1928 proudly advertised: "no passports are required, and there are no prohibition laws to annoy the visitor."[13] The Jewish Colonisation Association of Montreal, after having requested government information about entry regulations in January 1926, retained the belief until 1934 that there were practically no restrictions on European immigration except the provision that immigrants should be in good health and have means of supporting themselves.[14] The notion that Newfoundland was open and welcomed settlers stubbornly survived the imposition of drastic controls in the late 1920s and came to haunt the government and the public throughout the 1930s.

Newfoundland's apparent openness was actually an expression of the continued quest for "desirable," i.e. independent British settlers, which characterized the colony's prewar immigration policy. The beginning construction in 1923 of the combined paper mill and hydro-electric power project on the Humber River promised employment for 2,500 men and a growing demand for skilled labor.[15] However, even this huge industrial project did not bring the anticipated influx of immigrants. In 1924 the balance of immigration (consisting largely of returning Newfoundlanders) over emigration was only about 2,500.[16] In January 1925 the Colonial Secretary in St. John's still expected that the development of the work at the Humber would "no doubt attract people of other nationalities from the neighbouring Continent."[17]

The irony of the situation with regard to immigration was summed up in February 1925 in lawyer Gordon Bradley's plea to Justice Minister W.J. Higgins to adopt a more active policy of promoting immigration:

> In the past Newfoundland seems to have held out no attractions sufficient to induce prospective settlers to come amongst us. . .The acquiring of expert mechanics is needed in Newfoundland at present and in view of the industrial expansion which is now and will probably be hereafter taking place it will be a calamity if we are not able to meet their demand. It is now well known to you and me that there has been a shortage of skilled labour. . .during the past year or so and this shortage is likely to increase rather than to lessen unless we find additional men somewhere.[18]

As late as the spring of 1926 the management of the Power and Paper Company in Corner Brook confirmed this demand for foreign skilled labor at a time when the press hailed the island's paper industry as having "developed to an extent equal to the cod fishery."[19] A statement read to the House of Assembly revealed that 2,800 of the company's 3,200 employees were Newfoundlanders and that skilled operators still had to be imported from Canada. The largest proportion of imported labor was employed in the manufacturing process. Of course, it was always company policy to hire Newfoundlanders whenever possible, a company manager stated reassuringly. "It all depends how quickly they can adapt themselves to the special conditions required in our industry."[20]

THE IMPACT OF CANADIAN AND AMERICAN IMMIGRATION CONTROLS

By 1926, however, a combination of new pressures and old fears had prodded Newfoundland's immigration policy in the direction of excluding and deporting foreign immigrants. The pressures derived from the progressive tightening of Canadian and American immigration restrictions gave rise to old fears about the potential impact of an imagined foreign influx on the crisis-ridden Newfoundland economy. The nature of the pressures exerted by Canadian and American immigration policies became manifest as early as 1921 in two unrelated incidents: the deportation of Newfoundland-born residents and exclusion of transient workers, and the threat of

Canadian retaliation if Newfoundland admitted foreign immigrants who had been refused by Canada.

In June 1921 Newfoundland's Minister of Justice received word that more than 200 of his countrymen had been deported from Sydney. They had arrived in Canada by the steamer *Kyle* without being able to fulfill the requirements of the immigration law which was being thoroughly enforced. Only six months before, the St. John's press had greeted with equanimity a Canadian Order-in-Council which required that "no immigrant, of the mechanic artisan or laborer classes, shall be allowed to land in Canada, unless he possesses in his own right money to the amount of $250, and in addition transportation to his destination in Canada."[21] It was not expected to affect the traditional movement of labor from Newfoundland to Canada, especially Cape Breton, because it had been official Canadian policy to treat migrants and seasonal workers from Newfoundland "very much" as Canadians.[22] Now these men, having spent their last penny on transportation, had to return home destitute.[23] Recurring Canadian deportations of Newfoundlanders are documented at first sporadically—in 1923, 1925, 1928—and, after the Privy Council's 1927 resolution of the Labrador boundary dispute in favor of Newfoundland, as a chronic problem.

The United States, too, abandoned the practice, reaffirmed in the 1907 Act Regulating the Immigration of Aliens, of granting exemption to persons who had resided for at least one year in Newfoundland from its four dollar immigration head tax.[24] From 1922 on, Newfoundlanders were deported in increasing numbers from the United States, either on the grounds of coming in conflict with the law there, or entering a charitable institution, or becoming a public charge. In 1927 Newfoundland's Minister of Justice complained that he was troubled to an unprecedented degree with deportations from the United States, "where they attempt first to deport the person to Canada and Canada denies responsibility."[25] Before entering America, some of the deportees from there had even acquired Canadian nationality, but to no avail.

The closure of the American and Canadian gates reversed Newfoundland migration trends. While 1926 population statistics still showed a net loss by emigration of 2,818, returning Newfoundlanders were mainly responsible for the immigration gain of 2,867 in 1931. Unable to find work at home, these expatriates became a charge on the government at a time when the country could least afford to support them. On top of that, the local economy lost the cash remittances—estimated to amount to $1 million a year—which these former emigrants would normally have sent home.[26]

PUBLIC NOTICE

As a number of Newfoundlanders, proceeding to the United States of America, have recently been stopped at Vanceboro, on the American Border, and sent back to Newfoundland, being thereby subjected to inconvenience and expense, the following extract from the United States Immigration Laws is published for general information—

"That the following classes of aliens shall be excluded from admission into the United States: All idiots, imbeciles, feeble-minded persons, epileptics, insane persons; persons who have had one or more attacks of insanity at any time previously; persons of constitutional psychopathic inferiority; persons with chronic alcoholism; paupers; professional beggars; vagrants; persons afflicted with tuberculosis in any form or with a loathsome or dangerous contagious disease; persons not comprehended within any of the foregoing excluded classes who are found to be and are certified by the examining surgeon as being mentally or physically defective, such physical defect being of a nature which may affect the ability of such alien to earn a living; persons who have been convicted of or admit having committed a felony or other crime or misdemeanor involving moral turpiture; * * * * * persons hereinafter called contract laborers, who have been induced, assisted, encouraged, or solicited to migrate to this country by offers or promises of employment, whether such offers or promises are true or false, or in consequence of agreements, oral, written or printed, express or implied, to perform labor in this country of any kind, skilled or unskilled; persons who have come in consequence of advertisements for laborers printed, published, or distributed in a foreign country; persons likely to become a public charge; persons who have been deported under any of the provisions of this act, and who may seek admission again within one year from the date of such deportation, unless prior to their reembarkation at a foreign port or their attempt to be admitted from foreign contiguous territory the Secretary of Labor shall have consented to their re-applying for admission; persons whose tickets or passage is paid for with the money of another, or who are assisted by others to come, unless it is affirmatively and satisfactorily shown that such persons do not belong to one of the foregoing excluded classes; persons whose ticket or passage is paid for by any corporation, association, society, municipality or foreign Government, either directly or indirectly; stowaways, except that any such stowaway, if otherwise admissable, may be admitted in the discretion of the Secretary of Labor. * * * * * * * *"

In view of the above, Newfoundlanders who may contemplate proceeding to the United States should first satisfy themselves that they do not fall within any of the classes of Immigrants therein specified.

ARTHUR MEWS,
Deputy Colonial Secretary.

Department of the Colonial Secretary,
St. John's, Newfoundland,
June 20th, 1922,

PUBLIC NOTICE warning Newfoundlanders to heed United States immigration restrictions, 20 June 1922. Credit: PANL.

In 1929 Newfoundland authorities protested that American and Canadian deportation practices were very unfair to Newfoundland. Newfoundland families who had emigrated with small children were torn asunder when one child would be deported many years later for an infraction of the law. A typical case was that of a Newfoundlander who "goes to Canada, acquires Canadian nationality, stays there for years, then enters the United States illegally; Canada says he has lost Canadian nationality, and the States deport him back to us." A high-ranking Newfoundland government official lamented in March 1929 that "we are always in difficulties with U.S.A. and Canada, because both of them are willing to take all the good emigrants we can send them, but they pick out the bad ones and return them to us to fill our gaols and asylums."[27]

In dealing with the dilemma of having to take back destitute deportees who had emigrated long ago, the Newfoundland government had three choices: to retaliate in kind by deporting residents of Canadian and American origin, to refuse to take emigrated Newfoundlanders deported from the mainland back as citizens, and to enact barriers to immigration and provisions for deportations similar to those of Canada and the United States. Since emigration from Canada to Newfoundland was negligible compared with migrations in the opposite direction, retaliation in kind would be ineffective.[28] As to the possibility of refusing to receive direct deportations from Canada, the Canadian Minister of Immigration explicitly warned that such action "would of course, immediately necessitate the Government of Canada giving consideration to the necessity of prohibiting the admission to Canada of immigrants from Newfoundland."[29] That left only the choice of adopting American- or Canadian-type entry restrictions for migrants seeking admission to Newfoundland.

The pressure for restrictions was reinforced by a chain of events which originated in October 1921 with an inquiry from the British Passport Control Officer in Brussels. The official transmitted a message through the Secretary of State for the Colonies, Winston Churchill, wondering whether visas for Newfoundland may be granted to a "large number" of emigrants who had been refused permission to land in Canada. The immigrants, on their way back to Antwerp, were neither impoverished nor diseased, but apparently had arrived without the requisite visas shortly after new Canadian visa regulations had come into force. It was the idea of the shipping companies to get these people to Newfoundland and from there to Canada. Newfoundland's options in the matter were reduced by the non-British background of the immigrants in question and the danger that Canada might terminate the preferential treatment traditionally accorded to Newfoundland migrants. The Governor of Canada warned that

> If a movement of these people takes place to Newfoundland, it would compel the adoption of more rigid inspection of passengers travelling between Newfoundland and Canada. At present time Newfoundlanders are treated very much as Canadians and there is little hindrance put in their way in coming to Canada but it is intimated that the Immigration Department will absolutely exclude all Continental immigrants who land in Newfoundland and later seek entry into Canada.

The Newfoundland cabinet therefore agreed that "it is most undesirable for emigrants, and particularly alien emigrants, to be admitted to Newfoundland at this time, when it is becoming increasingly difficult for even our own people to find employment." And the Governor of Newfoundland hastened to reassure Churchill that "in no way would the Government of Newfoundland be a party to the attempt of agents or Aliens to encourage emigrants to evade the Canadian immigration regulations."[30]

Representations from Canadian immigration officials in January 1925 indicated that "quite a number of undesirables" had been entering Canada through Newfoundland and that they would welcome cooperation with Newfoundland officials to stop such practice. The Colonial Secretary commented that "Newfoundland seems to be the only country at the present time which has no definite immigration policy backed by legal enactment." At the same time inquiries were received from Furness Withy steamship agents and the American Vice Consul on behalf of American clients about entry and settlement requirements for prospective Italian, Greek, and Middle Eastern immigrants. Some of the queries had ominous implications: "Would it be necessary for a foreigner. . .to use his own name or could he book passage under whichever name he wishes? Are there any restrictions other than being healthy in body and character applicable to foreigners arriving at St. John's on a visit?"[31]

The realization of Newfoundland's easy accessibility added to the growing apprehensions. Newfoundland's coastline was dotted with many harbors with shipping connections to European countries, Canada, the United States, and St. Pierre, and immigrants determined to enter the island might do so through any one of them. Immigrants were known to have disembarked from ore boats coming to Bell Island and other vessels landing in Carbonear, Botwood, Corner Brook, Port aux Basques, Lamaline, and Fortune. Nonetheless, the volume of such immigration was acknowledged by the Newfoundland government to be negligible,[32] even from countries such as Spain, Portugal, Italy, and Greece with whom Newfoundland had long-established commercial ties.[33]

THE EXCLUSION AND EXPULSION OF ALIENS

Allegations and apprehensions over Newfoundland's role as a base for slipping undesirable migrants into the United States and Canada were brought to a head in September 1925 by the American consul. He complained that a local American agent named F.R. Lawrence was importing people from Lithuania and other Baltic provinces by Furness Withy steamers via Liverpool with the object of smuggling them into the United States by some secret method. Already ten of these people had arrived and according to their local solicitor F. Gordon Bradley, 200 more were to follow in groups of 20 to 25. Bradley had been given assurances by Lawrence that each immigrant would have at least $200 and "some will be in possession of a thousand or more dollars." On the assumption that they would form the basis of a welcome stock of productive settlers and skilled workers, Bradley had earlier lobbied successfully on behalf of Lawrence's Lithuanian settlement project with the Minister of Justice.

The ten Balts (nine men from Lithuania and one Red Cross nurse from Riga, Latvia), who arrived in August 1925 under the auspices of the Immigration Association of Lithuania, were apparently refugees. According to Bradley, they were "compelled to seek new lands because of conditions due to war." When the Inspector General of the Constabulary found some of them to be destitute Bradley dissociated himself from Lawrence and the planned official welcome turned sour. Preoccupied with the seriousness of this traffic growing to any proportions, Colonial Secretary J.R. Bennett intimated to Minister of Justice W.J. Higgins, that this "class of people. . .may give us untold trouble," especially if news gets around that they are seeking work as loggers. Higgins agreed that the Lithuanians had evidently obtained entry under false pretenses and stated that they would be deported as they "may become a charge on the colony."[34] The possibility that these immigrants might qualify for admission as refugees under the 1906 Aliens Act seems never seemed to have been considered by officials.

The local press greeted the arrival of these aliens as undesirable competitors for jobs in the thriving pulp and paper industry. The editor of the *Evening Telegram* (18 February 1926) pointed out that anyone who was in the "habit of scanning the train and boat passenger lists which appear in the press, cannot but have observed in recent months an unusually large influx of persons whose unfamiliar names offer little or no clue as to the country of origins of their owners." His enquiries showed that a considerable number of these new arrivals intended to be settlers and, "while no doubt Newfoundland would benefit by an influx of new settlers," these should be admitted only if they arrived "with sufficient capital to turn their attention to industries at present undeveloped." Newfoundland's first object, he continued, should be to provide for its own people and to enforce the immigration laws of the country against undesirables more rigidly.

In the 1926 session of the House of Assembly the case of the Lithuanians was presented as the most compelling reason for the speedy passage of a new immigration act. Bennett repeated his unproven fears and suspicions and peppered them with references to the "large numbers of Chinese" who before the introduction of the head tax were allegedly imported into Newfoundland for the purpose of being smuggled into the United States, "and they would disappear from here in cargoes over night." He demanded that an embargo be put on these types of undesirables. In the debate Bennett argued that destitution should not necessarily be the main criterion for the undesirability of an immigrant. In the case of those Lithuanians Bennett claimed to have information from "the other side" that

> one Lithuanian woman was very wealthy, and many of them are wealthy people, and this particular woman had engaged an agent to get her into the United States, and she was prepared to pay any money to attain that object, and he was employing this means by way of Nfld.

When two Opposition speakers accused Bennett of lobbying for a country which was legislating against Newfoundland and excluding its citizens, he shifted to the irrefutable argument that Newfoundland labor had to be protected, even against those who seek temporary work on the island. The object was to learn a lesson from the experience of 1906 and prevent Newfoundland from being used by those trying to get into the U.S. and Canada through the back door: "When we put on a Chinese head tax it was not merely for the purpose of taxing a few laundrymen but to prevent Newfoundland from being made a Chinese dumping ground." Higgins explained that the new act would only go into force through subsequent regulations which spelled out the undesirable and prohibited classes of immigrants.[35]

The instrument that enabled the Justice Department to exclude the Lithuanians and any immigrant in future was an innocuous sounding "amendment" to the Disembarkation of Paupers Act of 1924. The amendment provided, apart from the disqualifications of paupers, mentally diseased, and criminals, for the expulsion of any non-native considered an undesirable person in the opinion of the Minister of Justice. In February 1925, Higgins allayed apprehensions that he might exercise his powers of expulsion under the 1924 provision "capriciously." In response to F. Gordon Bradley's request for clarification, Higgins declared that

> a person would not have an expulsion order issued against him on the ground that he was "undesirable" unless there was something in his conduct or habits that would give rise to complaint against him, such as, for example, his being a labour agitator or a troublemaker in some other direction.[36]

To inquiries from immigrants unable to enter the United States or Canada and desirous of coming to Newfoundland to buy land for farming purposes, the Justice Department would reply that

> our immigration laws prohibit the entry into this Colony of all persons who may be classed as "undesirable aliens," such as paupers, lunatics, and people without any means of subsistence. All transportation companies bringing such persons into this country are subject to severe penalties. In addition, we have an Act passed in 1924 which gives the Minister of Justice very large powers respecting the expulsion of such persons.[37]

The people excluded or expelled under the authority of the 1924 act happened to be largely non-British. Apart from the above-mentioned party of Lithuanians, unfavorable reception is documented in the case of a second request to bring 200 Lithuanians to engage in lumbering and other work. It came from one Abe Gervitz who arrived in February 1926 from England, accompanied by five "Poles with German and Russian or Polish names." Although the steamship lines agreed to refuse passage to this group, Deputy Minister of Customs H.W. LeMessurier, Newfoundland's chief immigration official, impressed on Bennett the necessity of passing rules prohibiting the landing of aliens "as quickly as possible before further immigration takes place."[38]

In July 1926, ex-Magistrate Scott of Curling interceded on behalf of resident Abraham Sherman of Corner Brook who desired the admission of one Oscar Bercovitz from Cuba. The decision was deferred until regulations had been made under the new act. To deal effectively with cases like these, the Colonial Secretary and the Justice Department urged that Canada's tight regulations of 1920 "be adopted in large part in this country."[39] The specter of foreign immigration thus precipitated the passage of discriminating regulations in November 1926. The regulations, applicable only to non-British and non-American immigrants, were based on the 1926 Immigration Act and will be discussed below.

Official reactions to applications for sponsorship by local residents of non-British origin reveal the ethnocentric motivations of the designers and executors of Newfoundland's immigration policy. In June 1926, Assad S. Kyte of Corner Brook asked for permission to sponsor the immigration of his cousin and his cousin's immediate family from Beyrut, Syria. In forwarding the application to the Justice Department, the Deputy Colonial Secretary Arthur Mews volunteered the advice that such persons "are mostly peddlers of cheap jewellery and other common wares from whom it is questionable whether our people derive any benefit or profit."

Similar negative advice was proffered in the case of an application by Romanian-born David Cross, resident of Badger, Newfoundland, for the admission of a fellow countryman from Bessarabia with his wife, two children, and $800 cash. "I am personally inclined to think that there is no benefit to the country in encouraging this type of immigrant," wrote the Minister of Justice W.R. Howley to the Chief Commissioner of Immigration in September 1928. Not only was the application refused on the ground that "they were undesirable" but, since the Minister of Justice decided to accept the unproven argument that these Romanians were trying to use Newfoundland as a stepping stone to Canada, he recommended that no reasons be given for the rejection.[40]

Among the sponsorship applications approved were those submitted by pre-World War I Syrian and Jewish immigrants K. Noah, I.F. Perlin, and A.M. Tooton on behalf of relatives. The petitioners had become prominent local businessmen and each had, as official comments reveal, in the eyes of government officials "for all purposes become a Newfoundlander."[41] However, the presentation of Kalleem Noah's request to the Governor by the Deputy Minister of Agriculture revealed the colonial elite's cultural and social distance from foreign-born residents. Noah, the official explained, was

> the big chief of the Syrians in Newfoundland, most decent man, well to do, quiet but very interesting.
>
> I would like to suggest that H.E. send for him and have a chat. It would do no harm and possibly make for good with a class in Nfld not previously touched.[42]

In the case of two Italians, deported in October 1927 upon their arrival from Liverpool, the records indicate that the deportation was in defiance of assurances given in London by the British Consulate

and the High Commissioner that their passports were in order and
that monetary requirements were satisfied. The deportation appeared officially based on the unproven assumption "that if they
attempt to enter the United States—as it is suspected they may
do—they will probably be thrown back upon us." LeMessurier
argued to the Colonial Secretary and the Minister of Customs that
the two Italians were "undesirable in other ways." In defense of his
decision, LeMessurier advanced the general principle that "immigrants are not accepted because they have proper passports or
because they have a sufficient quantity of money. If so, we might
flood the country with undesirable people." Higgins endorsed the
deportation, although he insisted that for persons whom the
authorities may consider undesirable for reasons other than specifically provided for in the act, the Governor in Council would be the
proper authority. He "can exclude in his own unqualified discretion."[43]

THE IMMIGRATION ACT OF 1926 AND ITS ENFORCEMENT TO 1934

The Immigration Act of June 1926 was designed to supplement, but
not replace the 1906 Aliens Act. The 1926 act defined an immigrant
as any passenger on board any vessel arriving in Newfoundland. As
well, it provided for the examination of all immigrants at the point
of entry. An immigrant might be landed or rejected and kept in
custody pending deportation. Deportation orders were made by the
Minister or immigration officer and compelled the ship or its owner
to remove the immigrant. Grounds for refusal of an immigrant
included lack of means, mental or physical infirmity, conviction of
any crime abroad, prostitution or its procuration and professional
begging, and vagrancy or the likelihood of becoming a public charge.
The act, Higgins explained to the House of Assembly, was the
product of continuous requests from the Customs authorities on
account of difficulties they experienced in the handling of so-called
"undesirables." Customs authorities had now the right of rejection
in the first instance, instead of having to wait until persons were
proven undesirables. Officials would be able to board and inspect a
ship, and the onus was on the immigrant to report himself. One of
the act's main benefits was that it facilitated deportations and put
the liability for the return of undesirables on the steamship owners
and their agents. Undesirables no longer had to be deported at the
expense of Newfoundland.[44]

    Along with stringent immigration and deportation procedures,
the act established the structures necessary to implement these. It
enabled the government to prescribe, by regulation, the minimum

amount of money, depending on race, occupation or destination, that immigrants must possess on landing. Furthermore, it authorized the government, whenever it "deems it necessary or expedient," by regulation or order to prohibit "the landing of immigrants belonging to any race deemed unsuited to the climate or requirements of the Colony, or immigrants of any specified class, occupation or character." The new act, finally, empowered the Minister of Finance and Customs or Immigration Officer to deport "any immigrant rejected or landing without leave or landing contrary to any of the provisions of this Act."

The act had barely been passed when the Deputy Minister of Justice, with reference to the Bercovitz case, urged that it be enforced by immigration officers to be appointed outside Newfoundland and by Canadian-type restrictive regulations. Indicative of the minimal kind of threat which alien immigration actually constituted by September 1926, was LeMessurier's advice to Higgins: "It is not necessary to appoint Immigration Officers at either Sydney, Boston or New York, as the immigration of aliens into Newfoundland is not sufficient to warrant any large expenditure." However in connection with administering the new act, LeMessurier requested new and increased authority. As superintendent over the island's Collectors of Customs and their new duties as immigration officers, he was concerned that "legal action may be taken against me" if in the minister's absence he prohibited any future landing of immigrants. LeMessurier's request was granted and in October 1927 he was promoted to the new rank of Chief Commissioner of Immigration.[45]

Based on the authority of the 1926 act, regulations issued in November 1926 required every adult immigrant to have a valid passport and $250 (dependents needed half the amount), unless the immigrant was sponsored by a first-degree relative or going to assured employment and had the means to reach it. British, Dominion, and American subjects were exempted from these restrictions, as were the citizens of France, Italy, Spain, Switzerland, Liechtenstein, Holland, Denmark, Ireland, Norway, Sweden, Portugal, Belgium, and Luxembourg. These controls were soon considered insufficiently restrictive, especially in the light of Canadian orders of August 1930 barring the admission of laborers from Central Europe, and American measures of March 1931 limiting the immigration from quota countries to 10 percent of their quotas.[46] In addition, the Depression had hit Newfoundland badly.

In January 1932 the 1926 regulations were replaced by a proclamation (under the 1926 act) which prohibited the entry for

PUBLISHED BY AUTHORITY

On the recommendation of the Minister of Finance and Customs, and under the provisions of Section 11, of Chapter 29, 17 George V. (1926), entitled, "An Act respecting Immigration," His Excellency the Governor-in-Council has been pleased to approve the following Rules and Regulations, namely:—

The landing in Newfoundland is hereby prohibited of any immigrant who does not possess in his own right the minimum amount of money hereinafter prescribed;

In the case of an immigrant of the age of 18 years or upwards the sum of $250.00, and in the case of an immigrant of the age of five years and under the age of 18 years, the sum of $125.00; provided that in the case of an immigrant who is the head of a family and is accompanied by one or more members of his family, the money qualification shall be $250.00 for the head of the family, and $125.00 for each member of the family of the age of 18 years or upwards, and $50.00 for each member of the family of 5 years and under the age of 18 years; provided further that the Immigration Officer in charge may, notwithstanding anything hereinbefore contained, exempt any immigrant from the operation of the foregoing regulation if it is shown to his satisfaction that:

   (a) The immigrant, if a male, is going to assured employment, and has the means of reaching the place of such employment; or

   (b) The immigrant, if a female, is going to assured employment, at domestic or other service, and has the means of reaching the place of such employment; or

   (c) The immigrant, whether male or female, is of one of the following descriptions, and is going to reside with a relative of one of the following descriptions, who is able and willing to support such immigrant and has the means of reaching the place of residence of such relative:

      Wife going to husband.
      Child going to parent.
      Brother or sister going to brother.
      Minor going to married or independent sister.
      Parent going to son or daughter.

Acceptable Certificates being furnished and sworn to by the parties interested.

The entry or landing in Newfoundland is hereby prohibited of any person who is not in possession of a valid passport issued in, and by the Government of, the country of which such person is a subject or citizen, and for the purposes of this regulation, such passport must be presented within one year of the date of its issue, and if not a British passport, must carry the vise of a British Diplomatic or Consular Officer;

Provided that this regulation shall not apply to British subjects coming to Newfoundland directly or indirectly from the United Kingdom of Great Britain and Ireland; the United States of America; or any self-governing British Dominion; nor shall it apply to American citizens entering Newfoundland from the United States of America; nor to persons who have been resident in the United States of America for a period of at least two years immediately prior to their entry to or landing in Newfoundland, nor to citizens of France, Italy, Spain, Switzerland, Lichtenstein, Holland, Denmark and Iceland, Norway, Sweden, Portugal, Belgium and Luxemburg.

NOTE—In accordance with Section 5 of the Immigration Act, until such time as the Governor-in-Council may appoint Commissioners of Immigration, the Customs Department shall perform the duties of, and the Collectors of Customs shall be deemed to be, Immigration Officers.

J. R. BENNETT,
Colonial Secretary.

Dept. of the Colonial Secretary,
   November 2nd, 1926.

PUBLISHED BY AUTHORITY: Newfoundland immigration regulations of 2 November 1926. Credit: PANL.

two years of all central and east Europeans (excluding natives of countries to which Newfoundland was selling fish), persons belonging by race to any country in Asia or Africa, and all non-Newfoundlanders who were of the laboring classes. Immigrants even from non-prohibited countries had to satisfy the authorities that they would not likely become public charges. The new system resulted in steamship companies requiring European immigrants to obtain permits before sailing in order to avoid the risk of having to carry them back if refused on landing. In the 1930s, permits issued by the Chief Commissioner of Immigration became a prerequisite for anyone intending to enter Newfoundland for a period of more than six weeks. The issuing of advance permits to those eligible to land became the most effective way of controlling immigration.[47]

The immigration of the Sidel family is indicative of the direction in which immigration policy was moving in 1931. Moses Sidel was a Polish Jew who was admitted into Newfoundland in October 1930 upon the guarantee and assurance of his brother Otto, a pre-World War I immigrant to St. John's. Eight months later Moses Sidel requested that his bilingual (German and Latvian) wife Ida and two children (six and four years old), living at the time in Riga, Latvia, be permitted to join him. Sidel's lawyer argued that "it would seem only just and fair that Mr. Sidel. . .should not be separated from his family." The Acting Chief Commissioner of Immigration since 1928, H.V. Hutchings, complained to the Acting Minister of Justice that he had no legal right to refuse entry and requested "that something definite be done in connection with immigration to this country, so that I can legally refuse to admit this class of people."[48]

In preparing the 1932 proclamation, which went through various revised drafts from August 1930, the Department of Justice in conjunction with the Colonial Secretary's office ensured that the countries of origin of Newfoundland's non-British minorities—Syria, Armenia, Turkey, and Egypt were specifically singled out in the government memoranda, as well as Russia, Poland, and the Baltic countries—were in the prohibited category. Excluded also were persons belonging by race to a prohibited country, even though they may actually have been nationals of a non-prohibited country, for example a Russian who was a German national, or a Pole who was an American national. Germany incidentally, an importer of fish and iron ore from Newfoundland, ended up in the non-prohibited category, unlike Austria, Hungary or Czechoslovakia, countries that did not import from Newfoundland.[49]

The tightening of immigration restrictions from 1924 to 1932 occurred against the background of a chronic crisis in the fishery.

In part due to the failure of reform and ensuing marketing problems, it caused widespread unemployment and crippled retailers and local manufacturers. Beginning in 1926 Newfoundland's second largest export industry was hit hard when the world price for newsprint fell by half. Workers in the Grand Falls and Corner Brook pulp and paper mills were put on short time and logging operations were decreased.[50] By 1933, the number of destitute persons eligible for social assistance climbed to 90,000, almost one-third of the population.

The economic and political crisis was worsened by Newfoundland's own elite. The dominant class of fish merchants, used to looking upon the fishery as a resource to be exploited rather than developed, made no sustained attempts to find solutions to the island's problems. Newfoundland was to them a sinecure whose exploitation was taken for granted or, as one historian put it succinctly, a mere "projection of their balance sheets."[51] No more sympathy for immigration came therefore from Newfoundland's commercial, social, and professional elite of lawyers, doctors, and politicians, than from organized labor and occupational lobbies. They all viewed immigration as having only negative ramifications for them; they thought it would add to the competition for jobs, privileges, and profits,[52] and increase the number of relief recipients. The mood with regard to immigration was such that in St. John's the Minister of Finance and commentators in the press blamed the growing unemployment and dole problem on the migration of "baymen" to the city.[53]

Unlike in 1906, there was thus an obvious socio-economic rationale for the exclusion of immigrants after 1926. Ironically, only non-British "foreigners" were excluded, while native-born British, Canadians, and Americans continued to be welcome. The soliciting of British immigration until 1926 and its exemption from the exclusionist measures thereafter became a tradition which grew naturally out of the 1906 legislation. Canadian and American exclusionist legislation provided the catalyst as well as the model for Newfoundland's tight immigration controls. In none of the cases involving the exclusion or deportation of aliens did government records indicate any official inclination to test the applicability of the 1906 refugee law.

In 1933, news commentator Albert Perlin alone had the courage to identify the lack of immigration as one of the reasons for the degeneration of Newfoundland's political and economic life. Perlin, himself the son of Russian-Jewish immigrants, was then on his way to becoming Newfoundland's most outspoken public affairs critic.

He dared to postulate that there might actually be "a good living here for four times our present population if our economic life were properly planned." An infusion of fresh blood would "improve the stock" and have other fringe benefits.[54]

Part II

Newfoundland's Response to the Refugee Crisis, 1934-1939

"It would have been so beneficial to the country"   5

Refugee Settlement Projects and Economic Development, 1934-1939

The rise of the Third Reich created unprecedented masses of potential immigrants for Newfoundland in the form of refugees. In fact, the refugees knocking on Newfoundland's door from 1934 to 1939 constituted the largest tide of immigrants desiring entry during any comparable period in the island's history in more than a century. Several significant proposals for group settlement were advanced on behalf of the refugees. The proposals took into account the country's social and economic plight and presented the ruling elite with unique, challenging solutions in the search for economic rehabilitation, social reform, and the restoration of political sovereignty. Some of these proposals may have been inspired by promotional literature that portrayed Newfoundland as a country offering space, a favorable climate, undeveloped resources, and a myriad of challenges for economic development.

One article published in Germany in February 1937 under the title "Settlement Plans in Newfoundland" featured the colony as spacious and vastly underpopulated in comparison with Holland and England. Looking for ways to utilize its undeveloped resources, Newfoundland was allegedly interested in recruiting settlers from such countries as Switzerland, the Netherlands, and Belgium. Settlers from these countries were presumed to have expertise in areas particularly suited to Newfoundland's plans for economic and financial revitalization. Britain was allegedly not interested in resettling her own unemployed population in Newfoundland, since this required considerable capital; in view of the current economic crisis and danger of war, the British government could only afford to invest in dominions of strategic value, such as Australia and New Zealand. Instead, foreign capital investors would be allowed to underwrite the economic reconstruction of Newfoundland whose export markets were known to represent great risks. In this connection Newfoundland was expected to offer a new existence to immigrants from continental Europe, the article concluded.[1]

Like most promotional literature, this article painted a misleadingly rosy picture of settlement prospects while playing down the severity of the economic crisis in Newfoundland and the staggering problems confronting its Commission of Government. At the same time that Adolf Hitler took power in Germany in 1933, the British and Canadian governments intervened to save Newfoundland from complete financial collapse. The price for their support was the suspension of democracy and the appointment by Britain of a government by commission for an undetermined period. Composed of three British and three Newfoundland commissioners, with a British-appointed governor presiding, the Commission assumed office in February 1934. It had legislative as well as executive functions and its proceedings were subject to the supervision of the Dominions Office in London. The mandate of the Commission of Government was to develop policies for Newfoundland's immediate and long-range reconstruction.

The commissioners, some of whose only qualifications for the job were skills as administrators and bureaucrats,[2] had a mandate for reform but were pressured to solve problems as much as possible within a traditional frame of reference. Until the war began, numerous conflicts among the commissioners persisted and affected the consideration of proposals for immigration and refugee settlement. The conflicts encompassed such topics as long- and short-term reconstruction objectives, land settlement or alternate sources of employment for the unemployed, and the extent of British government control. The question was whether the Commission of Government would be willing to consider immigration and be able to accept the challenge of refugee settlement as an instrument of socio-economic reform or whether it would share the preceding governments' apprehensions about immigration and base its policy on the assumptions of its predecessors.

Refugee settlement proposals do not appear to have been the only projects for group immigration considered by the Commission among the available options for reconstruction. If credence can be given to a St. John's-based economist claiming to be reliably informed, the Commission entertained plans for Dutch, Swiss, and Belgian group settlement between 1934 and 1936. He disclosed that a Dutch delegation had visited Newfoundland in 1934 and proposed the settlement of a considerable number of Dutch families in conjunction with the establishment of a fish-oil industry financed with Dutch capital. In 1936 the Commission apparently undertook steps to recruit Swiss cattle breeders with experience in developing such secondary industries as dairying and wool spinning. In 1936 an official inquiry by the Belgian government about the possibility of Belgian immigration was also under consideration in St. John's in connection with the planned expansion of iron ore mining on the east coast and of coal mining on the west coast of Newfoundland. Even Japan reportedly offered to invest in Newfoundland's economic reconstruction and skilled Japanese workers requested admission.[3] None of these projects were brought to fruition.

SIMON BELKIN AND THE ICA PROPOSAL OF 1934

The Commission of Government received its first proposal for a group settlement of German-Jewish refugees in March 1934 when it had held office barely a month. The proposal's sponsor was the Jewish Colonization Association (ICA). The ICA had its headquarters in Paris (see chapter 2), and branches in Canada and other countries. Inquiries with the Newfoundland government in 1926 had revealed to the ICA of Montreal that Newfoundland immigration laws were comparatively liberal. When early in 1934 the Canadian Jewish Congress began receiving appeals to help German Jews in distress, as well as a request from ICA headquarters in Paris to explore immigration possibilities for them in Newfoundland, the Secretary of the Canadian ICA committee, Simon Belkin, was sent to St. John's.[4]

Belkin was aware that Newfoundland immigration laws were "very liberal" towards persons seeking admission "to avoid persecution or punishment on religious or political grounds." He was also informed that under the 1932 Proclamation a German citizen would not be admitted "unless he shall show to the satisfaction of the Chief Commissioner of Immigration . . . that he will be in a position to support himself and those dependent upon him . . . and that neither he nor they is or are likely at any future time to become a public charge." Furthermore, Belkin realized that the Commission was still too preoccupied with reorganizing the government administration to consider the desirability of immigration, and that it would be guided by the fact that 25 percent of the population were on the dole. There were therefore possibilities for only a limited and select number of refugees, and none for workers (unskilled, skilled or white collar), engineers, mechanics, and merchants, he concluded.[5]

Belkin had been advised that there might be a few openings for doctors, provided they agreed to live in outports and answered calls up to forty miles away, using open motor boats during the summer and sleighs during the winter. Such doctors and their families "would have to live under primitive conditions, receive their mail only once a week, and have their daily contact with the outside world by means of radio only." A demand for two specialists at the Grace Hospital in St. John's and for dentists in the towns of Grand Falls and Corner Brook had been suggested to him, as well as a need for five travelling clinics operating from small boats travelling along the coast to take care of the isolated population and devoted particularly to the relief of tuberculosis. Belkin saw in these suggestions an "opportunity of giving employment to some doctors and nurses and, at the same time, to serve the vital interests of the population of Newfoundland."

After interviewing leading personalities in government, business, and industry, as well as in the local Jewish community, Belkin carefully selected forty refugee families "who would be very useful to the country in its predicament and who would at no time become a public charge." The refugee families were to be settled at ICA expense and included the following: five doctors in outports that had lost their medical services; five doctors with two nurses each in five travelling clinics of the kind offered earlier by the Commonwealth Fund; two specialists for the Grace Hospital in St. John's; and dentists for Grand Falls and Corner Brook. Two German Jewish scientists would be employed at Memorial University College, an idea which the President of the college, Professor A.G. Hatcher, welcomed. There were also provisions for agricultural and industrial development. Since only one modern poultry farm operated near St. John's and Belkin found farming conditions in the most deplorable state, he felt there was room for ten to fifteen new poultry farmers producing eggs and broilers, and engaging in truck farming on the side. The remaining refugees would come with capital to start factories for items that were imported but could be produced locally, such as bed springs, stoves, castings, toilet articles, brushes, paints, soaps, washing powders, fish meal, condensed milk, and flour. Belkin had made a list of twenty-eight different items which should have been produced in Newfoundland instead of being imported.[6]

Belkin sought an interview with Sir John Hope Simpson who controlled the economic life in the country. As Commissioner for Natural Resources he was the strongest and most important of the six commissioners. The conference lasted for one hour. Hope Simpson was moved by the idea of the travelling clinics, indicated additional prospects for resource development, and impressed his willingness to be of assistance. Surprised that a Jewish resident owned the only poultry farm near St. John's, he

> expressed his admiration for the cooperative spirit of the Jewish people, citing some of his experiences in Palestine, and stated that if a group of qualified dairymen and poultry farmers would be established in Newfoundland, if possible on a cooperative basis as practised in Palestine, they would be a good example to the rest of the community.[7]

In a memorandum prepared for the Commission's deliberations, Hope Simpson pointed out that opening the gates to Jewish settlement entailed a question of general policy which the Commission ought to decide by ascertaining public opinion. To obtain the views "of any persons interested, either in favour of the policy or opposed to it," he proposed that the Commission issue an official communiqué. His memorandum brought out the positive aspects of the proposal and underlined the absence of any risk for the government. "I know the Association," Hope Simpson concluded. "It has spent millions in settling Jews in the Argentine and in Russia and is a very wealthy foundation."[8]

In the 67-year-old senior British Commissioner, Belkin could not have found a more sympathetic advocate. Commonly recognized in the late 1930s as the outstanding international authority on the refugee question, Hope Simpson was a man of vision and cosmopolitan experience. A former Liberal Member of Parliament and civil servant in India, he had acquired a worldwide reputation as Director General of the National Flood Relief Commission in China. As Vice-President of the League of Nations Refugee Settlement Commission from 1926 to 1930, he had been involved in refugee resettlement in Greece. As early as the summer of 1933, he is reported to have expressed to the General Secretary of the League of Nations High Commissioner for Refugees his concern with the fate of the victims of racial and political persecution in Germany.[9]

Hope Simpson was particularly eager to prove his goodwill towards the Jewish people by promoting the admission of German Jews to Newfoundland because he wanted to refute the charge that he was anti-Semitic. That charge had arisen from his report of August 1930 to the Passfield commission on economic conditions in Palestine. (The Passfield commission of inquiry had been appointed to investigate the 1929 anti-Jewish uprising in Palestine.) In this report Hope Simpson had considered the area suitable for agricultural settlement so overcrowded that, as he put it, you "cannot swing a cat." The Hope Simpson Report was attacked by

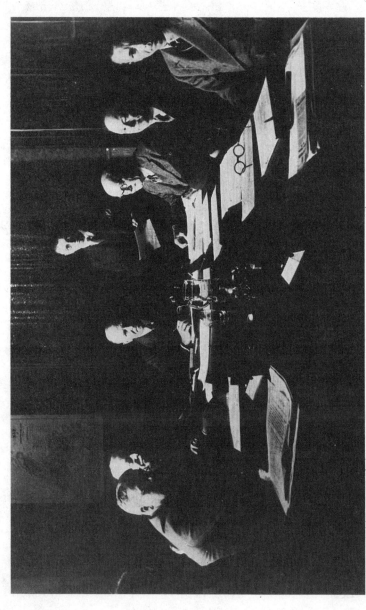

Commission of Government of Newfoundland, February 1934. Left to right: W.R. Howley, Commissioner for Justice; Thomas Lodge, Commissioner for Public Utilities, F.C. Alderdice, Commissioner for Home Affairs and Education; David Murray Anderson, Governor; W.J. Carew, Secretary; J. Hope Simpson, Commissioner for Natural Resources; J.C. Puddester, Commissioner for Public Health and Welfare; E.N.R. Trentham, Commissioner for Finance. Credit: PANL.

Zionists because it had recommended the *de facto* closure of Palestine to further Jewish settlement. Belkin noted that Hope Simpson raised the problem of Palestine to defend himself, that he was extremely cordial throughout the interview, met Belkin twice at the hotel, and made a point of stopping and talking to him in a friendly manner.[10]

The minutes of the tenth meeting of the Commission of Government, held on 31 March 1934, record that it was decided to refer Belkin's plan to the editors of the city's daily newspapers with a view to sounding public opinion. However, no publicity was given to the plan in any of the papers until after the Commission had reached a decision.[11] Instead, Belkin received an unsigned letter dated 16 April 1934 from Hope Simpson informing him that "after careful investigation of the whole question, the Commission . . . could not see its way to accepting the proposal you made." The Commission, he admitted, realized quite clearly that there was no chance the immigrants could become a charge on the state and that Belkin's foundation would perform a badly needed service in the outports. But, after considering the matter in all its aspects, the Commission decided "that at the present time it would not be desirable that we should allow immigration and settlement of any kind."

How "can one interpret the refusal of proposals which would have been so beneficial to the country," Belkin wondered. The lack of a signature on the reply did not seem simply an oversight and he returned the letter for official signing. The whole episode was to Belkin a sad epilogue to Hope Simpson's anti-Zionist report on Palestine.[12] Belkin could not know that Hope Simpson, although the Commission's dominant figure and eager to embark on reform, was unable to prevail over the opposition of the medical profession and was forced to retreat as he "stepped onto the sacred ground of local interest groups who were able to defend themselves."[13] It was because of "the difficulties with which professional men in this island are contending at the present time," as Governor Humphrey T. Walwyn later put it, that the government "could not view with equanimity immigration of Jews of this class."[14]

The chief influence that evidently was at work to kill Belkin's proposal came from the Medical Board whose Secretary-Treasurer Belkin had interviewed. The Board immediately became alarmed and succeeded in blocking the plan before the media had a chance to publicize it. Had not a prominent member of the Medical Board been displeased over the government's simultaneous bypassing of local nurses in favor of nurses from England for the St. John's Clinic, the Board's opposition to Belkin's proposal might not have been publicized at all. In the *Evening Telegram* (11 May 1934) an indignant Dr. N.S. Fraser disclosed:

> Be it widely known that the Newfoundland Medical Association interfered . . . and prevented the importation of a number of doctors. It was proposed to settle a colony of German Jews in Newfoundland, including 8 or 10 doctors, and backed by enough money to keep them for two years. But the President and Secretary of the Newfoundland Medical Association heard of it in time and were successful in stopping it.

Referring to this statement, Registered Nurse Lana M. Clement in Burgeo demanded to know in *Observer's Weekly* (14 July 1934) why German Jewish doctors were prevented from coming. Burgeo was an isolated outport where one of the refugee doctors was expected to fill a vacancy. The Registrar of the Newfoundland Medical Board replied that the President and Secretary of the Medical Association had warned the authorities that registration would be refused to foreign doctors because reciprocity did not exist between Great Britain and Germany. Explaining the concerns of the local medical profession, the paper elaborated that these foreign doctors and professors would ultimately be left to fend for themselves, that they might leave their assigned places and seek practices where medical men were already established, and that the refugees would thus end up competing actively with local professional men. The bottom line was that there was no adequate means "to check upon these German doctors' qualifications."[15]

Clement's rejoinder countered the Registrar's arguments and reflected the mood among people outside St. John's. It objected strongly to the professional elite's manipulation of their needs with regard to refugee settlement:

> I see no comparison between Great Britain with her oversupply of doctors and Newfoundland with her great shortage. Would it not have been an easy matter to write to the German universities from which these doctors received their degrees in order to check up on their qualifications and since there is no reciprocity between this country and Germany to require the passing of the Newfoundland Medical Examination to determine their eligibility for practicing medicine here. The Royal Commission Report says that the number of doctors has decreased from 119 in 1911 to 83 in 1933 so there should not be much reason to fear competition. Is it right for 83 Newfoundland citizens to prevent thousands of other Newfoundland citizens from receiving medical care?[16]

FRANK BANIKHIN'S PROPOSAL OF 1936

The second proposal for group settlement of German Jewish refugees was initiated in March 1936 by Frank Banikhin, a member of the St. John's Jewish community and a close friend of John Hope Simpson. Banikhin proposed to industrialize Newfoundland by settling thousands of skilled refugees in Labrador. The idea of colonizing the barely explored interior of Labrador in combination with some industrial development had already been vented in 1934 as "the salvation of many of those now on the dole."[17] As a matter of fact, from 1927 to 1932 American investors had been proposing to pay off Newfoundland's debts in return for the right to develop Labrador's hydro-electric potential. Unverifiable rumour had it that at the same time Zionist organizations had tried "to purchase a large part of the southern section [of Labrador, but] had been sidetracked to Palestine."[18] After the British Privy Council's judgement of 1927 had confirmed Newfoundland's historic claims over those of Canada to Labrador, the Newfoundland government on several occasions, the last time in 1932, had considered selling Labrador to Canada, intimating that the United States, various private American interests, the Zionists, and even "the Germans" would be prepared to buy or lease it.[19]

Banikhin had come with his family to Newfoundland in 1917 at the age of 29, after having migrated from his native Ukraine via Germany to Saint John, New Brunswick, in 1907. Considering himself a reform Jew in St. John's, he remained an outsider in the Jewish community and had no intimate social contact with it. His Ukrainian background, education (he spoke seven European languages), cosmopolitan interests, and secular frame of mind set Banikhin's world off from the Polish roots, the liturgical orthodoxy, and the total integration into the local economy that the inner core of Newfoundland's Jewish community shared.

A shipowner and world trader in various commodities, such as hides, metals, and fish, and with eighteen commercial establishments all over the island and in Labrador, Banikhin had business connections with Canada, the United States and Germany. As an exporter of pitprops to Germany, he had frequent dealings with German sea captains who showed him ore samples given to them by natives and prospectors on their voyages to the Lake Melville area in Labrador. On his business trips to the United States, Banikhin took the ore samples with him for assay. The economic potential of Labrador and the possibility of exploring the deposits intrigued him. When his American contacts verified the high ore content of the samples but refused to consider investing capital in such a distant and inaccessible region, Banikhin decided to tackle the job himself with the help of refugees from the Third Reich.[20]

Although Banikhin, according to the recollections of his son Cyril, had no personal connections with German Jews, he knew that among the growing exodus of refugees there was a high percentage of "skilled workmen, craftsmen, engineers, manufacturers, mechanics, etc." and that there were many Jewish agencies providing financial aid for their resettlement. There is some evidence that Banikhin may have been encouraged by Hope Simpson to submit a proposal to enable the latter to prove that he cared for the Jews. It seems that Hope Simpson incorrectly attributed the growing public disenchantment with his policies of reconstruction to the anger among local Jews for recommending in 1930 the prohibition of Jewish immigration to Palestine.[21]

Banikhin suggested to Hope Simpson that if a concession were given enabling Jewish immigrants to develop the water power of the Grand Falls (now called Churchill Falls) on the Hamilton (now called Churchill) River in Labrador, it would be possible to organize a settlement in the vicinity entirely financed by international Jewish funds. There would, thus, be established in an area hitherto vacant "a manufacturing centre which might conceivably grow to proportions almost beyond belief." Once the not insuperable difficulties of contact with the coast were surmounted, the proposed site would be centrally located as regards the United States and Canada, for which the Hudson Bay route was available part of the year. It would be nearer Europe than either Canada or the United States. Such a development would bring out "millions of dollars worth of hidden resources," and it "would necessarily use up our unemployed population and would in addition provide a market for a great deal of our produces as it would be purely a manufacturing centre." Banikhin expressed the conviction that if German Jews—known for their industriousness, self-reliance and talent for manufacturing and invention—were brought to Labrador, "the results would be almost staggering."[22]

Hope Simpson warmly recommended the scheme to his fellow Commissioners as a proposal that "may sound fantastic" but in reality was not "so fantastic as it would appear to be on the surface." The Commission decided to request the views of the British government on the political aspects of the proposal before taking any further action. The Commission was prepared to give serious consideration to the settlement of Jews on the Labrador "on a considerable scale" on three conditions: first, that the British government raise no political objection; second, that it be endorsed by public opinion; and third, that no financial burden fall on the Newfoundland government.

In a memorandum of 25 March 1936 to Malcolm MacDonald, Secretary of State for Dominion Affairs, the Governor of Newfoundland stressed that Banikhin's proposal was "of an entirely different nature" than other plans for settling Jewish refugees that had been proposed earlier by a Zionist organization in Canada. Jewish professional refugees would not compete with professional groups in Newfoundland according to Banikhin's proposal, which "would have as its object industrial development in a country which is vacant at present." The Governor believed the Grand Falls on the Hamilton River to be the most important water power on the North American continent still available for hydroelectric development. Such development would be financed entirely by funds subscribed by Jews in other countries.[23]

The Dominions Office decided to consult with Newfoundland's two other British Commissioners E.N.R. Trentham and Thomas Lodge who happened to be visiting London. Trentham's views are not known but Lodge stated that he personally welcomed some Jewish settlement in Newfoundland or Labrador but did not think that the Commission would endorse it. The desired introduction of doctors "would almost certainly be very unpopular," he warned and only "a colony of Jews ready and able to work in the woods" under the auspices of the Labrador Development Co. ought to be considered. However, as long as there were "power rights going abegging in Newfoundland much nearer civilization," Lodge could not see Banikhin's suggestion to be "at all practical." To the Newfoundland expert in the Dominions Office P.A. Clutterbuck, the scheme was "a brain wave of a local Jew who apparently wants to found a second Palestine in Labrador." What would these Jewish settlers manufacture once they had the water power rights? Clutterbuck characterized the project as "entirely visionary and unsubstantial, typical of those constantly put up in Newfoundland."[24]

Dominions Secretary MacDonald did not object in principle to the settlement of Jews in Labrador, subject to the second and third conditions of the Commission of Government being satisfied. But in his reply of 10 July 1936 he let it be known that Commissioner for Public Utilities Thomas Lodge had considered the scheme "not a practical one, since the Grand Falls on the Hamilton River are very inaccessible and at present there is nothing to which the power obtainable from the Falls could be applied." Furthermore, a concurrent application by Weaver (Minerals) Ltd. covered water power

rights which included the Grand Falls. The scale on which a settlement would be possible or desirable would depend on the working
out of some practical scheme.[25] The Dominions Office expected to
receive further suggestions on how to overcome these difficulties,
but the Newfoundland government seemed to have found a con-
venient excuse to abandon the project.

Years later Cyril Banikhin did not attribute the failure of his
father's scheme to any lack of support from the British or Newfoundland governments, but rather to the refusal of Zionist
organizations in New York to fund the project. The Zionists,
Banikhin's son contended, made a living from sending Jewish
refugees to Palestine, and they were not willing to support any
alternative places of settlement: "Dad went to New York full of hope
and optimism, but they [the Zionists] were not very receptive and
wouldn't budge. They called him a traitor to the Jewish people. So
he came back very disappointed and disillusioned, and forgot the
whole matter."[26]

The Newfoundland government's dissociation from Banikhin's
proposal coincided with Hope Simpson's resignation from the Commission in June 1936 and his return to England. Hope Simpson was
viewed by contemporaries as "a popular commissioner, and his
departure, when he had ripened by local experience, was a loss to
the colony."[27] Refugee settlement was part of his strategy to reform
the old order in Newfoundland and he departed thoroughly disillusioned about the prospects for prosperity there. In his personal
correspondence with the Dominions Secretary and his memoirs he
attributed Newfoundland's intractable problems to its commercial
elite. The St. John's merchants, their partners, and directors, he
wrote in September 1935

> live in luxury and seem to have money for everything they want. I
> was dining last night at the home of one of these merchants and
> after dinner . . . I raised the problem of the fishermen. The three
> merchants were agreed that the standard of comfort was very low
> but that the fisherman wanted nothing more, and was happy
> struggling along the circumstances in which he found himself. My
> Newfoundland colleague took the opportunity to warn me that we
> (that is the U.K. Commissioners) must be careful not to attempt to
> create in the minds of the people of this country a demand for a
> higher standard of comfort. The opinion of the merchants there,
> and the remarks of my colleague, are typical of the St. John's
> attitude towards this problem.[28]

For 300 years, Hope Simpson remarked, the earnings of the
woodsmen and fishermen had gone into creating about 300 wealthy

families. These "see no further than the end of their noses and have no interest outside their own profits. They dislike me and they dislike the Commission Government, because our main interest is prosperity among the common folk."[29]

PROPOSALS BY HENRY KLAPISCH AND OTHERS, 1936–1939

Hope Simpson's resignation removed from the scene Newfoundland's most influential spokesman for accepting refugees from the Third Reich. This became clear when the Commission received a request on 12 June 1936 from A.L. Wurfbain, General Secretary for the League of Nations High Commissioner for Refugees from Germany, asking whether Newfoundland would accept, "for settlement on the land," a small number of non-Jewish refugees from Germany. The Commission rejected it outright, even though it was accompanied with an offer of possible financial support as the result of a special international appeal.[30]

The spontaneous mass flight of Jews since the spring of 1938, following the annexations of Austria and the Czech Sudetenland, and the pogrom of *Kristallnacht*, revived modified versions of the settlement proposals of 1934 and 1936 in Montreal, London, and New York. From Montreal Charles E. Chaisson, a native Newfoundlander, called on Dominions Secretary MacDonald in July 1938 to "open the immigration doors without seventeen restrictions, esp. to German Jews and others looking for a prosperous home." This was a unique opportunity to make this Island Colony "equal to any nation." Newfoundland had an abundance of natural resources of all kinds and manufacturing possibilities and could support millions of people if properly administered.

> In years to come Newfoundland will develop as our Island Centre of the Empire, why not start it now. Immigration on a large scale means new homes, new developments, new manufacturing, new exports and imports. Whenever you have Jewish immigration you have business, you will have the support of the entire world. I mean the democracies, especially the Jews scattered throughout the world.
>
> By developing Newfoundland on a British Isles basis you will have relief of Newfoundland's present problems, help the British Empire in general, especially the shipping industries and numerous others. It is going to be done some day, why not start now. The opportunity is awaiting. Strike now and strike heavy, it will solve more problems than one.

In a letter to the British War Secretary three months later, Chaisson proposed the opening of a naval base in Newfoundland in conjunction with the transporting of hundreds of thousands of suffering and oppressed European peoples to the island so that they could start life anew and give the Empire within a few years a well trained army equal to any. "Seldom does such an opportunity lie open." Clutterbuck of the Dominions Office considered Chaisson's proposals "all rubbish" not worth forwarding to St. John's.[31]

In London, Hope Simpson in November 1938 urged the settlement of a large number of refugees in the dominions and colonies. He was now, in the words of Sir Neill Malcolm, High Commissioner for Refugees since 1936, "commonly recognized to be the outstanding authority on the refugee problem, on which he has been at work for the last twenty years."[32] Under the auspices of the Royal Institute of International affairs, Hope Simpson had just published a comprehensive study on refugees.[33] In a major policy statement of 22 November 1938, Prime Minister Chamberlain promised British aid in settling Jewish refugees in the Colonial Empire. He proposed Tanganyika, Kenya and British Guyana as suitable areas. On 11 January 1939 the *Times* of London suggested that Newfoundland should be included in the list of areas under investigation by the Inter-Governmental Refugee Committee, established at the Evian Conference in the summer of 1938 to explore refugee immigration possibilities.

Apparently at the request of Norman Bentwich, assistant to the League of Nations High Commissioner for Refugees, the Dominions Office reconsidered refugee settlement possibilities in Newfoundland and Labrador on 16 November 1938. Clutterbuck restated his conviction that Labrador was *prima facie* unsuitable for large scale settlement because of its harsh climate and inaccessibility. Even "a settlement of Jews to work in the woods there would probably be resented by the Newfoundland public, who would almost certainly argue, and not without reason, that the unemployed Newfoundlander should have the first claim on such work." Agricultural and employment conditions on the island of Newfoundland did not offer encouraging prospects either. "The introduction of alien breadwinners would be resented locally and might indeed be politically impossible," Dominions Office assistant secretary Eric Machtig pointed out, "*unless* [emphasis in the original] outside funds were available to finance the settlers throughout. If some sort of industry could be set up involving employment for imported Jews and additional employment for local Newfoundlanders, this would seem to offer the best prospects." In any case, it was agreed that the government of Newfoundland would have to be consulted and concrete proposals would have to be solicited from Jewish interests on the spot.[34]

In November 1938 New York civil engineer Saul Bernstein had completed an 80-page survey of Newfoundland's potentialities on behalf of Jewish welfare organizations in New York. He stressed that "the Jews can take little from a country that is practically bankrupt. On the contrary, with undeveloped resources and small population, much can be contributed by them. . . Jewish ingenuity will certainly develop these resources."[35] While traveling incognito across the island for a month, Bernstein had been amazed at the unsolicited suggestions uttered to him that "the oppressed people of Europe would be welcomed." In the light of his findings, "serious consideration" was being given to settle thousands of Jewish refugees in Newfoundland, the *New York Journal* (31 January 1939) announced. The newspaper stated that Newfoundland offered "definite possibilities" for refugees because of its "absolute need" for doctors and dentists and its opportunities for farming. Each family would require $2,000 to $3,000 to start life there. The only quota rule was that newcomers could not enter as paupers or become public charges.[36]

A major settlement plan was announced at the beginning of March 1939, when the local press carried the startling headline: "Proposal to Place Refugees in Labrador; Provides For Admission of 5,000 Emigrants; $10,000,000 AVAILABLE."[37] It was reported that Henry Klapisch, a Jewish fish merchant from Seattle, had secured an option to purchase certain timber limits in the St. Lewis Bay and Alexis Bay areas as a preliminary to settlement. He had under consideration a proposal to export timber as well as to process it in a new furniture factory, to set up a fish cannery, and to transfer entire new industries from Germany and Czechoslovakia. The development would rely heavily on Newfoundland labor and make St. John's its base for purchases and clearing. At least three large Jewish organizations in the United States were apparently prepared to fund the entire project. It was proposed to settle about 5,000 selected immigrants, adequately financed, during the first year and increase the number year by year as the settlement developed. The three American backers of the project were, according to the local press, waiting for assurances that the Newfoundland government would entertain such a scheme.

The fate of Klapisch's refugee scheme at a time when a similar American scheme for settling Jewish Refugees in Alaska received some publicity remains somewhat of a mystery. In 1939 Klapisch was a resident of New York and represented the Santa Cruz Oil

Has Plan To Settle Labrador

Provides For Admission of 5,000 Emigrants From Germany and Czechoslovakia

$10,000,000 AVAILABLE

Plans are now on foot for the development of the Labrador by means of labour and capital from the United States and European countries, Mr. Henry Klapisch told a **Daily News** representative yesterday. No cut and dried plans have as yet been absolutely developed. Mr. Klapisch is now visiting Newfoundland on other business but at the same time is active in the matter of the settlement of European refugees on he Labrador Coast.

On his last visit to Newfoundland in December he secured an option to purchase certain timber limits in St. Lewis Bay and Alexis Bay as a preliminary to a settlement and has under consideration the development of the timber resources, both for export and for use in a furniture factory, the setting up of a fish cannery, and entirely new industries which are now carried on in Germany and Czechoslovakia.

Mr. Klapisch states that at least $10,000,000 can be raised immediately by a vast organization in the United States. The proposed development would draw most of its labour, such as the fisheries and timber industry, from Newfoundland labour and make St. John's its base for purchases and for clearing.

United States Interested

During this week Mr. Klapisch has received the following cables:

From Philip Novik, Attorney, 291 Broadway, New York.

"With reference to your scheme for settling and developing Labrador for refugees I am legal council for three large Jewish organizations. If we can be assured by the Newfoundland Government that they are prepared and willing to entertain such a scheme I can get these three organizations to back the project."

From Bialystoker Centre, David S. Sohn secretary, 228 Broadway, New York:

"I understand you have a certain scheme for settling and developing of Labrador for refugees. We wish to state that we are interested in such a scheme and would like to have the opportunity of going into the matter further with you, but before doing so we would like to have some assurance from the Newfoundland Government that they are prepared and willing to entertain such a scheme. Our organization has 40,000 members and are vitally interested in the refugee problem."

Dr. Spiegal and Mr. Liepsen of Boston have stated that they have a tremendous interest in the Labrador refugee proposition and all they are waiting for before proceeding further is an assurance from the Newfoundland Government that they will entertain such a scheme.

If satisfactory arrangements should be made it is tentatively proposed to settle about 5,000 picked emigrants, adequately financed, during the first year and increase the number year by year as the settlement develops.

The Daily News, 2 March 1939. Front page headline "Has Plan to Settle Labrador."

Company, the biggest producer of herring and pilchard oil and meal in California. He had come to Newfoundland in 1937 with a proposal to launch three plants for herring reduction into oil and meal on Newfoundland's south coast and a floating herring-reduction plant on the coast of Labrador. In April 1939 he travelled to New York to firm up this proposal and other deals.[38] During his absence the Newfoundland Chief of Police inquired about Klapisch's criminal record in the United States. FBI Director J. Edgar Hoover replied that "one Henry Klapisch Jewish fish dealer" had been indicted in Alaska in 1930 charged with uttering worthless checks but that the outcome of this case was not known.[39] When Klapisch returned in July 1939, there were public references only to his floating herring-factory project on the Labrador coast.[40] The herring project was launched by the ratification of an agreement with the Commission of Government on 31 August 1939.[41]

By 1939, the public had become alerted to the possibility that Newfoundland might derive advantage from the refugee situation. A report featuring the economic benefits of refugee settlement, published on 16 January 1939 in Ottawa by the Canadian National Committee on Refugees and Victims of Political Persecution, found a remarkable echo in St. John's. The report called for an initiative in economic development through new industries not operating in Canada at the time to be launched by refugees. The skills of the Czechoslovak refugees from the Sudeten areas were characterized as being "based upon long training in one of the finest technical systems in the world," while the Jewish emigrants consisted of the "most highly educated, cultured section of Germany's population." The immigration of "carefully selected individuals or groups of refugees" would bring skills, new arts, crafts, and industries and thus prove of inestimable value to Canada's national economy.[42]

"Why should not Newfoundland also avail of the opportunity to reap the benefit?" wondered the editor of the *Evening Telegram* on 18 January 1939. The editorial recalled the industrial benefits to Britain from the influx of French Huguenots with their arts and crafts and the effect upon Palestine of the return of the Jews. It drew the readers' attention to the fact that the 11,000 Jews permitted to settle provisionally in England since 1933 had not only managed to establish new industries and to remove the center of the fur industry from Leipzig to London, but were also employing 15,000 Englishmen. Australia, it was reported earlier,[43] would admit 15,000 refugees within the next three years, giving preference to those able to establish new industries.

JOHN H. PENSON'S INITIATIVES IN 1939

Government records reveal that since April 1937 Newfoundland's newly appointed British Commissioner of Finance John Hubert Penson had been quietly pursuing a strategy aimed at bringing some economically beneficial refugee settlement to fruition. Penson, a British treasury official, had served in 1931 as an assistant to Percy Thompson (Newfoundland's British financial advisor) and later as Newfoundland's Acting Deputy Minister of Finance. Interested in proposals for promoting new secondary industries, especially for processing local products, and in developing appropriate schemes of financial assistance, Penson became a driving force behind the launching of a new industries committee in cooperation with the Board of Trade.

The pursuit of such an industrial development strategy was in accordance with the Commission's long-range reconstruction plan as articulated in the Gorvin Interim Report of November 1938.[44] Gorvin was a principal attached to the Ministry of Agriculture and Fisheries in England who was seconded to the Commission to advise on development prospects. In his Interim Report J.H. Gorvin deplored the low standards of education and the lack of apprenticeship for trades in Newfoundland. Although the thrust of his recommendations was on schemes of rural reconstruction, he urged an offensive "over a wide front by a combination of the best brains the trade and industry of the country and the Departments of Government can produce." He suggested new industries on the model of Norway and the recruitment of experts. "Let us invite to our shores . . . those men and women who can best help—scientists, engineers, agriculturists, economists, social workers," he told the St. John's Rotary. "Let us develop organized effort to suit Newfoundland."[45]

Penson was aware that in November 1938 the Dominions Office was considering sending representatives of refugee organizations to Newfoundland to examine settlement possibilities. On 6 February 1939 Penson, after consultation with fellow British Commissioner Robert B. Ewbank (who had succeeded Hope Simpson to head the Department of Natural Resources), confidentially approached the Dominions Office about suitable refugee enterprises. As industrial projects Penson tentatively suggested a newsprint mill in Labrador, a wall-board factory, fish canning or preparation, and the development of mineral resources. At the same time he attached five conditions to such settlement: (1) the industry must be established in a thinly populated part, (2) it must not compete with existing industries, (3) it must be self-supporting, (4) it should give employment not only to the refugees but also, directly and indirectly, to Newfoundlanders, and (5) it required capital for starting up the factory and for housing its employees. The pressure to find a home even for small numbers of refugees may be so great, Penson figured, "that even very exacting terms—provided they are not wholly unreasonable—may very possibly be accepted."

Penson acknowledged that "the policy adopted has for long been very definitely unfavourable to anything like general immigration of foreigners." Certainly Newfoundland, with unoccupied territory and many undeveloped resources, was under a certain degree of obligation to consider the possibility of permitting controlled refugee immigration. But he decided not to stress that aspect. Rather, he was guided by the question "whether advantage could not be gained from the present refugee situation" since large funds were being collected in the United States and elsewhere for the settlement of Jewish emigrants from Germany. The main social objections to be anticipated and against which precautions had to be taken from the outset were (1) that the refugees might end up in heavily populated regions, (2) that they might form a substantial part of the population in areas already occupied or where Newfoundlanders themselves would like to develop, and (3) "that they might enter this country in such numbers that they would form a substantial part of the population of the country as a whole."

To forestall these dangers, immigrants would be allowed to enter only in limited numbers and only under an approved scheme for thinly populated areas. The scheme must provide an organization through which the immigrants would secure their livelihood and which would be responsible for keeping them from spreading to other parts of the country. Penson did not think that local feeling would necessarily be opposed if the proposal could be shown to be of sufficient advantage to the country itself by bringing in opportunities for new industries, new chances of employment, etc. He proposed an initial quota of one thousand families.[46]

The Dominions Office could not help but be skeptical of Penson's petty terms and in his introductory remarks C.R. Price anticipated nothing but problems for refugee industries in the absence of a local market as a backbone. Any proposal for a new industry would be beset with local and political difficulties and its examination would have to be exhaustive, assistant secretaries Price and Clutterbuck agreed. A new industry could not be expected to be self-supporting and not in competition with existing industries unless it would be one which it would be natural and reasonable to establish (in which case local opinion would no doubt demand to know why such an industry had not been established for the benefit of Newfoundlanders) or it would be an artificially created industry, in which case its prospects of success would be small.

Location in a remote area would mean that starting capital was required not only for the factory but also for the housing of its employees. "Settlement in a new country is difficult enough in itself, harder still for foreign refugees," R. Wiseman commented. "To couple it with banishment to a remote district would make it virtually impracticable from the outset." Concerning funding, Price feared that, even if British-held Czechoslovak government money were used for settling Czech refugees in Newfoundland, it might be "resented by the Newfoundlanders who might be expected to claim that if any United Kingdom money is to be spent in the Island it should be spent on them and not on aliens."

To gauge the support Penson's initiative might enjoy in the Commission, Sir Eric Machtig of the Dominions Office decided to solicit confidentially the opinion of Commissioner for Public Utilities Wilfrid Woods, the third British Commissioner besides Penson and Ewbank (and successor to Lodge since January 1937), who was on a visit to London to discuss the Gorvin report. Woods believed that getting a small number of refugees into Newfoundland would be "a very good thing," provided of course, that they were adequately financed from other than Newfoundland sources. Newfoundland public opinion would not react unfavorably under this condition. It did not matter whether the refugees came in for industrial or agricultural purposes, and Woods thought "it would be very interesting and instructive to see what people of alien stock made of N'land conditions." Woods was sure that, had Penson put his suggestions before the Commission, they would have been sympathetically received. In fact, Woods personally believed that the terms stipulated by Penson were "almost absurdly stiff," but he was "all in favor of our initiating enquiries on the basis of Mr. Penson's suggestions." There would be no need to worry that possible leaks might become embarrassing to the Commission.

> On the contrary, they might gain some credit, for they would be able to show that they had made it clear that they could only consider such proposals on terms which would ensure no conflict with N'land interests, and indeed that it was their duty to make clear that the present refugee situation did not provide an opportunity of devising a scheme which, while serving humanitarian purposes, would also be of direct benefit to the Island.[47]

Woods' positive evaluation prompted the Dominions Office to signal to Newfoundland on 22 May 1939 that enquiries would be initiated as soon as a telegraph had been received confirming that the Commission as a whole had concurred with the proposal. The Dominions Secretary proposed to proceed by sending representatives of refugee interests or organizations to Newfoundland with a view to examination of possibilities and discussion with the Commission of Government.[48]

Penson presented his initiative to the Commission on 27 May as "a purely tentative outline indicating no more than the terms on which, in my opinion, we could consider the question of admitting assisted immigrants into Labrador or possibly (at a later stage) into sparsely populated districts of Newfoundland." The essential first step, furthermore, was to be made by the interested organization, and not by the Government of Newfoundland. "We would then be entirely uncommitted on our side, and would then be free to lay down such terms as we thought fit, or alternatively to reject the proposal altogether if it did not seem sufficiently advantageous." Penson merely wanted the Commission to commit itself in principle to the consideration of the reception of a body of refugee settlers.[49]

The support which Penson received from his fellow Newfoundland Commissioners was just as noncommittal as the way he presented his plans to them. On 12 June he replied to Clutterbuck that in view of the experience of other countries, the Commission wanted for consideration an outline of the terms on which the refugee organization was prepared to put forward proposals before an indication of Newfoundland's attitude could be given. Penson wondered whether "it would be possible to gather information without disclosing that Newfoundland was in any way interested."[50]

The Dominions Office interpreted Penson's reply as an indication "that the Commission as a whole are not enamoured of the idea" and Assistant Secretary Price had "the strongest doubts as to the practicability of any of Mr. Penson's proposals." Clutterbuck felt that the Dominions Office could hardly refuse to make some enquiry, but no organization, however much interested, could be expected to put forward specific proposals without first sending someone out to study possibilities on the spot. The prevailing opinion was that without an indication as to the possibilities or the attitude of Newfoundland any enquiries among refugee organizations would be futile and a waste of time. The Dominions Secretary therefore informed the Commission by telegram of 5 July 1939 that he would be unable to make enquiries among refugee organizations unless he had assurances that their representatives would be welcome in Newfoundland to make investigations on the spot.[51]

The Newfoundland government did not react until it had received a second telegram from the Dominions Office dated 21 July. This telegram concerned enquiries which had been received from the London office of the German Jewish Aid Committee in response to a report in the *Times* of 20 April. It had disclosed that "in spite of the heavy unemployment in Newfoundland, there has been some discussion in the island about the advisability of welcoming the immigration of a limited number of craftsmen who could establish new industries." The Overseas Settlement Department of the Committee, indicating that it had a number of skilled craftsmen on hand, desired to know if these openings would be available for refugees and what types would be suitable.[52] The Governor of Newfoundland answered on 27 July that a limited number of specialists or professional workers proposing to establish new industries would be permitted to enter as individuals, provided they had recognized qualifications as such and no less than $250 in their possession or could otherwise prove that they were able to support themselves. The same would apply to farmers, but not to medical professionals who would have to obtain permission to practice from the local Medical Council.

As to the Dominion Secretary's request of 5 July 1939, Penson was pleased that Whitehall endorsed the course of action he had in mind. On 24 July he proposed to reply that

> we should be glad of an investigation of certain parts of New-foundland territory as a possible location for a controlled immigration scheme. Actually area to which investigation would probably be directed is Labrador. For guidance of organization it might be mentioned that industries which appear most likely to be worth consideration in that region are lumbering and paper manufacture, fish canning or curing, and agriculture.[53]

The reply which was actually sent to London on 27 July indicates that the majority in the Commission insisted on a significant qualifying addition to the first sentence, namely "cost of investigation falling, of course, on this Organisation."[54] This was the closest the Newfoundland government ever came to offering asylum to refugees from the Third Reich. In September 1939 Commissioner Woods inquired with Finnish geographer Väinö Tanner, who had led scientific expeditions to Labrador in 1937 and 1939, about the chances for colonization to succeed there. Tanner expressed views "very favourable to the prospects of economic development in Labrador." In a short memorandum to the Commission, he considered the total area available for colonization "considerable," and he particularly recommended mixed farming in southern Labrador.[55]

Unfortunately, all this was too little too late. R. Wiseman of the Dominions Office pointed out that refugee organizations in Britain had no money and therefore it would be useless to approach them. There was no need for a reply and the Dominions Office decided to put Newfoundland's proposal "into cold storage."[56]

In the summer of 1939 the promotion of new industries in accordance with the Gorvin Report had become official policy. The cooperation between government and private business in pursuit of this objective found its expression in the creation of the New Industries Committee (the predecessor of the Newfoundland Industrial Development Board) with Penson as chairman. The seriousness of the Commission's intent to stimulate domestic industrial activity is indicated by the allocation for this purpose of nearly one quarter of the overall expenditures envisaged for the implementation of Gorvin's rehabilitation program.[57] In May, the British reconstruction advisor John H. Gorvin himself became Commissioner for Natural Resources. He was known as an outspoken advocate of soliciting refugee industrial skills and expertise.

Despite the government's quest for economic rehabilitation through the development of new industries, nothing concrete came of Penson's timid and half-hearted search for refugee industries. In June 1939 two German refugee merchants visited Newfoundland at the recommendation of the Newfoundland Trade Commissioner in London on a combined business and pleasure trip, according to the Criminal Investigation Bureau of the Newfoundland Constabulary.[58] Earlier, in 1934 and possibly in 1936, refugee group settlement with independent funding and the prospect for significant industrial development had been available had the government pursued Belkin's and Banikhin's proposals. When in 1939 the Commission squeamishly tried to solicit the very type of offer it had rejected earlier, refugee organizations had no more capital to invest or no longer wanted to invest it in Labrador. In the memory of the advocates of industrial development, the Commission of Government had "missed the opportunity of a lifetime."[59]

"We should first look to British stock"   **6**

Public Perceptions and Reactions, 1933-1939

THE PRESS AND THE REFUGEE CRISIS OF THE 1930S

An analysis of the proposals for economically beneficial refugee group settlement in Newfoundland and Labrador reveals the important role the media and public opinion played or were assigned to play. Belkin's proposal is a case in point. In this first confrontation between one Commissioner's reforming tendencies and the conservative establishment's opposition to any change that affected its own vested interest, the newly appointed and still insecure Commission of Government felt that, with regard to the contentious issue of reversing immigration policy, the local press should call upon public opinion to be the arbiter. Although the Newfoundland Medical Board decided the issue in its favor and prevented public opinion from playing the assigned role, the few comments that appeared in the press in 1934 indicated that, outside St. John's, opinion was anything but hostile to the proposed settlement of Jewish professional and business people. By the beginning of 1939 the pros and cons of the refugee question had been vented sufficiently for Klapisch to consider it advantageous to resort to the press to announce his scheme. Penson's approaches in the summer of 1939, as well, were encouraged by a certain amount of public support for refugee industries.

Judged by editorial comments expressed in St. John's in January 1934, the cards seemed to be stacked against any refugee immigration. "Inasmuch as our industrial and commercial activity is not great enough to absorb the local labour surplus," a leading

St. John's paper summed up the standard argument, "it would be in the nature of folly to import more population." The editorial declared that Newfoundland did not want the type of central European immigrant who was attracted to Canada by the schemes of the Canadian railways. Immigration on any scale would be conceivable only if it were British and carefully planned.[1]

Five years later the *Evening Telegram's* editor confirmed the continued prevalence of the traditionally dichotomous attitude towards immigration when he hailed the publication of a handbook on Newfoundland,[2] written in the summer of 1939 by the director of the Newfoundland Information Bureau in New York, Robert H. Tait, and distributed to tourists and prospective settlers. The handbook informed readers that

> Newfoundland does not bar the entry for temporary or permanent residence of a desirable immigrant, i.e. one who can show that he is capable of supporting decently himself and his dependents and is not likely to become a public charge, who is of good reputation and character, and who is not suffering from any mental or bodily disease.

At the same time the handbook promoted Newfoundland's ethnic homogeneity as an asset. With non-British residents forming a "negligible" minority of 653, the colony was spared the kind of "racial problems that confront the countries on the mainland or in other parts of the Empire."

The yearning, on the one hand, for "desirable" settlers to develop the island's resources and, on the other hand, the country's *de facto* closure to any foreign immigration in general and the rejection of all prospective refugee farmers in particular, became such a standard pattern of behavior that its absurdity was not questioned. Tait could not resist the temptation of reiterating the traditional lure that "all through the island are potential farm lands which could be rendered capable of supporting a population many times as great as that which now occupies it." Although exposing Newfoundland's social and economic plight, the handbook declared that "every inducement is given to promote the settlement of the country and encourage development of its natural resources." The laws regulating the purchase or leasing of Crown lands were presented as very liberal in character, and the government was reported to be encouraging agricultural development by offering a land clearing bonus of $25 an acre and a freight bonus on limestone fertilizer.[3]

As long as the number of requests for asylum seemed negligible, public opinion on the refugee question was not articulated although the media recognized the seriousness of the refugee-generating

developments in the Third Reich and gave it considerable publicity.
When in 1938 the refugee crisis suddenly made headlines, Newfoundland was preoccupied with a renewed economic crisis. The
surge in able-bodied relief, whose recipients were more numerous
in the winter of 1938–39 than at any other time since March 1934,
indicates the gravity of the economic situation.[4] Aggravated by the
country's economic plight, the terrifying and well-publicized spec-
tacle of an escalating demand for asylum thus played into the hands
of those who, out of traditional conviction, advocated a comprehensive policy of exclusion.

The strong and controversial sentiments expressed in the public
debate over the desirability of opening the doors to refugees were
exacerbated by the frightening image the media transmitted of the
international refugee situation. The editors of the three main newspapers articulated conflicting perceptions of and responses to the
refugee crisis, and they sought with unequal degrees of determination to tip the scales of government policy. The advocates of refugee
immigration and settlement experienced on more than one occasion
the "making" of public opinion in St. John's by those newspaper
editors who traditionally acted as mouthpieces for political,
religious, or other divisions among the elite. The most influential St.
John's paper's editorial stance and public impact on refugee policy
remained true to the reputation the local press was said to have
acquired as a factor in Newfoundland's political life, namely the
reputation that it "makes for mischief, not good."[5] Newspapers were
not representative of opinions in the outports since—largely due to
transportation problems—they were not widely circulated outside
the capital city area.

Most effective, judged by the numerous concurring anti-refugee
comments it evoked, seems to have been the nativist stance promoted by Charles E.A. Jeffery, editor from 1923 to 1959 of the
Evening Telegram, Newfoundland's oldest daily newspaper. Jeffery's
outlook reflected his vita: his upbringing as the son of an Anglican
priest who had immigrated in 1874 from England, his occupation
as a schoolteacher from 1901–13, his volunteer service in the
Canadian Expeditionary Force from 1914–18 (which seconded him
in 1917–18 to the Canadian High Commissioner's Office in London),
and his headship of the Ex-Servicemen's Rehabilitation School in
St. John's from 1919–21. Stubborn, provocative, and righteous,
Jeffery remained even to co-workers the typical schoolteacher.
During his term as editor, Jeffery singlehandedly determined the
paper's editorial stance without any interference from the paper's
owner. He wrote all of his paper's editorials himself, except during

his absence when he subscribed to a "canned" mainland editorial service.[6] In the 1930s the *Evening Telegram* had an estimated circulation of 20,000 and was known to have the best advertising patronage of any paper in Newfoundland. It grew steadily in importance and size and was seen "acquiring decided political influence."[7]

Jeffery's chief competitor was John S. Currie, editor of the conservative *Daily News* from 1916–1956. A member of the House of Assembly (1913–19), of the government in 1919, and the Legislative Council (1932–34), Currie and his paper rallied the opposition to Confederation in 1948. Harold Horwood's depiction of Currie as "almost painfully respectable" and "a pillar of the United Church" adequately reflects the *Daily News'* reticent and sympathetic editorial posture with regard to refugee settlement. Currie's editorials were critical of Jeffery's often provocative stance. "It is not too much to say that no newspaper ever published in the colony has done more for its social, moral and political uplift," judged Alfred B. Morine in the 1930s.[8] However, the smaller number of supportive letters to the editor indicated that Currie's viewpoint was less popular.[9]

The third, and least influential, opinion maker was Albert B. Perlin. The son of Israel Perlin, the acknowledged founder of the local Jewish community and an astute, successful wholesale dealer in St. John's, Albert aspired from the beginning to upward social mobility.[10] From 1934 to 1978 Perlin was associate editor of the *Daily News* and wrote daily editorial columns for it. As a journalist and public affairs critic, he emerged in 1934 as a leading spokesman of a small but vociferous and growing segment of the public that expected from the Commission of Government entirely new initiatives in economic development. Perlin wanted to see not only more efficient government and a reform of the crisis-ridden fishing industry, but also the development of new industries as well as selective immigration. Although a convert to Protestantism, he acknowledged and appreciated his Jewish roots; the combination enabled him to view Newfoundland society insightfully from the dual perspective of an insider as well as an outsider. In his 1933 testimony to the Amulree Commission's inquiry into the reasons for Newfoundland's economic collapse, Perlin denounced what he termed the "small mind" that is opposed to experts. Experts provide "the progressive brain that our people do not have," he said. For the same reasons he favored immigration as a necessary infusion of fresh blood.[11]

In 1934 Perlin launched his news magazine *Observer's Weekly* as the advocate of a more open, progressive, and industrially diversified Newfoundland. Perlin's editorials challenged the government and the public to overcome Newfoundland's handicaps. What was needed was less respect for tradition, he asserted, and more courage to take appropriate and prompt action in emergencies. Decrying government schemes of agricultural cooperation, Perlin demanded that the Commission be chaired by a business executive. What, he asked, "is keeping this country alive today? Four great industrial enterprises, employing perhaps no more than a total of 10,000 men."[12] While Perlin's *Observer's Weekly* never openly espoused the cause of admitting Jewish or other refugees to Newfoundland, he acted on the correct premise that, with a quarter of the population on the dole and tuberculosis rampant in the outports, a campaign for industrial diversification and hence new employment oppor-tunities would have a greater chance of convincing Newfound-landers to open their doors to skilled refugees than would outright appeals for charity.

MEDIA PERCEPTIONS OF REFUGEE-GENERATING CONDITIONS IN EUROPE

What kind of image did the Newfoundland media present to their reading public about the conditions generating refugees and their plight? Anyone gleaning the Newfoundland press of the 1930s cannot overlook the extensive news coverage devoted to the refugee problem and the conditions that caused it. The media provided particularly rich information on virtually every aspect of the mass flight caused by the establishment of the Third Reich in 1933 and the acute persecutions beginning in 1938. Thus, the contemporary newspaper reading public could have been reasonably well informed on these developments.

The *Daily News* one month after the Nazi takeover noted (8 and 21 March) the departure of "many" newspaper men, an "embarrass-ing" exodus of political exiles to Austria, the Netherlands, and Belgium, and the expulsion of Jewish doctors from Berlin hospitals. The front page headline of the 1 April issue read "Acute Persecution of Jews Seen in Germany: Germany Boycotts all Jewish Stores . . . Jewish Doctors, Lawyers and Judges Dismissed." The editor inter-preted the boycott of Jewish stores and the removal of all judges, lawyers, officials, and professors as "excesses" that he attributed to "underlying and primary causes." The situation was a passing one, which would right itself when Hitler's intoxication with his newly acquired power had cooled down. On 11 September readers were informed, that of the 40,000 Jews who had left Germany since Hitlerism had begun, most had gone to France.

The *Evening Telegram* (21 September 1933) reported the arrival of 4,000 Jewish refugees in Czechoslovakia, some with substantial sums of money, others unable to support themselves and cared for by a Czech central welfare committee. The paper took a dim view of Nazi Germany's agenda in general and the kind of future it held in store for Jews in particular. Its readers could learn (29 September 1933) that some 300 German professors had been dismissed, that many of the most distinguished German intellectuals were in exile, and that thousands of students were denied the prospect of further study. Europe, the paper quoted Harold Laski, "has seen nothing like it since the policy inaugurated by Louis XIV in the grim years of relentless persecution which preceded the Revocation of the Edict of Nantes."

Comments and editorials in 1933 in the two St. John's daily papers did not always agree on what sense to make of persecutions and expulsions in Germany. On 5 May, the *Daily News* published E. Hickman's positive impressions of a visit to Germany, suggesting that the "recent Jewish outbreak" had been confined to Berlin "where the greater number of lawyers are Jews." In the 11 July issue of the *Daily News* Lord Rothermere spread the anti-Semitic fable that "Israelites of international attachment were insinuating them-selves in key positions in the German administration." Hitler had allegedly saved a country which was rapidly falling under the control of its alien elements. Rothermere warned Newfoundlanders

> not to be misled by any misrepresentation of Hitler's opponents who launched a clamorous campaign against 'Nazi atrocities' which consist merely of a few isolated acts of violence such as are inevitable among a nation half as big as ours, and which have been generalized, multiplied, and exaggerated in order to convey the impression that Nazi rule is a blood-thirsty tyranny.

Perspectives offered by men like Rothermere seem to have sug-gested to some members of Newfoundland's elite that certain lessons might be learned from Germany's new order. In February 1934 a judge in Corner Brook was reported to have censured a father of ten children who could not pay his bills with these words: "Men of your type ought to be treated as they are treating them in Germany. You ought to be sterilized. More animal than brains, that is the trouble."[13]

Refugees returned to the public limelight in the summer and fall of 1938 as one of the manifestations of an international crisis heading inexorably for war. Media condemnation of Hitler as a ruthless fanatic was now unanimous in light of the anti-Semitic violence descending on annexed Austria and spreading to Czechoslovakia and beyond. Throughout the fall of 1938 the plight of more than 100,000 "absolutely destitute" refugees from the ceded Czech territories made headlines. Many of these refugees were desperate to enter Canada.[14] Two refugee-related issues preoccupied the local media until the outbreak of the war: the steady deterioration of the refugee situation and the urgent search for sanctuary set in motion by the Evian Conference in July 1938 and the newly created IGCR (see chapter 2).

The failure of Evian was blamed partly on the Third Reich's successful instigation of anti-Semitism in other countries, such as Poland and Romania, partly on the refugees' destitution. The crux of the problem, the editor of the *Evening Telegram* (27 July 1938) quoted *The Times* of London, is that "the Nazis take the bulk of the Jewish fortunes into their custody . . . and seek to fling their own impoverished subjects . . . on the benevolence of other countries." But he also reminded readers that every country, not just Germany, which adopted the stance of "Am I my brother's keeper?" bore responsibility for "the utter inhumanity let loose in Vienna," and he drew attention both to Canada's closed doors and to Australia's refusal to depart from its practice of bringing in only settlers of British nationality.

The brutality of German anti-Semitic persecution was unequivocally condemned by the Newfoundland media. The Jews' continued subjection to violence following *Kristallnacht*, their expulsion from their last remaining positions in Germany's social and economic life, the detention of 60,000 in concentration camps, and the confiscation of one-fifth of personal assets above $2,000 as down payment of a $400 million fine imposed upon them, was featured in considerable detail in the local press.[15] The barbarism of *Kristallnacht* had so alienated public opinion in the democracies, was the consensus of the *Evening Telegram* (12 November 1938) and *Observer's Weekly* (29 November 1938), that there could be little common ground of understanding with the Nazi regime since "intolerance of differences of race, creed or colour finds no favour under the rule of democracy." Opinions voiced in these papers agreed that this anti-Semitic terrorism like "every act of the people and even their thoughts are directed by the head of the State."

A number of prominent Newfoundlanders returned from visits to Germany in 1938–39 conveying conflicting impressions. Among them were Alan Gillingham, A.E. Hickman, O.L. Vardy, and C.E.A. Jeffery. Some, like Memorial University College Professor Gillingham, were careful to distinguish between the Nazi regime and the German people. His Rotary address, published in the *Daily News* of

27 January 1939, emphasized the point that the great mass of the German people are "utterly innocent" of Nazi convictions.

> Most Germans listen to the speeches of the Nazi leaders or read them in the press, not with enthusiasm, but with care, sorrow and resentment. The Nazis have forgotten too that deeds speak louder than words. Enlightened Germans, probably a majority of the population, dissociate themselves from the policy and practice of the Government.

Gillingham stressed that with regard to their love for peace, patriotism, and morality, Germans differed little from any other people. He found it hard to believe that the English had a monopoly on righteousness.

Rotarian A.E. Hickman stated that all Germans he met, both Jews and Christians, were kind and subservient. They put up with the regime's restrictions and regulations because they were never free. "Almost every German is a spy, not necessarily a Government paid spy, but ready to catch any word dropped against Hitler and report it." The most unfortunate Germans were Jews born in Germany whose ancestors had lived there for a century or more. Hickman recounted the ordeals of an old Jewish acquaintance of his who was taken from his office after *Kristallnacht* and placed in a jail. His house was ransacked, and his wife ordered to leave. In jail that Jewish friend witnessed the murder of fellow inmates. Released after six months, he was broken in health. Jews had to surrender 95 percent of their property, and no lawyer would defend them. Hickman left no doubt that it was the "general opinion of Jewish people still living in Germany that in the event of war by Germany every Jew would forthwith be shot."[16]

Local broadcaster and journalist O.L. Vardy was impressed by the extent to which Nazi propaganda had brainwashed Germans. The only persons he found questioning official propaganda were people of 40 years and older. "Youths from 20 to 25 hold down practically all the important positions and they believe that Hitler can do no wrong." Vardy nevertheless concluded categorically that the German people would "rise as one man and sweep Hitler and his gang back to the oblivion whence they came" if they were free to judge Hitler's policies.[17] *Evening Telegram* editor Jeffery, on the other hand, appears to have witnessed nothing but "happy and contented" people on a visit to Vienna where he tried to ascertain reactions to the Nazi regime. Spending most of his time in indoor and outdoor places of amusement and entertainment, Jeffery saw people enjoying full employment, spending money freely, and crowding cafés, beer or wine gardens and "never saw fitter or healthier looking children." Although Jeffery reported observing plenty of uniformed officials in Vienna—police, SA, and SS men, the most disturbing experience he found worth recording was being the solitary occupant on the Royal Dutch Line flight to Vienna. The assertion that "on no occasion did I experience any unpleasantness" characterized his report.[18]

Throughout 1939, the St. John's press kept its reading public extremely well informed about the direction in which the steadily worsening European refugee crisis was heading. On the one hand, there were the weekly accounts of ever tightening restrictions on Germany's remaining Jews—their elimination from the roster of registered handicraftsmen, the liquidation of Jewish retail stores, the issuing of special ID cards with Israel and Sarah as first names, the confiscation of radios, and the ousting of one hundred Berlin Jews daily from that city—alternating with news of purges and expulsions of Jews from Italy, anti-Semitic riots in Romania, anti-Jewish legislation in Hungary, the impossibility of German Jews emigrating with the $400 million Nazi levy hanging over their heads, and increasing numbers of Jewish suicides in Germany.[19] The editor of *Observer's Weekly* (6 December 1938) aptly compared the situation of Jews brought on by the snowballing restrictions with that of "a cage in which they live the lives of complete outcasts."

At the same time, headlines conveyed the specter of an exploding exodus of refugees from Europe seeking a haven: 200 of a projected contingent of 5,000 German refugee children leaving for England via Holland (2 December 1938); 350 Austrian refugee children reach England (16 December 1938); 4,000 Danzig Jews unable to go to Palestine (24 December 1938); 6,000 Germans entering Britain since September 1938 (3 February 1939); wandering band of 165 Austrian Jews, thrice refused, admitted to Venezuela (4 April 1939); Britain receiving 1,500 more refugees (13 June 1939); Britain haven for 44,909 German, Austrian, and Czech refugees (20 June 1939); Sudeten refugees in Canada (11 August 1939); Nazis proscribe life for 265,000 Jews, etc. (25 August 1939). With the gates of the traditional refugee-receiving countries closed or closing, newspaper articles from September 1938 through August 1939 featured the British Government, the IGCR, and Jewish relief agencies scanning the world map for real and potential refugee havens. From Mexico, Australia, Canada, and Finland, the search was reported moving on to more and more exotic places like British Guyana, Tanganyika, the South Pacific Islands, Cuba, the Dominican Republic, and Alaska. Newfoundland and Labrador are also mentioned in this context.

Press portrayals of the ordeals of the refugees scrambling for a haven in 1939 leave little doubt that their journey was heading inexorably for catastrophe. An eminent example was the ill-fated trip of the German liner *St. Louis* with 907 German Jewish refugees on board (see chapter 2). The *Evening Telegram* related its odyssey in four articles[20] and the *Daily News* even devoted three headlines and a large photograph to it over a period of 26 days.[21] The ship had left Hamburg for Cuba on 15 May 1939 but was not allowed to land there due to alleged visa problems and the lack of a bond of $500 for each refugee. When the Cuban president ordered at gunpoint the ship's return to Hamburg, the ship's crew apparently feared a "collective suicide pact" among the disheartened refugees. "Unless some other nation offers to give asylum to the 917 [sic] refugees they will have to return to Germany where in all probability they will be put into concentration camps," stated the paper on 2 June 1939. Anchoring off Miami on 5 June and "easily visible from the shore," the *St. Louis* was kept at a safe distance by the American Coast Guard.

The *St. Louis* was reported "steaming in aimless circles" while her unwanted cargo of refugees waited for an offer of asylum from Latin American or North American countries. Belgium, Holland, and France, already overcrowded with thousands of refugees, finally agreed to take 623, and England the rest. A cablephoto in the *Daily News* (29 June 1939) showed the hapless passengers debarking in Antwerp "jubilant at finding even a temporary haven after wandering for five weeks." Of those 623 incidentally, only 40 are known to have survived the war.[22] Although the plight of the *St. Louis* was widely publicized, Jewish refugee organizations were unsuccessful in their attempts to have any of its passengers admitted by Argentina, Paraguay, Uruguay, Panama, the United States, or Canada.

As the *St. Louis* passed by Newfoundland on its way back to Europe, the local press response was characterized by a notable lack of any editorials or expressions of humanitarian concern of the kind voiced on the occasion of *Kristallnacht*. After having drawn attention to the ship's desperate pleas for sanctuary, the *Evening Telegram* did not consider the *St. Louis* story even important enough to feature in its weekly recapitulation of "News of the Week" section on 3, 10 or 17 June. Unlike *Kristallnacht*, the *St. Louis* tragedy came uncomfortably close to North America's shores and it would have been difficult to show empathy for the victimized refugees without offering help. Of course, Newfoundland had more than its own share of problems and if Latin America, the United States, or Canada were not prepared to come to the aid of the *St. Louis*, why should

Newfoundland? The *St. Louis* episode epitomized the general perception of the refugee crisis as a distant event, emotionally removed
from the concerns of Newfoundlanders. A review of the public
response to a possible influx of refugees confirms this impression.

REACTIONS AND OPINIONS

Opinions expressed in the columns of the local press reveal that only
the outports would have welcomed refugees. In St. John's, although
there seemed to be some support for admitting refugees with capital
to start viable new industries, the prevailing mood was hostile.
Objections to the refugees on the grounds of social class and adverse
economic impact went hand in hand with the contention that these
people constituted a threat to the ethnic identity of the host society
and were useless castaways for any country. It was alleged that in
business, labor, and other activities there was no room for increased
numbers. Even among Newfoundland's small Jewish community of
some 120 members, Simon Belkin observed concern in 1934 over
the prospect of further Jewish immigration. "It was the usual fear
that the increase in the number of Jews would prejudice the position
of the older residents in the Jewish community."[23]

The week after *Kristallnacht*, the editor of the *Evening Telegram*
(16 November 1939) voiced concern over the increase in the number
of Newfoundland's foreign-born (excluding natives of the United
Kingdom, Ireland, and the Dominions) from 731 in 1911 to 1,601 in
1935. Suggesting that most of the refugees, probably unskilled as
well as penniless, would become a burden to any country accepting
them, he urged a considerable stiffening of the immigration regulations to prevent the country from "being overrun by peoples who
could not possibly be absorbed in the population, for whom occupation is not available, or who, living on a lower standard, could
compete unfairly with residents, or who for other reasons would not
be desirable immigrants." When Newfoundland needs a larger population, responded one commentator approvingly in the *Evening
Telegram* on 17 November 1939, "we should first look to British
stock." He hoped that the public as well as the authorities would
realize "the danger of throwing this country open indiscriminately
to aliens."

Opposing the *Evening Telegram's* kowtowing to xenophobic prejudice, the editor of the *Daily News* (1 November 1938) wondered,
"Does all the world contain no land upon which refugees may be
settled to work out their own salvation as pioneer communities?" He
found it hard to believe that even completely unsettled and climati-
cally unfavorable tracts would be refused. "Some such tracts there

must be, Labrador might even be one of them, in which refugees willing to work and financed during the period of reestablishment may be able to work out a new destiny far removed from their birth where political, religious, and racial intolerance have made life unlivable," he concluded.

Shocked by the *Kristallnacht* tragedy, an anonymous resident of St. John's pleaded in the *Daily News* for Newfoundland to do something. "It is not often that Newfoundland is able to assist others. We think we have so little to offer. But we have the present of freedom . . . And we need doctors badly." The writer pointed out that New-foundland, Canadian, English, and American doctors were very reluctant to accept the conditions of living in Newfoundland outports where everything was lacking and that it should be possible to bring in German-Jewish doctors through some Jewish refugee organiza-tion and assign them to certain territories so they would not interfere with local doctors. Extending a helping hand to refugees in distress would, at the same time, mean recruiting for Newfoundland a class of badly needed people. "History has shown that any country which has extended ordinary rights to Jews has never lost by it."[24]

As expected, the *Evening Telegram* did not take kindly to the Inter-Governmental Refugee Committee's suggestion that New-foundland be added to the list of prospective havens within the Empire. "The opinion is general," maintained one of its editorial columnists on 16 January 1939, "that Newfoundland is more or less an open field for those who feel inclined to come in from other countries and settle or work here. The number of occasions on which Newfoundlanders have been fleeced by outsiders taking advantage of this laxity on the part of our immigration laws is apparent from a perusal of back issues of the local newspapers." While admitting that "Newfoundland for Newfoundlanders" was too narrow a posture, he nonetheless urged that immigration laws be tightened to the same extent as those facing Newfoundlanders entering other countries.

The next day the *Evening Telegram's* editor reiterated the warn-ing that the possibility of settling "some" of the refugees in Newfoundland was "not without danger" in view of the fact that the immigration laws of the country imposed little or no restrictions upon anyone choosing to come here. However, he would not be opposed to the establishment of industrial undertakings by carefully selected refugees skilled in some promising trade or handicraft, especially if assisted by some of the "immense" international funds allegedly available to resettle refugees. The sympathy the editor suddenly felt for "saving these people from the suffering they are undergoing and from the even worse fate that may be in store for

The Daily News

THE DAILY NEWS is a morning paper established
in 1894 and published daily at the News Building, 325-329 Duckworth Street, St. John's, New-
oundland, by ROBINSON & COMPANY, LIMITED.

TELEPHONE NUMBERS...........178 and 179

All Press services and Feature articles in this
paper are copyright and their reproduction is
prohibited.

ST. JOHN'S, NOVEMBER 1, 1938.

NO PLACE TO GO

The wide open spaces of the most
sparsely-settled of Empire countries have no
room for the hundreds of thousands of refugees who for political or racial reasons are
now existing in Europe in helpless and hope-
less misery. This fact has been ascertained
by Mr. George Rublee who has undertaken
the almost superhuman task of directing the
activities of the International Refugee Committee.

The British dominions want only trained farmers. They cannot be blamed for that.
The world already has too many white col-
lared workers. And even the vast spaces of
South America will not provide a home for
an appreciable number of these human
derelicts of Europe for a similar reason.

But is there no possible solution to this
unprecedented problem.? Does all the world
contain no land areas upon which refugees
may be settled to work out their own salvation as pioneer communities? After the
miseries they have endured or are now enduring, it would seem reasonable to imagine
that the opportunity to build anew in some
completely unsettled tract, even where
climatic and other hardships have to be suffered, would be refused. Some such tracts
there must be, Labrador might even be one
of them, in which refugees willing to work
and financed during the period of re-establishment may be able to work out a new
destiny far removed from the lands of their
birth where political, religious, and racial
intolerance have made life unlivable.

them, should they be left to the mercy of their persecutors," was admittedly influenced by "our minds filled with the dream of industries which would absorb thousands of workers." Thanks to a Canadian report on economic benefits associated with refugees, it dawned on the *Evening Telegram* editor that in Newfoundland these people might contribute to the economy by, for example, utilizing tree and fish wastes, producing for export preserves and syrups from the presently scarcely touched acres of wild fruit, and harnessing some of the numerous streams for electrical power to operate commercial undertakings. "These things we have so far failed to use." Any such scheme, the editor conceded, might of course nevertheless be opposed on the ground that newcomers would be taking the bread out of the mouths of the local people. But the chief idea was that, using Newfoundland's many resources, they would apply themselves to some new form of occupation and thereby employ locals. Since the bulk of the refugees were reported to be highly skilled, the editorial was optimistic that it was "not merely possible, it is highly probable" that a select few of them might "make the utmost of the things that are available."

On 20 January 1939 a Newfoundlander, who claimed to have fifty years' personal experience in the fisheries, wrote the *Evening Telegram* that he "cannot see what help or knowledge any refugee from Central Europe can bring to us in Newfoundland." Ronald Martin, commercial agent and secretary of the Great War Veteran's Association, worried about the effect of refugees on both the wage scale and unemployment. "Hold fast Newfoundland to what little you have left. You are fast losing your identity," was his motto. In the *Daily News* (21 January 1939) he urged that Newfoundland impose a $500 tax on each admitted alien, $250 on each commercial traveller, "exclude the unfit," and adopt American-type immigration restrictions. In the *Evening Telegram* (9 February 1939) he characterized Newfoundland as "one of the few countries where the only bar to the ragtail and bobtail of the world is the cursory glance of officialdom."

On the other hand, public opinion was undeniably exerting pressure on Penson and the Commission in favor of refugee industries. That became obvious when the local press urged the recruitment of such world-famous manufacturers as the Czech Bata shoe company, whose intended relocation to Canada was initially opposed by the Canadian shoe industry. Such a business, the *Evening Telegram* of 22 June 1939 reasoned, might utilize local animal hides and seal skins, which were, at the time, all sent abroad for processing. Newfoundland, the *Daily News* of 7 July 1939 agreed,

THE EVENING TELEGRAM

Newfoundland's Oldest Newspaper
Founded in 1879 by W. J. Herder

Owned and Published by
THE EVENING TELEGRAM LIMITED
Address:
Water Street, St. John's, Newfoundland

Private Branch Exchange Connecting
All Departments
2900 — 2901 — 2902

The rights of reproduction in newspapers or in radio broadcasts, of Canadian Press despatches and other news items not credited appearing in this paper are strictly reserved.

Wednesday, November 16, 1938.

IMMIGRATION LAWS

With upheavals going on in many parts of the world and armies of refugees fleeing from their former homes to escape persecution, the question as to what is to become of them has created a serious problem. Japan has over-run a considerable part of China and untold thousands of Chinese have been rendered homeless and destitute. Fleeing from the wrath to come, many in Sudetenland and other parts of Czechoslovakia became outcasts rather than risk persecution under their new masters. In Germany and Austria, the Jews have been only too painfully made to understand that there is no place for them within the boundaries of the Reich. Exiles, they are compelled to become wanderers on the face of the earth, and to-day unfortunately there are no longer to be found promised lands into which they may enter in and take possession.

While no doubt many countries would extend a welcome to some of these exiles whose knowledge of science, arts and industries would make them useful settlers, by far the larger number, probably not only unskilled in any trade or profession but penniless as well, would become a burden to any country accepting them, and no state in these days is anxious to increase its non-supporting population. In addition, there are other good reasons why a country would consider it necessary to keep the door firmly closed against some refugee elements.

Because of the possibility of attempts being made by some of the latter to gain an entry into this country, it becomes all the more necessary to overhaul our immigration laws. On more than one occasion it has been pointed out in this column that the loopholes in the laws or the ease with which in other ways they permit undesirables to enter the country make the tightening up of the regulations necessary. According to the 1935 Census, the foreign-born population in that year was 1,601. (This is exclusive of persons born in the United Kingdom, Ireland and the British dominions and colonies). The total in 1911 was 731. To-day, more than ever before, the right to come in and settle is likely to be pressed, and unless the regulations are very considerably stiffened, the country runs the risk of being over-run by peoples who could not possibly be absorbed into the population, for whom occupation is not available, or who, living on a lower standard, could compete unfairly with residents, or who for other reasons would not be desirable immigrants.

The Evening Telegram, 16 November 1938. Editorial "Immigration Laws."

would welcome refugees of the kind reported to be setting up some twenty new industries in Montreal manufacturing glassware, chemicals, plastics, textile specialties, and food products, and employing a total capital of $2 million. "The opportunity is one that may be short-lived, and is certainly too good an opportunity to be lost for want of trying," the editorial concluded.

Opinions expressed in the local press in 1939 reveal that there was a groundswell of support for refugees if they brought new industries. On the other hand, opposition to the immigration of refugees without such industries was as strong and outspoken as ever. The reason Newfoundland cannot get any doctors but refugees to come here, charged an anonymous "Native" in the *Evening Telegram* of 11 February 1939, was that British doctors were not given a living wage, or the necessary things to work with. Those refugee doctors would be "followed by all their relations, good, bad and indifferent until we fail to remain predominantly British." Newfoundlanders should "strongly object to our country being the dumping ground of people who have been turned out of their own country."

The arrival in St. John's of two refugee physicians under contract to serve as nurses in the outports (see chapters 7 and 9), was greeted by the *Evening Telegram* (7 July 1939) with a stinging editorial. It criticized the admission of these refugees on every conceivable ground. "The foreigners" were suspected of taking away jobs from eligible Newfoundlanders, or lacking proper qualifications as doctors and nurses, and of being spies and fifth columnists entering the country under the guise of refugees. They were reproached for not being immigrants with the capital and skills necessary to establish badly needed new industry or a rare trade that would not interfere with any local industries. The editorial warned:

> Who vouches for the bona fides of these newcomers, and what steps are taken to prevent the entry of persons who in the capacity of doctors or nurses would have a great opportunity—in fact the best opportunity—to inculcate ideas inimical to the best interests of a British community?

PREJUDICE TOWARDS JEWS

Some of the critical comments were clearly motivated by a more or less overt anti-Semitism. For readers of the *Evening Telegram* this type of prejudice was evident in the frequency with which Jews figured in the paper's regular joke column as early as 1934, for instance, on 22 January, 5, 6, 14, 18, 26 April, 19 May, and 21 June. The joke on 14 April 1934 read: "A Jew repeatedly returned home

The Daily News, 15 November 1938. Letter to the editor "Asylum for German Jews."

LETTERS to the Editor

This Paper Assumes No Responsibility for the Opinions of its Correspondents

ASYLUM FOR GERMAN JEWS

Editor Daily News,

Dear Sir,—It is not often that Newfoundland is able to assist others. We think we have so little to offer.

But we have the blessing of freedom, and that at the present time is something to be greatly prized by one class of persecuted people.

And we need doctors badly.

Newfoundland, Canadian, English and American doctors are very reluctant to accept the conditions of living in our outports, with the small money to be earned and the lack of anything but elementary schools.

Is it not possible to make arrangements through some Jewish Refugee organization to bring German-Jewish doctors into this country? Undoubtedly practically all can speak a fair amount of English, and their co-religionists could purchase suitable dwelling houses and provide sufficient funds to establish them. Certain territories might be assigned to them so that they do not interfere with doctors now practising here.

History has shown that any country which has extended ordinary rights to Jews has never lost by it.

In this case, by holding out a helping hand in so far as it lies in our power we shall show that we are not entirely deaf to the cries of the persecuted, and our country, while alleviating in some small measure their distress, will reap a great benefit by bringing to our shores a class of people whom above all we need at this time.

Yours truly,
LISTENER-IN

St. John's,
November 14, 1938.

The Telegram Forum

THE EVENING TELEGRAM, while providing a means of venting matters of public import, accepts no responsibility for correspondents' opinions.

WOULD EXCLUDE REFUGEES.

Editor Evening Telegram.

Dear Sir,—Evidently a Mr. Paul Bernstein—who has a fantastic article in New York Journal American—is kind enough to propose dumping a number of refugees in this country. He says he posed as a geologist. It is a pity Mr. Bernstein did not confine his efforts to settling refugees in his own country. For too long have our emigration laws been too lax, anybody and everybody can get into the country, evidently. It is said that the Government is looking for refugee doctors and they can't get others to take up work here. If Doctors were given a living wage and were able to get the necessary things to do their work with, there would be no reason to think of importing non-British persons. Furthermore, if it is that people of our own race cannot live and do the work on salaries offered, how can we expect efficient work done by others, unless they are of the wrong type? We shall have some refugee doctors coming here followed by all their relations, good, bad, and indifferent until we shall fail to remain predominently British. It is said that some refugees who got into England employed thousands of people. That may be so in one case, but if one takes up trade papers he notices refugees advertising for jobs. For one, I hope that the people of Newfoundland will strongly object to our country being the dumping ground of people who have been turned out of their own country, and that rather than emigration laws being relaxed, Newfoundlanders will insist on a general tightening up. As things are, almost anything can happen overnight, so we—the people of Newfoundland—should be on our guard.

Yours truly,
NATIVE.

Rotary Address

The following is a synopsis of the address delivered to the Rotary Club on Thursday by Rev. Canon Howitt of St. Thomas's Church:—

After expressing his pleasure at being present the Reverend Gentleman continued; "When the history of these hectic years is written by historians in the future I am inclined to think they will set down as one of Germany's greatest mistakes her brutal treatment of her Jewish population. As soon as Herr Hitler gained the reins of power he began a campaign against the Jews. Last November, the 7th day of that month, a young Polish Jew driven almost insane by the hardships which his people were suffering, went to the German Consulate in Paris and shot a German secretary. His death was the signal for a campaign of brutality which other ages have not witnessed. Under the guidance of Goebbels the full terror of Nazi prosecution was loosed upon the Jews. Hundreds of Jewish stores were looted while the police stood looking on. Thousands of Jews, many of whom had occupied positions of importance were forced to the humiliating task of cleaning the streets of the city. Then to cap it all a fine of four hundred million dollars was levied upon the Jews throughout Germany. The same thing is continuing with increasing force today. The following is a quotation from a letter received by American friends from a Jew living in Germany, "We have a wonderful life, not a hair on the head of any Jew is being harmed, Uncle Maurice, who expressed a contrary view, is being hanged tomorrow." Alongside the prosecution there is a world-wide wave of anti-semiticism. Italy is adopting similar measures. Largely because of Nazi propaganda even on this side of the Atlantic there are signs of anti-Jewish feeling. What is the cause of this anti-semitic spirit? First of all there is national antipathy. Jews are to be found in all parts of the world, they always remain Jews, they are never of the people. Another cause is personal jealousy. Jews are exceedingly gifted and capable people and they have been remarkably successful. They are simply paying the price which every successful man has to pay. Another reason is financial capability. How much do we owe the Jews from a Christian standpoint? First from race meetings with empty pockets. 'How is it, Abe, that you always win at cards and never on the horses?' asked his wife anxiously. 'Vell, you see, my dear, I don't shuffle the race horses,' was the reply." Jews were the scapegoats in Lewis E. Emerson's railing in the 1929 legislative session against Canadian "Jew bootleggers" who were allegedly eager to control Newfoundland's liquor sales so that they "would then have the opportunity to pollute the liquor" sold in Newfoundland and rake in "huge profits."[25] Even at Memorial University College a faculty member's Jewish religion "could be a difficulty," wrote President John L. Paton to an American Jewish scientist applying for a position in 1931.[26]

On the occasion of the Royal visit to Newfoundland in June 1939, an unidentified Jewish Water Street businessman refused to give his employees an extra holiday. He led them to understand that he was not a millionaire and that the Royal visit meant nothing to him. Thereupon, he and his "race" were attacked in an anonymous letter to the *Evening Telegram* (26 June 1939) for being ungrateful while his kind was being persecuted in Germany. "Quite a lot of these people play their employees for a bunch of suckers," the writer said, when they ought to "crawl on hands and knees before the flag of the world's greatest Empire—where freedom is given to all regardless of creed and color."

On behalf of the Newfoundland Board of Trade, a director of Job Brothers & Co. Ltd., one of Newfoundland's oldest and largest firms, conveyed to the St. John's immigration agent his concern that in the past too many foreigners had come with the intention of competing in established lines of business. "I quite realize that there are not really so very many people coming into Newfoundland, and, on looking over the business on the street it would seem to me that the principal cause of worry is the Jews in the retail trade. These people do not carry their load as citizens of the Country and are serious competitors in the retail trade."[27]

It was apparently assumed in some quarters that Jewish refugees from Nazi persecution, if they were allowed in, would earn their livelihoods like Newfoundland's pre-World War I Jewish immigrants —"Jewish tailors, cheap furniture and clothing makers and vendors, ice cream and fish parlour keepers, and the like." Commissioner Penson had been told, as he informed the Commission in 1938, that "most persons of Jewish origin who landed here to take up residence commenced business as peddlars of dry goods. It is of this type that I imagine we should get the larger number were the door to emigrants opened." Penson admitted that "the attitude of the general public to any change in the present policy of exclusion cannot be ignored, and it is highly probable that it would be hostile."[28]

Aerial view of downtown St. John's, about 1949, showing the harbor, Court House, and Anglican Cathedral (both in the center). The first street parallel to the harbor is Water Street, Credit: PANL.

Water Street, St. John's, in June 1939, decorated on occasion of the Royal visit. Credit: Nora Gut.

"There is no prospect of room being found"　　7

Immigration Regulations and the Fate of Individual Refugee Applications, 1934-1939

IMMIGRATION LAW AND PRACTICE, 1934-1938

From 1934 to 1939 the Commission not only entertained significant proposals for refugee group settlement but also received numerous applications for entry from and on behalf of individual refugees. Newfoundland's officially distributed promotional literature and information sent to certain immigrants indicated to those who managed to access it that Newfoundland was seeking settlers with skills and capital.

Regulations for taking up farming operations on the island were apparently quite flexible for "desirable" settlers. In June 1936, for example, the Commission of Government found no objection to the settlement of a "suitable" Dutch family of five persons wishing to farm in Newfoundland. There were still areas of good virgin soil available, although starting funds of $2,500 would be needed for clearing the land, stocking the farm, and feeding a family of five. The cost of living was somewhat high, Governor Walwyn conceded, but the climate was "quite favorable for the growth of the most common farm crops found on the Atlantic seaboard of Canada and northern U.S.A."[1]

The generosity of Newfoundland's refugee laws, furthermore, were matched only by those of the United Kingdom. The island appeared enticing as an escape route, i.e., a temporary refuge, as well as a permanent sanctuary for refugees from the Third Reich. While some of the applicants chose Newfoundland because they had friends and relatives there, the choice for most of them was dictated by Newfoundland's proximity both to Europe and to North American traditional refugee receiving countries. Unable to enter the United States or Canada, either because they failed to obtain a visa or because the quota for their country was oversubscribed and they were placed on a long waiting list, refugees decided that sanctuary in Newfoundland would be preferable to whatever was offered by Shanghai and the few Latin American countries still open to refugees in 1939.

Little did refugees looking to Newfoundland for a haven know of the confusion characterizing the state of immigration law and practice since the Commission of Government took office in February 1934. Nor were they aware of the extent to which adverse public reaction to the refugee crisis affected the charting of immigration policy. On 19 January 1934 the proclamation of 1932 lapsed and was not renewed because the Dominions Office objected to any discrimination against specific countries or class of countries as likely leading to retaliatory action. The 1932 proclamation had prohibited immigration from most of Europe, all of Asia, Africa, and Latin America, as well as of all persons of the wage-earning or laboring classes. When the proclamation expired, the most discriminatory provisions of the 1926 Act were unenforceable, and the state of the law should have allowed a return to a rather more liberal practice. In reality, however, the immigration authorities continued to act—without fully apprising the public of the fact—in the spirit of the 1932 proclamation.

In 1934 and 1935 officials discussed the available alternatives to keeping the severe restrictions of the 1932 proclamation in effect. The choices before them were: a quota system, judged unsuitable to a country "where immigration is infinitesimal;" a general prohibition of immigration, save with special permission; or the issuing of permits through British consular officers. In the ensuing debate opposing positions emerged between British and Newfoundland officials in the various departments responsible for aspects of immigration. Differences developed particularly between the Departments of Finance (in charge of customs and immigration procedures under the 1906 and 1926 acts) and Justice (in charge of interpreting and revising the law and of administering deportations under the 1924 act).

The Commissioner for Finance E.N.R. Trentham endorsed the argument of his advisor on customs, P.D.H. Dunn (Chairman of the Board of Customs from 1935) in favor of a permit system. Intending settlers and visitors should apply to the Board of Customs, which acted as immigration authority, for a permit to land. Those favoring the enactment of a revised law allowing for exclusion by specified racial and national criteria included the Commissioner for Justice, W.R. Howley, his Secretary Brian E.S. Dunfield, and the Chief Commissioner of Immigration H.V. Hutchings. Howley considered it "a comparatively easy matter to make effective prohibition on such terms as will not in any way be embarrassing to international relations" and expected the Dominions Office to cooperate in drafting an appropriate proclamation.[2]

Dunfield and Hutchings, who had administered immigration and deportation before 1934, took up the defense of Newfoundland's traditional immigration policy. The 1926 act gave them the authority to declare "undesirable" any person "likely to become a public charge." They could also fall back on a doctrine which the Department of Justice, in connection with the deportation of two Italian immigrants, had communicated to the Customs Department as early as October 1927. It provided as follows:

> In the case of an immigrant who was not an undesirable person within the provision of the Acts, the Governor in Council may be the proper authority to decide on his exclusion, which the Governor in Council can do on any ground, or on no ground whatever if he thought fit.[3]

Dunfield, a lawyer and economics lecturer at Memorial University College, had been Acting Deputy Minister of Justice since 1927.[4] The government's legal expert on exclusion and deportation, Dunfield was highly critical of Dunn's prescription for an "ultra-generous" immigration policy which he considered appropriate for Britain but unsuitable for Newfoundland. He pointed out to Hope Simpson in 1935 that the 1924 and 1926 acts established "good expulsion procedure for use at any time." Dunfield explained that the 1924 provisions for expelling undesirable aliens were drawn up "to exclude Communists or others of suspected undesirable activities that we could not prove, at any rate, in our Courts."[5] Characterized by Commissioner Thomas Lodge as "an odd bird, an ex-associate of Squires, intelligent, very hard working but with a kink in his brain somewhere," Dunfield remained at his post until 1939. After a brief interlude in early 1937 as head of the Department of Rural Reconstruction (where he apparently clashed with British Commissioner Ewbank),[6] he became Commissioner L.E. Emerson's right hand man in the Department of Justice until he was appointed a judge of the Supreme Court in November 1939. Years after he retired from the Department of Justice, Dunfield found it amusing to scare a refugee immigrant whom he met socially with the taunt: "You shall be deported."[7]

H.V. Hutchings, who had served at his post since 1928, also stood for continuity in the administration of immigration rules and procedures. Guided by the spirit of the 1932 proclamation, he refused landing permits to aliens whenever possible. His practice was challenged in 1935 and 1936 by the solicitors of two residents who applied for admission of their fiancees from Poland and Lithuania respectively. In each case Hutchings was advised by a Justice Department official that his practices were not in accordance with the law and that he had the options of issuing new restrictive regulations prior to the arrival of these fiancees or, failing this, of deporting them.[8]

Dunfield's and Hutchings' practices served the interests of the business community as represented by the Newfoundland Board of Trade. Formed in 1909 to coordinate the interests of fish merchants, manufacturers, importers, and industrialists, the Board of Trade had, according to the *Newfoundland Quarterly* (Spring 1916), soon "come to play such a large part in the activities of the community that its presiding officer had come to be regarded as second only to the prime minister himself." In view of the exclusion of Newfoundlanders from Canada as a result of Canadian immigration laws, the Board in 1936 was eager to see the Commission introduce new restrictive regulations and negotiate the establishment of a reciprocal arrangement "whereby Newfoundlanders entering Canada may encounter equal facilities with Canadians entering this country."[9]

The Board of Trade lobby manifested distinct nativist overtones. By 1938 one Board member maintained he saw "a much greater number of Orientals walking the street than there were some few years ago" and entering all activities, while another one expressed concern about the "Jews in the retail trade." Worried that in the absence of new controls it was "possible for undesirable businessmen to enter the country and go into business," the Board demanded that "our immigration laws should be tightened very considerably indeed." Since there was unemployment in all lines of production, except qualified farming, a Board spokesman doubted in January 1939 if it was "wise for the Government to encourage immigrants, even though they be trained."[10]

THE PURSUIT OF "WATERTIGHT" CONTROLS

Addressing these concerns became a prime objective of L.E. Emerson who succeeded W.R. Howley as Commissioner for Justice in September 1937. Emerson had been a cabinet member in 1924 and

Minister of Justice from 1932 to 1934. The 1932 Proclamation was passed during his term in office over and against the objections of the Dominions Office. Intelligent, experienced and ambitious, Emerson quickly became a key figure on the Commission. He had not been invited to join the Commission in 1934 because, as historian Peter Neary has revealed, Governor D.M. Anderson had "certain doubts about Emerson's strict honesty" and saw him as a man who "is not popular, is very inclined to split hair and I am told is very bumptious and self-opinionated." Married to the daughter of a prominent Water Street business family and an intimate of Roman Catholic Archbishop E.P. Roche, Emerson was highly regarded and "well connected in the small, tightly knit elite that dominated local society." Neary has interpreted Emerson's elevation to the government in 1937 as a demonstration of British willingness and ability "to head off establishment opposition by bringing key members of it on board."[11] As Commissioner for Justice (and from September 1939 also for Defence) until 1944, he stood for the protection of the interests of that elite against British reforming zeal whether it came from within the Commission or from Whitehall.

The four-year search for a solution to the unsettled state of immigration and deportation policy was brought to a head by the coincidence of three developments: Germany's annexation of Austria, the British reintroduction of visa requirements for holders of German and Austrian passports in April 1938, and the receipt by the Customs Department and the local German Vice-Consul of a number of applications from Germans and Austrians to take up permanent residence in Newfoundland. Since it might "not be desirable to admit" these persons and some action was imperative, Emerson requested that the Commission agree in principle on a new act "on Canadian lines, establishing a Newfoundland citizenship and leaving the power of deportation to be exercised departmentally, as at present, against any undesirable not a holder of such citizenship, whether technically British or alien."

Emerson emphasized that Canadian law, apart from prohibiting persons of undesirable political opinions and illiterates, had a

> very broad provision against persons who do not fulfill the requirements of regulations. The regulations may require a money qualification and prohibit or limit the number of immigrants of any nationality or race or any class or occupation or immigrants whose customs or modes of life are deemed undesirable, or who are considered not readily assimilable by Canada.

Canadian law also allowed for any person not being a Canadian citizen to be deported with his dependents, if any, upon the Order

Commissioner L.E. Emerson inspects Newfoundland troops, March 1941.
Credit: PANL.

of the Governor in Council. Regretting that Newfoundland law did not exclude classes of economically or racially undesirable persons, Emerson singled out the provision of the 1906 Aliens Act "that a political or religious refugee is not to be refused leave to land merely on the ground of the probability of his becoming a charge on the public funds" as being "too liberal in present circumstances."[12]

Commissioner Penson countered Emerson's plans on the basis "that we are bound to follow the United Kingdom and should in any case wish to do so." Great Britain, he argued, was densely populated and suffering from unemployment but pursuing a policy of offering asylum as far as practicable. Newfoundland should admit a limited number of qualified immigrants with assured employment and possessing no less than $250. A policy of total exclusion was harmful. Penson singled out the rejection of Belkin's 1934 proposal and the Commission's compliance with the pressures of the New-foundland Medical Council as a mistake. "The need of the country should override the interests of individuals," Penson maintained:

> we could well and profitably allow the settlement on the Island of well qualified professional men and other specialists. It may be too in the common interest if farmers and agriculturists of the industrious and well informed type so common on the Continent, took up permanent residence in this country.[13]

At its 13 April 1938 meeting the Commission agreed on a compromise solution. Until the passing of new legislation, Penson's proposal would be adopted. It permitted a limited immigration controlled by the Commission's prior approval of visas granted by British consular authorities. With regard to the proposed legislation, the minutes state that "the Commissioner for Justice will, after consultation with the Commissioner for Finance, communicate semi-officially with the Dominions Office recommending that in the treatment of British subjects and aliens, Newfoundland should follow the same practice as Canada."[14] In a covering statement to London, Emerson contended that the kind of legislation he proposed "would certainly be enacted" if self-government were restored.

The Dominions Office did not reply for six months, and then only in response to a reminder from St. John's. It asked for more time to consider "the rather complicated issues" raised by Emerson and suggested other interim measures, such as a permit system for aliens or an Order under the 1926 act. Although Newfoundland could not be prevented from introducing Canadian-type legislation, Emerson had raised "a good many thorny subjects" which had troubled the Dominions Office in the past. One official, C.R. Price, believed the main difficulty with the proposed legislation was how to control the entry of political refugees without discriminatory regulations. The best solution would be a permit system for aliens. A "less watertight solution" would be a repeal of the 1906 refugee clause, but this would perhaps "not be politically desirable at the present time."[15]

At the end of November 1938 Emerson made his next move. The Customs Department was "flooded with applications, mainly from Continental Jews, who desire to settle in Newfoundland," he cabled London, and apart from the permit system proposed by the Dominions Secretary, legislation was necessary. He proposed amending the 1926 act,[16] as well as issuing a proclamation to prohibit for two years the landing for residence of persons being natives of or belonging by race to any country other than the United Kingdom, unless they had received a special permit. The legislation, he explained to the Dominions Office, followed strictly Canadian precedents and would be acted upon only with great discretion.[17]

The Dominions Office was concerned and confused about Emerson's real intentions and wanted his proposed comprehensive legislation "on somewhat drastic lines" to be "allowed to sleep," until it could be ascertained how the permit system worked. The main question was whether Newfoundland immigration and deportation legislation should follow the exclusionist stance embraced by the self-governing dominions, or the less restrictive approach adopted by British colonies without self-government on the instruction of Whitehall. Price singled out four difficulties the Dominions Office had with Emerson's proposal: the Dominions Secretary had to be able to defend to foreign representatives and British public opinion the effect of Newfoundland's legislation on aliens, British subjects, and alien refugees; second, the proposed legislation, if adopted with Dominion Office assent, would be reactionary from the colonies' point of view and might induce them to adopt "Dominion" legislation themselves; third, there was the specter of a self-governing Newfoundland enacting even more drastic legislation which might be forestalled by assisting in working out "reasonable legislation on Dominion lines now;" finally, new legislation on Canadian lines establishing Newfoundland citizenship with a rule as to how it would be acquired or lost might, as in Canada, lead to wholesale deportations of people—"whether technically British or alien"—if they became public charges before they became eligible for citizenship. Price realized that "under existing legislation an expulsion order may be made on grounds *inter alia* of public charge or of mere undesirability, against any person not born in Newfoundland." Therefore, and in view of Emerson's warning that this kind of legislation "would certainly be enacted" if self-government were restored, Price felt the United Kingdom had little choice but to promote the adoption of a moderate rather than an extreme course.[18]

The Dominion Office's apprehensions were not entirely unfounded because Emerson had also considered legislation compelling Newfoundland's resident German nationals, among whom were several refugees (see below), to register with the German consul, so they could be deported to their country of origin, if desirable. Reacting to a German law of 3 February 1938, which provided that German nationals abroad who failed to register with the appropriate German consul could be deprived of German citizenship, Emerson proposed legislation in April 1938 "compelling German nationals residing here to register with a view to avoiding or limiting number likely to become stateless." This course of action was abandoned on the advice of the Dominions Secretary who urged the Governor of Newfoundland in July 1938 to allow aliens affected by the German law complete freedom to comply with it or not. Emerson was satisfied that Whitehall complied with his request to instruct all British consular and passport control officers (as published in a circular despatch of 13 June 1938) that

> in the case of Newfoundland, applications by holders of German and Austrian passports proceeding to that country otherwise than for a limited period not exceeding six weeks should be referred to the Chief Commissioner, St. John's, for approval before a visa is given.[19]

In his official replies to St. John's of 2 and 12 December 1938, the Dominions Secretary did not discuss the contents of the draft proclamation. He acknowledged with relief the Commission's decision to use the permit system to control the influx of aliens but asked that British subjects be omitted from it: "We should have felt considerable difficulty about provision for unqualified exclusion especially at the present moment when refugee question is so much in the minds of governments and public." As a useful adjunct for controlling would-be settlers and temporary visitors who presumably did not need a permit, Whitehall recommended the visa system. What kind of instructions regarding visa requirements should be forwarded to British Consular Officers? Visas could be granted only to holders of valid passports and persons with legitimate reasons for visiting. Non-Aryans in Germany, for example, now rarely held documents valid for return.[20]

Although distinguishing between British citizens and United Kingdom natives and insisting that only the latter should be exempted from the permit system, Emerson admitted that his draft proclamation was unnecessarily arbitrary and had to be modified. However, no revised proclamation was ever submitted and the promulgation of new legislation was no longer a priority in St. John's. After December 1938 London received no further communication concerning this matter. Although Newfoundland's immigration legislation was viewed in London as being in "a state of considerable confusion," the tightening of the existing permit system achieved the effect of new restrictive laws. The Commission continued to depend on the prerogative power to exclude undesirable aliens—or "indeed any aliens whom they did not wish to admit."[21]

In April 1939 the Chairman of the Board of Customs G.C. Price summarized the existing procedures for the benefit of the Council of the Newfoundland Board of Trade. The Board was worried that in the absence of new regulations "peddlars, company promoters and others find their way to St. John's, and in some cases subject the public to fraud, or exert other undesirable influences." The Council also wondered "whether or not there was a system in use for the registration of alien visitors so that their whereabouts and activities can be known to the authorities."[22] Price reassured the Council that

> the Immigration Department is not only restricting the admission of aliens of the prohibited classes as commonly understood, but it is not permitting the landing in this country . . . of any person who proposes to engage in any trade or business which would be in competition with any established concern.

The authorities were, nevertheless, "prepared to consider, on their merits, applications to take up permanent residence from a limited number of persons (a) of the professional classes, (b) possessing specialist qualifications, or (c) who purpose to set up a new business or undertaking." During the previous 18 months, Price revealed, "only a very few permits have in fact been accorded" to prospective settlers and these had been "strictly confined" to the specified classes.[23]

The Council was left in little doubt that the whereabouts and activities of any aliens permitted to enter the country was known to the authorities. All visitors had to disclose their purpose, length of stay, and nature of business to the police. Foreign consuls had instructions not to issue permits or visas to "certain nationals" without the prior concurrence of the Chief Commissioner of Immigration who also conveyed information about the landing of any alien to the police. Price's reply to the Board of Trade was released to the local press.[24] The description of immigration procedures confirmed that access to Newfoundland for refugees from the Third

Reich was entirely at the discretion of the Chief Commissioner of Immigration and unqualified exclusion was the practice, as the following cases illustrate.

INDIVIDUAL APPLICATIONS FOR SANCTUARY, 1938–1939

A married couple, both of whom were Czech-born doctors and held British passports, were the only immigrants of alien background identified by Penson as having been granted temporary entry in the summer of 1938 while "numerous applications from aliens (mainly Jews from Central Europe)" had been turned down. Applications had almost invariably been from persons "who would be employed in the dry goods trade, e.g. furriers, watch makers." Practically no applications were received from the kind of professional workers and small farmers whom Penson was prepared to consider on their merits.[25]

Foreign-born seamen who had traditionally found asylum on the island after deserting from ships docked in Newfoundland were also deported without much ado. In mid-July 1938 two 18-year-old sailors deserted from two different German freight vessels in Botwood and in Corner Brook. One of the seamen, Johann Miltzon, was ordered to be sent back by the next German ore boat leaving Bell Island. The other one, Hendrich Rozany (or Haranzy), was granted a temporary permit "subject to deportation if and when ordered." Although a Newfoundland Board of Trade memo urged that "he should be treated as deserters have always been treated," the local Jewish congregation interceded on his behalf and offered a bond guaranteeing that he would not become a charge on the colony.[26] The Danzig-born seaman claimed that he had been very harshly dealt with by the ship's crew and was in fear for his life because he belonged "to the race persecuted by the Nazis." He is alleged to have left Newfoundland in February 1939 as a stowaway on one of the ore boats.[27]

Beginning in the fall of 1938, increasing sharply in January 1939, and continuing until after the outbreak of the war, personal inquiries and applications for visas forwarded by British consular officers began to pour into St. John's from actual and prospective refugees in Germany, Austria, Czechoslovakia, Poland, Hungary, Romania, Slovakia, the Netherlands, the United Kingdom, the United States, Cuba, and even Japan. Most of the applicants appeared to be highly qualified professionals and skilled workers. Among those who petitioned for temporary or permanent admission were not only refugees from the Third Reich whose lives were in imminent danger or who had managed to find temporary refuge in another country, but also several close relatives (i.e., parents, brothers, and sisters) of Newfoundlanders with every conceivable guarantee provided by their local sponsors.

Prior to 1936 no cases are known where admission to the country had been denied close relatives of a Newfoundland resident or a British subject. In 1938, however, the Commission turned down on alleged economic grounds two petitions from Nochau Goldman (a Jewish citizen of Poland) and his starving family of four (including children aged one and four) to join his sister in Corner Brook. She had immigrated seven years earlier to be married to Ernest Swirsky, a Newfoundland dry goods store owner of Polish-Jewish descent. Although the applicant's qualifications included a variety of trades in short demand, such as bookkeeping, farming, cement finishing and tile laying, he was given to understand that while the Commission

> are prepared sympathetically to consider any applications made on behalf of doctors, specialists, skilled and professional workers, they are not anxious to encourage the immigration of persons not possessing such qualifications and for whom suitable employment is [not] proved to exist. We have therefore further decided that permission shall not be accorded to applicants whose intention is to engage in any employment for which suitable persons of New-foundland birth are available.

Disappointed at his rejection by the Newfoundland government, Goldman appealed to the Secretary of State at the Dominions Office in London:

> I would very much like to say that I recently received a letter from my sister in Newfoundland informing me that seeing they had only one child, that both she and her husband were quite willing to take us to live with them, and share with each other as one united family, and that such would not have any effect regarding the employment in the Island.

> Lord Stanley, if it's not too much of me to ask, I do plead with you, that you will do all in your power by the help of God and through faith in Him, and your unfailing kindness to assist me, in obtaining papers to immigrate if not to Newfoundland, then please God to England, Canada, or wherever it would be permissible for me to immigrate, and if such could be granted, then my brother-in-law and sister will do all in their power to help us in any way.

At the Dominions Office it was "thought right that Mr. Goldman's further representations should be brought to the notice of the Newfoundland Government" and it was suggested, in view "particularly" of the statement in the second paragraph, that "his application should be regarded as meriting further consideration." In the Commission's judgement, however, Goldman was "a book-keeper, admittedly in very poor circumstances, who desires to be employed in a small dry goods store." A review of his appeal, Governor Walwyn replied to London on 22 October 1938, did "not disclose any grounds for varying the decision already conveyed to you, and the Commission of Government does not desire that permission should be granted him to enter Newfoundland."[28]

The shifting criteria for the rejection of refugees left little doubt that their access was not subject to any law or more or less clearly defined or consistent policy, but entirely at the discretion of the Commission, i.e., its Chief Commissioner of Immigration in St. John's. Typical is the treatment accorded to the application by a group of one thousand families of Hungarian Jews, and the well-documented cases of Erich Gruenberg, James N. Rosenberg and Rose R. Zuber.

In February 1939 the Commission received a submission by Budapest lawyer Dr. George Lichtenstern on behalf of one thousand Jewish families eager to take up farming and a variety of subsidiary occupations in Newfoundland. The party consisted of a mixed contingent of refugees including educated farmers, engineers, and young merchants, who had lost their livelihood as a result of the application of anti-Semitic legislation. They didn't expect any help and offered as security the value of the properties they were leaving behind in their homeland. They were attracted to Newfoundland because they had learned that it had nearly the same climate as central Europe.

> The group wishes to earn a territory large enough to nourish [a] thousand families by farm-working and would take along with them economical machines, mill equipment, the same for the proper physicians, several automobiles (tractors for the farm), various manufacturer's fittings and so on for civilized living.

Judged by Lichtenstern's petition, these refugees were the very type from whom, as Penson indicated in October 1938, no applications had been forthcoming during 1938 and whose admission the Commission was prepared to consider favorably. Now the Commission, after discussing the application at its meeting of 6 April 1939, resorted to the incredible argument that "there is no prospect of room being found" on the island for such settlers. The total area of land suitable for agriculture, Lichtenstern was informed, "is very limited indeed" and the known areas had already been reserved for resettling unemployed fishermen and others on the land.[29]

Not much time seems to have been wasted on Erich Gruenberg's petition from Berlin, which was forwarded by Dominions Secretary MacDonald on 17 January 1939. A former accountant in the Berlin bank of Alfred Freund, Gruenberg stated that he had been forced during the last months to work on roads and other construction sites in Berlin and that the police had ordered him recently to "leave my home and country in the shortest period." This was very likely a disguised reference to his subjection to forced labor in a concentration camp (which was the treatment accorded to a large number of German Jews after *Kristallnacht*) and the prospect of release on condition that he leave the country. Enclosing two certificates of conduct from his former employer and the police, as well as assurance of sufficient funds available from a friend in Stockholm for landing and subsistence, Gruenberg asked for urgent consideration that he and his wife be allowed to reside in Newfoundland while his application for an American visa was being processed. On 8 February 1939, the Newfoundland Department of Home Affairs received a telegram from Gruenberg in Berlin with a voucher for a prepaid reply: "Urge application M 651/5 in awaiting cable answer. Have to depart immediately. Please send permit." A week later the department cabled back: "No application received. Regret permits for residency in Newfoundland cannot be granted."[30] His fate can only be surmised.

A case that dragged on for months involved James N. Rosenberg, senior member of the New York law firm of Rosenberg, Goldmark & Colin. Rosenberg was a director of the American Joint Jewish Distribution Committee (JDC), the chief charitable organization helping Jews during the Holocaust. As chairman of Agro-Joint, a JDC subsidiary, which between 1924 and 1938 had successfully settled 50,000 Jewish families, Rosenberg in 1939 founded the Dominican Republic Settlement Association to take up Dominican dictator Rafael L. Trujillo's generous offer to accept 100,000 Jewish refugees.[31] In mid-December 1938 Rosenberg inquired of Major R.H. Tait, Director of the Newfoundland Information Bureau in New York, whether a cousin of his could come to Newfoundland and bring his mother from Germany to live there with him. The cousin from Germany had unexpectedly turned up in New York as a refugee on his way to Cuba. "Because he was a strong courageous fellow who had withstood Nazi persecution without letting it break his nerve, I determined that I would try to find a decent life for him," Rosenberg wrote. Rosenberg intended to buy a tract of land on the west coast of the island, where his family could spend the summer fishing, and have the refugee cousin and his mother look after the place year-round. He undertook to see to it that neither the cousin nor his mother would become charges on the public. Their coming would instead "bring money into Newfoundland."

The Commissioner for Home Affairs, after conferring with the Commissioner for Natural Resources and the Chief Commissioner of Immigration, turned thumbs down on the request, although they had ascertained from a New York bank that Rosenberg was worth a million dollars. The following grounds were given for the rejection: first, having been "faced with a considerable problem in dealing with applications from persons mainly of Jewish extraction who desire to leave central Europe," a visa was not to be issued to any person holding a German, Austrian, or Czechoslovakian passport without the prior approval of the Chief Commissioner of Immigration; second, owing to high unemployment, such approval would not be granted to anyone proposing to engage in an occupation for which qualified Newfoundlanders were available or who might become a public charge; third, only applications from a limited number of the professional class or those with specialist qualifications would be considered—each case to be decided on its own merits; finally, since the occupations or qualifications of Rosenberg's relatives were not indicated, "we should find it very difficult to grant permission for the settlement in this country of a man and his mother merely to look after a stretch of salmon river."[32]

THE ZUBER CASE

The case of Rose R. Zuber of St. John's confirms that neither financial security, nor first-degree family relationship, nor British citizenship, nor any other legally defined criterion was a sufficient ground for admitting a central European refugee. Rather, as Zuber's solicitor charged, "the Commissioner or other Official designated for this purpose has an unfettered and discretionary power, which may be arbitrarily and secretly exercised, to deal with each case as he thinks fit."[33] The Zuber case shows the absurd and tragic extreme to which those responsible for administering immigration were prepared to go, and it affords a revealing glimpse of a little known side of the relations between Newfoundland's ruling elite and its small Jewish community.

Mrs. Zuber and her husband, who had been married for nine years and were naturalized British subjects, carried on a successful business as ladies' costumiers in St. John's. Over a period of two years, starting in March 1937, Mrs. Zuber made five futile attempts to obtain permission for her parents as well as her two brothers (aged 21 and 18, and certified mechanics) from Pruzana, Poland, to join her in St. John's. "My family are all Polish Jews, and it is because of their increasing fear of persecution, and the possible confiscation of their property, that they are looking to Newfoundland," she wrote. "They have no relatives or friends elsewhere outside Poland."[34]

The Commission's motives for refusing Mrs. Zuber's request are revealed in a memorandum of October 1938 by the Chairman of the Board of Customs, G.C. Price, warning the Secretary for Justice that "if we show any sign of weakening in this case, there is no doubt that we shall be flooded with applications of a similar type." The Newfoundland immigration authorities insisted repeatedly that not only had the Commission of Government "the absolute right to refuse to receive any alien into this country," but also that "an alien has no legal right to be informed of the grounds upon which it is proposed to exclude him from landing here." The legal basis for the Commission's position, Secretary Dunfield argued, was the case of Musgrove vs. Chun Teong Toy, heard in the Privy Council in 1891. That decision reaffirmed the right of the Australian Colony of Victoria to turn back a number of Chinese which a ship attempted to land, because they exceeded the limit permitted to land by that colony's Chinese Immigration Act.[35]

After Zuber's first application had been rejected she engaged the services of Harry A. Winter K.C. of the law firm Winter & Higgins. Winter—a former newspaper editor, speaker of the House of Assembly, and cabinet minister, and a future Commissioner for Home Affairs and Education (1941–1944), and for Justice and Defence (1944–1947)—insisted that his client was at least entitled to be informed of the reasons for the exclusion of her family and to know their legal status in this respect. "We cannot believe," he wrote Secretary for Commission W.J. Carew in May 1938, "that the question of the admissibility of aliens must be left in the last instance to the arbitrary discretion of some official or officials." He wondered what rules, if any, under the 1926 Immigration Act had been applied to this case. Information supplied by Mrs. Zuber to him and to the Commission was sufficient, in his opinion, "to remove these applicants altogether from the class of immigrants regarded, for one reason or another, as undesirable." Winter inquired whether the same objections would be made if she omitted her parents and confined the application to the case of her two brothers. He advised that any doubt as to the future status of these men could be met by granting them conditional permission to land for a limited period, as is a common practice in most states, and "that such guarantees and other assurances could be given in this case as to make the requirements a mere formality."

Price at first contended that the Zuber case "has no features to differentiate it from numerous others which the Department has received." Dunfield reassured him that the legal precedent of Musgrove vs. Chun Teong Toy of 1891 entitled the government "to refuse to receive the Polish immigrants in question, and its right being absolute, it need not give any reasons." Penson granted Winter a personal interview and wrote him in June 1938 that he did not think "it would be in the general interest to require that the Department of Immigration should state the specific reasons on which a given application is refused."[36]

In October 1938 Winter protested that he was "still at a loss to know just what the policy of the Government is in this important matter or just what is considered to be the law of this country relating to it." Winter's renewed representation to the Commission came to the heart of the matter. He charged that in the legislation referred to by government officials he could not find "any authority for, what we cannot help thinking, the extreme view taken by the Department." Since 1934 no regulation or order had been published allowing exclusion on any grounds, and in the individual treatment of his client's application "on its merits" no hint had been given what those merits were. According to Winter, the case of Musgrove vs. Chun Teong Toy of 1891, cited in support of the Commission position, was irrelevant because the latter was a notorious criminal who would have been excluded under the statutes in any case.

Winter pointed to the serious consequences that would follow if the law on this subject was in fact what the Commission assumed it to be. He listed five objections that could be made to such a state of affairs. First, it represented a departure from the rule that laws should be general in their scope and application. Second, the refusal to give a reason for a decision in any particular case made the procedure even more objectionable. Third, it virtually repealed or aborted the statutory law on the subject, "since none of its conditions need be considered if they can be arbitrarily discounted." Fourth, no alien, regardless how desirable, could know just where he stood or whether he would be allowed to land until he reached Newfoundland and was actually permitted to land. Finally, there could be very serious repercussions as a matter of practical policy:

> Newfoundland has always had far more emigrants than immigrants and if such arbitrary power can be used in this country it can be similarly used in other countries greatly to the detriment of Newfoundland. We think that this is not at all an unlikely event if it should become known that no reliance can be placed upon

general rules and regulations such as laid down by the Acts and in use in practically all countries.[37]

In a confidential memorandum G.C. Price could not help concede that he agreed "to some slight extent with certain of the sentiments expressed," but confided to Dunfield that until a new Aliens Act was in fact made operative "I do not see that we can depart from the stand we have taken even if we have to place ourselves on the unsatisfactory ground that the Government of this Island has refused to receive any aliens in its absolute right." Emerson directed that the ruling of June 1938 should stand and that the matter was "one for the consideration of the Commission of Government as to policy."[38]

Suffering "great anxiety and distress" and feeling that she deserved better treatment as a British subject, Mrs. Zuber on 2 March 1939 made a final appeal to the Secretary of State for Dominion Affairs in London. She insisted that there was not the slightest danger of members of her family becoming a charge upon the state or engaging in business detrimental to any Newfoundlanders. She argued that the case of her family deserved to be considered on its own merits and distinguished from the general, and broad, class of "Jewish refugees." Finally, she feared that further delays "may be serious or even fatal" so far as her family was concerned and that "they may not be allowed to leave Poland at all, or only after confiscation of the whole or most of their property."

> The reports I receive of the trend of affairs in Poland, and the increasing hostility of the ruling class there towards people of my race fill me with apprehension, and the fear of what may happen at any moment. If the utmost you can do is to ask the proper authorities in this country to reconsider this case, or to bring to their attention any aspects of it which may justify prompt and favourable treatment, I shall be most deeply grateful.

At the Dominions Office C.R. Price [no relation to G.C. Price] reasoned that Jews resident in Poland could not, "at present at any rate, be properly regarded as having the same claim to special consideration as refugees proper." However, judged by the large number of applications from Polish Jews in the past two or three years, there was little doubt that most were suffering from considerable disabilities in obtaining employment and from being victimized by anti-Semitic measures. What made this case a special one was that the petitioner and her husband were naturalized in Newfoundland. Clutterbuck thought that, provided this applicant and her husband were in reasonably good circumstances, the Commission might well have "softened their hearts sufficiently to let in the father and mother," but not knowing the special circumstances of this application, the Commission must be the judge. C.R. Price and Clutterbuck agreed to return Zuber's appeal to the Commission "for such consideration as may be deemed appropriate," and to request that in any reply sent to Mrs. Zuber it may be explained that her letter was transmitted by the Secretary of State.[39]

Zuber's appeal was submitted for reconsideration to the Newfoundland government. Its Chief Commissioner for Immigration replied tersely on 8 July 1939 that there were "no grounds whatever to justify a reconsideration of the case, and the decision already conveyed to you cannot be varied."[40] The Dominions Office was stunned by the Commission's inflexibility and refusal to explain its harsh stand. "Very firm, and they did not explain as requested," Clutterbuck noted, and he concluded helplessly that "we can clearly do no more."[41]

In light of the depressing experiences of the Goldman and Zuber families, other Jewish residents in Newfoundland sought sanctuary elsewhere for their first-degree relatives threatened in Europe. Frederick William Ottenheimer, a German Jew who in 1932 married the daughter of a well-to-do Newfoundland fish supply merchant, was allowed to immigrate in 1934 at the age of 31 although upon her marriage Ottenheimer's wife automatically (i.e., under British law) lost her legal status as a British subject and became an alien. She reacquired her British citizenship in March 1939 when Ottenheimer's May 1937 application for a certificate of naturalization was granted. In 1940 Ottenheimer informed the Newfoundland Constabulary that he no longer had any connections to Germany after he did "everything possible to get my mother and sister out of Germany and succeeded in getting them to South Africa."[42]

GROUNDS FOR THE ADMISSION OF TEN REFUGEES

That the Commission was not interested in admitting individuals and really only cared to consider "assisted" group settlement of refugees in areas remote from civilization, was revealed in its response of 30 March 1939 to an inquiry from the National Co-ordinating Committee in New York for Aid to Refugees and Emigrants Coming from Germany. This body worked in close cooperation with the German Jewish Aid Committee in London which was authorized by the British government to process all applications of refugees wishing to proceed to England. The New York Committee was eager to place specially selected cases and wanted to minimize the likelihood of these refugees being refused upon landing, since the adequacy of their financial support would be guaranteed by the

Committee. It was proposed "that full details of each case be reported to you first by the Committee with a view to your granting some form of provisional permit to land, subject to confirmation on arrival."

The Committee, presented by the British Passport Control Officer in New York as a "thoroughly responsible organisation," expressed its "earnest desire to fulfill whatever instructions you may issue" concerning the requirements for admission of the following three categories of refugees: a) intending immigrants to the U.S.A. with adequate financial support and U.S. immigration quota numbers, awaiting receipt of their visas; b) intending immigrants with adequate financial support who will not seek employment; and c) intending immigrants who will seek employment or establishment of businesses. The Commission declared category "A" not admissible because it might not be possible for such persons "to be deported from Newfoundland, if allowed to enter, if for any reason such a course was found to be necessary or desirable." With regard to category "B" "there would be considerable difficulty in assuring ourselves that such persons do not in fact violate any given undertakings," and with regard to category "C," applications "may" be considered from persons with specialist qualifications or the desire to engage in a new industry.

Regardless of any intending immigrant's *prima facie* eligibility for admission, all cases would have to be referred for consideration to the discretion of the local authorities, with fullest particulars concerning the applicant, his family, his resources and intended employment. "A decision on his case would then be given." In concluding his reply, the Chief Commissioner for Immigration wondered why the question of assisted group settlement "in areas of the country hitherto unsettled, e.g. Labrador" had not been raised since "certain unofficial inquiries have been made by bodies or persons purporting to represent Jewish refugees."[43] The Commission thus deliberately rejected a potentially large supply of carefully pre-selected refugees whose adequate financial support was guaranteed by a reputable American refugee organization.

The only refugees from Central Europe whose arrival in Newfoundland prior to the outbreak of the war can be confirmed were Rabbi Max Katz with his wife and two sons, six doctors recruited to serve as nurses in outports, and one female designer and weaver employed by the International Grenfell Association in St. Anthony. Rabbi Katz, who had left Germany in April 1937 to look for a position in the United States, was referred in Montreal to the congregation in St. John's, where he arrived on 31 August 1937 for a three weeks' trial period. The St. John's Jewish congregation provided Katz with the security of a three-year contract, enabling him to travel to Germany in March 1938 so he could rescue his wife and two sons. In St. John's his and his family's passports were confiscated by the German consul on behalf of the German Consulate General in Ottawa and not replaced. Katz was not fluent in English and his background and training did not suit the local situation. His wartime experience will be related in chapter 9.[44]

The Commission had been exploring since November 1938 the possibility of using a few refugee doctors for its district services. The shortage of trained personnel was seriously hampering plans to control tuberculosis and to initiate a program of midwifery training as part of a newly inaugurated health care system to be dispensed by six new cottage hospitals and additional nursing stations across the island. Through the British Federation of University Women, the Newfoundland Department of Public Health was directed to the availability in London of refugee female physicians from Germany and Austria, ready for placement in the nursing services of countries of the Empire. After his encounter with them in London, Secretary for Justice Dunfield cabled the Commissioners assuringly: "Type frequently hardly distinguishable from Aryan type. Various ages unmarried. Ready take any job."

In January 1939 the Commission decided to set up a committee of Newfoundlanders in London for the selection of "a suitable type of recruit" from among those available. The intention was to contract refugees for nursing services only and to forbid them to represent themselves as doctors or practice as such. As officials were apprehensive of adverse public reaction, it was thought prudent not "to bring any considerable number of these people here at any one time," but to get them to the country in small numbers, "say one or two together." In this fashion and through the mediation of the German Jewish Refugee Committee in London, five Jewish refugee doctors were brought to Newfoundland in 1939, and one non-Jewish refugee physician in 1940. They were employed by the Department of Health on three-year contracts in cottage hospitals and outport nursing stations across Newfoundland.[45]

Newfoundland's six refugee physicians were hired to assume duties as nurses in the outports because they were the only qualified persons available in 1939. The Department of Health would have preferred trained English or Newfoundland nurses had they been obtainable.[46] Similarly, Rabbi Max Katz and his family were sponsored by the St. John's Jewish congregation because it needed a minister. He was admitted because no English or Canadian rabbi could be found. Of Newfoundland's one dozen refugees resident by the end of 1939, none was offered sanctuary because he or she was a refugee, regardless of their merits and their sponsorship as first degree relatives by Newfoundland residents. The search for ways to make Newfoundland "watertight" against refugees seems to have been one of the chief preoccupations of the Commissioner for Justice, despite his awareness of Newfoundland's uniquely generous refugee legislation.

Prior to the war, American, Canadian, and British subjects were allowed freely to enter Newfoundland as tourists for periods of up to six weeks, and neither permits nor visas or even passports were required of them. However, European refugees, despite assurances of adequate financial resources and eventual entry into the United States, (i.e., those already assigned a waiting list number for an American quota visa), were refused even temporary asylum in Newfoundland. The Commission was "not prepared to allow aliens to enter Newfoundland, when such persons during the period of their stay propose either to endeavour to obtain a visa permitting them to enter the United States or to reside until the date when a visa, of which they may be in possession, will permit them to enter that country," Governor Walwyn informed the British Consul General in New York, and he listed the following reasons for this policy: his government had been "faced with a considerable problem in dealing with applications from persons, mainly of Jewish extraction, who desire to leave Central Europe," these might not obtain their visas, "difficulties regarding repatriation might conceivably arise," making certain they would not engage in gainful occupations might cause administrative difficulties, and they might become a public charge.[47]

Latin American countries, by comparison, which suffered as hard from the Depression as Canada and Newfoundland, granted permanent or temporary sanctuary to 130,000 refugees. According to available statistics, Argentina took 50,000, Brazil 25,000, Chile 14,000, Bolivia 12,000, Uruguay 7,000, Cuba 6,000, Mexico several thousand, etc. Even Venezuela is known to have taken in at least 165, Jamaica 152, and tiny Curacao 86. The Dominican Republic, even poorer and more underdeveloped than Newfoundland, was willing to take 100,000 but due to the outbreak of the war was only able to serve as an emergency haven to some 3,000 Jews, most of whom resettled after the war in the United States or Israel.[48] The Newfoundland authorities refused even to consider the possibility that their country might actually profit as much from the transit traffic of middle-class refugees on their way to the United States as it did from American and Canadian tourists. That Newfoundland might have saved thousands of lives by letting in European refugees is a sad realization.

Canada—a country richly endowed, sparsely populated, and traditionally proud to accept the oppressed and dispossessed—admitted fewer than 4,000 Jewish refugees by the end of 1939. This record has been termed "arguably the worst of all possible refugee-receiving states." Can one avoid the conclusion that Newfoundland's record vies with that of Canada? Such countries, in the words of historians Irving Abella and Harold Troper, "share responsibility for the fate of the Jews of Europe."[49]

Part III

The War and Postwar Aftermath, 1939–1949

"Dangerous" Internees Who Never Were   8

The Victoria Camp and Paterson Schemes, 1940–1943

Even after the outbreak of the war, a significant refugee influx into Newfoundland nearly occurred in two ways, albeit not on the initiative of Commissioner L.E. Emerson. The first was in 1940 in connection with the construction of a large camp located at Victoria near Carbonear about eighty miles northeast of St. John's and two miles inland from the shore of Conception Bay. This camp was planned for 1,000 allegedly "dangerous" civilian internees who were in reality refugees about to be relocated from the United Kingdom. They never arrived. In their search for a purposeful utilization of the camp, the Newfoundland and British governments alternated plans for refugee internment with POW schemes, and the brief history of the camp contains the history of Newfoundland's recurring anticipation of receiving interned refugees. Second, in 1941 Newfoundland was scheduled to be the place where refugees released from Canadian internment and desiring to move to the United States obtained their freedom. The following chapter traces the origins and fate of these two stillborn wartime schemes for bringing interned refugees to Newfoundland.

BRITAIN'S INTERNED REFUGEES AND VICTORIA CAMP

An urgent despatch from the British government on 14 June 1940 pleading with Newfoundland to take 1,000 of Britain's civilian internees "at earliest possible date" led to construction beginning on Victoria Camp. (Heart's Content, Argentia, Port au Port, Whitbourne, and Random Island had also been considered as possible sites.) German male internees in Britain exceeded 12,000, and Italian male internees numbered about 10,000, the despatch reported, not counting prisoners of war and German seamen taken off ships. The despatch characterized the large number of internees in Britain as "dangerous or potentially dangerous" and as a serious security risk. In the event of an attack on England, "if given opportunity, they might assist the enemy." Furthermore, they were tying down a considerable number of service personnel who were needed for other, more essential purposes. Britain reassured Newfoundland that she was prepared to meet all expenditures and supply initial guards. Furthermore, Britain communicated that Canada had also agreed to take immediately 4,000 civilian internees and 3,000 POWs. The British government issued the request to Newfoundland despite reservations about the adequacy of Newfoundland's military resources to guard a camp of 1,000 "potentially dangerous persons." Newfoundland had become part of a hastily improvised British arrangement, which initially envisaged 8,000 internees—accompanied by guards—to be sent to Canada, 9,000 to Australia (and New Zealand), and 2,000 to Newfoundland by the beginning of July 1940.[1]

What the Secretary of State for Dominion Affairs had concealed from the governments of the dominions was that most of the allegedly dangerous enemy aliens to be dispatched to the colonies were innocent refugees fleeing from Nazi persecution. After the outbreak of the war in 1939 the British government had not contemplated general internment of enemy aliens as in World War I. Instead, tribunals were established to categorize all enemy aliens according to the level of danger they represented—"A" to be interned; "B" not to be interned but subject to restrictions; and "C" to remain at liberty. By the end of October 1939, the tribunals had interned some 600 of the 74,000 persons over the age of sixteen who were registered as German citizens in Britain.[2]

Among the growing number of interned Germans were German Jewish refugees like Ernst Deutsch. As related in chapter 2, at the age of fifteen he managed to flee Germany three months before the outbreak of the war with the help of a passport obtained on the black market. (He and his parents, Austrian citizens until the *Anschluss* of March 1938, were refused official passports on the grounds that his physicist father had done war-related work.) Even though Ernst's parents were classified as "C" aliens and not interned, he was below the minimum age for admission to the tribunal that would have exempted him from internment. As a result, he was treated as a class "B" alien and interned in May 1940.[3]

The sudden change from *Sitzkrieg* (phony war) to German *Blitzkrieg* in western Europe and the surrender of the Low Countries and France in May 1940 had intensified anti-alien feeling in Britain. The swiftness of German victories in western Europe was erroneously attributed everywhere to the subversive activities of a German fifth column which had allegedly paved the way for the invading forces.[4] In the weeks following the Dunkirk evacuations, the fifth column panic gained such wide currency that even Jewish refugees from Germany and Austria were suspected of aiding and abetting the enemy. Prime Minister Winston Churchill thought he had evidence of the existence of 20,000 German Nazis in England, and the British public demanded that all of England's 80,000 refugees from German-speaking and German-occupied Europe be put in concentration camps. Even though the German espionage network in England was negligible and so penetrated by British security services that it was actually run in the service of the British war effort, the British government began mass internment of category B Germans in May and category C Germans in June 1940. The great majority of those interned in May and June 1940 were Jewish refugees.[5]

Readers of the *Evening Telegram* of 4 June 1940 learned that the British government was planning to "export" interned aliens and prisoners of war to places remote from the British Isles, out of fear that they might collaborate with German aircraft or parachute troops. The British government's sudden impatient urge to deport a large portion of its suspected fifth column is indicated by Churchill's frequently quoted question to his Cabinet Secretary on 3 June:

> Has anything been done about sending 20,000 internees to New-foundland or St. Helena? . . . I should like to get them on the high seas as soon as possible, but I suppose considerable arrangements have to be made at the other end. Is it all going forward?[6]

Although Newfoundland was never approached to take 20,000 internees, a surprisingly well informed letter in the *Daily News* of 29 June 1940 by Charles F. Garland (a commercial agent, former Secretary of the Great War Veteran's Association, and early advocate of Confederation with Canada) declared that "we have plenty of space to accommodate hundreds of thousands." Proposing that Newfoundland help relieve congestion in the British Isles by taking large numbers of interned aliens, prisoners of war, refugees, and evacuees, the writer claimed to have the support of a large number of citizens. He suggested that lots of smaller islands around the coast could be utilized for that purpose, provided the British government would pay all the expenses incurred. Random Island, he estimated, could accommodate 50,000 interned aliens. The prisoners would create a lot of trade, jobs, and profit for Newfoundland. "There are so many angles to advantage they become more evident with thinking about the scheme."

On 18 June Governor Walwyn said he was prepared to receive "all German or all Italian" internees within two weeks, provided sufficient tents and wood floors were sent ahead of them. "And please send any further information as to regulations governing general treatment and discipline of internees not already here," he reminded the Dominions Secretary, adding "You will no doubt realize that construction in great haste of a camp for 1,000 men will present considerable difficulties which we shall have to overcome by improvised methods which may not in all cases be the best from the point of view of economy." The governor had every reason to expect real or potential enemy agents of the A category interned in Britain to be sent to Newfoundland. He therefore warned that, since Newfoundland would be unable to provide military guards for about two months, it would gladly accept an offer to have the accompanying British officers train local forces. He also requested advice on design and construction of a camp for 1,000 internees and received from External Affairs in Ottawa detailed plans and photographs of Petawawa (Ontario) and Kananaskis (Alberta) camps.

On 19 June Newfoundland was ready to receive up to 1,000 internees within three days, provided their disembarkation could be delayed for three days in St. John's while the canvas camp was being erected. On 29 June the shipping date for the tents was announced to be 30 June, and on 1 July 1940 the sailing date for Newfoundland's 1,000 German internees was set for 4 July. The internees were to arrive in St. John's on 10 July in the company of 7 officers and 148 NCOs and men. Fate kept the announced internees from arriving. The 15,000 ton luxury liner *Arandora Star* was supposed to bring fifty tons of tentage to Newfoundland and then continue on with 1,200 category A, mostly Italian, internees to Canada. However, it was torpedoed off the Irish coast where it sank with heavy loss of life. The 11,000 ton former Polish passenger liner *Sobieski* was originally scheduled to follow the *Arandora Star* with internees destined for Newfoundland. But with no tents to accommodate them in Newfoundland, the *Sobieski* was rerouted to Canada. The *Sobieski* with Ernst Deutsch on board—he had been separated from his parents and had no idea where he was being sent—departed from England as planned on 4 July and reached Quebec on 15 July.[7]

On its way to Canada the *Sobieski* entered St. John's harbor for three hours (allegedly for repairs) without docking or allowing anyone to disembark and without identifying the port to its passengers.

Had it not been for Ernst's ability to decipher the Morse code signals and the negative recollections of visits to Newfoundland of a German sailor on board the *Sobieski*, Ernst Deutsch would not have known he was in St. John's. He wrote in his diary that he saw kids pulling fish out of the harbor from boats, lots of British patriotism – it turned out that he saw school children waving the Union Jack on the occasion of Orangemen's Day – and fog.[8] Ernst's sixteen year-old refugee friend, the late Henry Kreisel, who became famous as an author of English-language novels and short stories in post-World War II Canada,[9] noted that "the harbour is beautiful but the town itself seems very primitive." Other refugee internees on board the *Sobieski* found St. John's rather gloomy and desolate and were glad they did not have to debark there.[10]

The real reason the *Sobieski* anchored in the middle of St. John's harbor was unknown to Deutsch and Kreisel: on 16 May 1940 the Commission had instructed the steamship agencies that the nationals of any non-Empire country in Europe (except France) were prohibited from landing in Newfoundland *"for any purpose"* [emphasis in the original] without the prior permission of the Chief Commissioner for Immigration.[11] The instruction originated with Commissioner for Justice and Defence L.E. Emerson who on behalf of the police conveyed his consternation to Penson on 13 February 1940 that refugees arriving from England in St. John's were permitted to step on land while in transit to the United States. While Emerson admitted "that it may cause a little inconvenience to these passengers that they have to remain on board the steamer for a couple of days," he asked Penson to instruct his immigration officers to cooperate for the sake of security and the "over-burdened" Registry of Aliens. Penson's reply speaks for itself: "I very much regret this decision, but feel that I cannot do otherwise than fall in with your wishes in this matter."[12] Clearly, the *Sobieski's* passengers would have been welcomed in Newfoundland only under guard and behind barbed wire.

The *Sobieski's* cargo consisted of 982 internees, a large number of them boys, as well as 584 POW who had from the outset been destined for Canada. The ship's crew was Polish and "very" anti-Semitic.[13] The internees were not the expected dangerous category A type spies, but category B and C internees, i.e., mostly refugees who had fled Nazi oppression. Had they been sent to Victoria camp as planned Newfoundland would ironically have – as Canada did – become a haven for refugees from the Third Reich despite official efforts to exclude them. Here they would undoubtedly have caused as much consternation and confusion as they did on their landing

in Canada. Assumed to be spies and saboteurs of the kind to be
delivered by the *Arandora Star*, they were at first put with merchant
seamen and category A pro-Nazis in a makeshift camp at Trois
Rivières. There the French Canadian guards robbed them of valu-
ables and their pro-Nazi fellow prisoners inflicted anti-Semitic
threats and insults on them. The Canadian authorities did not
realize their mistake for nearly one month; they then transferred the
interned refugees to a camp built at Fredericton.[14]

Like Ernst Deutsch, many of the 2,284 B and C internees
deported to Canada on the *Sobieski* and on two other ships remained
imprisoned in Canadian internment camps as late as January 1943.
Ernst Deutsch was moved from Trois Rivières to camps at Fredericton, Farnham, Sherbrooke, and finally Ile aux Noix. In Farnham
near Oka, Quebec, the mostly Jewish and other anti-Nazi inmates
organized a hunger strike to press their long-standing demands for
separation from the camp's provocative pro-Nazi minority and for
the right to be recognized as "friendly aliens" instead of as enemy
aliens. Deutsch remembers vividly how the Canadian armed forces
were ordered to mount machine guns, move in against the internees,
and suppress the strike by arresting its five ringleaders. It was not
until after the hunger strike, Deutsch recalled, that the first refugee
internees were released and allowed to return to England, while the
status of all refugee internees in Canada was changed to that of
"friendly aliens."

The visit of H.M. Commissioner of Prisons in the United
Kingdom, Alexander Paterson, to Canada in 1941 confirmed that
the treatment of the refugees was not merely due to their being
confused with "dangerous" enemy civilian internees. In Fredericton
and Farnham Paterson observed "a wealth of wire, three banks
thick, with machine-guns, pass-words and fixed bayonets to dis-
courage the bespectacled professor and the perky schoolboy from
showing any violence."[15] Canada's Director of Internment Operations was reported to have "despised, disliked and distrusted" the
refugees. As a result of Paterson's sympathetic intercession, anti-
Semitic insults and petty persecution by the guards were stopped,
conditions of internment in Canada were eased, and some refugees
were permitted to return to Britain.[16]

ALTERNATE PLANS FOR VICTORIA CAMP

In London, England, meanwhile, "serious difficulty" was anticipated
over the accommodation of internees in Newfoundland, owing not
only to the "unsatisfactory climate and the necessity of erecting
huts" but also to the scarcity of guards because of the "very small

military resources of the Island," as Canada's High Commissioner in Great Britain, Vincent Massey, reported to Ottawa on 22 July 1940. While awaiting new dates for the shipment of tents and internees, Newfoundland on 16 July sent London an estimate of $150,000 for the erection of the camp and a projected cost of $2,500 weekly for food. Payment was requested immediately. In reply, on 3 August, the Dominions Secretary cancelled all plans to send internees to Newfoundland and asked that no further expenditure be incurred in connection with the camp. Worried about its ability to collect the amount it claimed in alleged disbursements, the Commission of Government demanded £20,000 "at once" instead of the £40,000 originally asked for. Payment of £20,000 was confirmed on 19 August 1940. At the same time the Commission of Government inquired twice in London whether the camp should not be finished before winter in case "present decision not to send internees here was reversed before 1 September next."[17]

In response to these inquiries on 27 September 1940 the Dominions Secretary proposed a new scheme for Victoria Camp, namely its utilization as a POW camp for 1,000 captured enemy airmen. England already had some 850 captured enemy airmen and the total was increasing daily, the Secretary of State for Dominion Affairs explained. The British government considered it desirable to move them overseas. The Newfoundland contingent would consist of 250 officers and 750 other ranks, mostly NCOs. The officers would need to have a separate camp from the other ranks. Arrangements as to guards would be the same as those proposed for internees, except that militia guards would not be appropriate for POWs. Newfoundland signified that work on the camp would restart on 1 October and that everything would be ready to receive the 1,000 airmen by 15 November. However, as a result of rearrangements, the cost for completing the camp had increased to £50,000, including equipment and a two-week supply of provisions. The new layout provided for officers to be separated from the other ranks by a fifteen-foot road with a strong wire fence on both sides. The two sets of prisoners would be able to see each other when outdoors, but they would share no common area. According to a blueprint from London of 8 October 1940, the camp required 153 guards and an administrative staff of 24, including four nursing orderlies, three batmen and three clerks, two interpreters, two electricians, and a hospital cook. Newfoundland's offer relieved Britain of the need to send POWs to Australia for some time.[18]

While construction was proceeding to modify and complete Victoria camp, the Permanent Joint Defence Board (PJDB) learned

of the plans for a POW camp at Victoria and objected to the scheme.
The PJDB had been created on 17 August 1940 at a meeting between
Canadian Prime Minister W.L. Mackenzie King and American President Franklin D. Roosevelt. It consisted of representatives from each
of the two countries; its mandate was to recommend to the Canadian
and American governments courses of action for the joint defense of
the northern half of the Western Hemisphere, such as the stationing
of troops and the establishment in Newfoundland and Labrador of
American bases at St. John's, Argentia and Goose Bay, in addition
to the Canadian bases at Gander and Botwood. Although half of the
PJDB's recommendations during its first year of existence dealt with
Newfoundland, members of the Commission of Government were
not invited to attend PJDB meetings until early October.[19]

Commissioners L.E. Emerson and J.H. Penson appear to have
had the first opportunity to inform the PJDB of their plans for
Victoria on 7 October. "The Board feel strongly," Canada's Secretary
of State for External Affairs warned Governor Walwyn on 9 October,
"that incarceration of German prisoners in Newfoundland would
present a serious military hazard which might jeopardize the defence
scheme for Newfoundland which the Board is now preparing and
thus menace the safety of Canada and the United States." PJDB
members feared in particular that German forces might be prepared
to take grave risks to liberate captured airmen and might make the
geographically vulnerable island subject to attacks, against which
the neutral United States might find it difficult to intervene.

Neither the British nor the Commission of Government had good
reason to persist with their POW project in the face of such determined and irrefutable representations, especially since Canada
offered to take the German airmen destined for Newfoundland. In
the fall of 1940, however, Victoria camp was nearing completion just
as a German invasion of the British Isles appeared imminent,
making it more desirable than ever for the British to transfer their
growing number of German POWs overseas. The Dominions
Secretary, therefore, on 12 October proposed a third scheme for the
utilization of Victoria camp. The 1,000 enemy airmen intended for
Newfoundland would be diverted to Canada which would in turn
send 1,000 of its interned merchant seamen to Newfoundland.
Governor Walwyn eagerly seized upon the proposal and was confident that the Canadian government, while it might perhaps be able
to object to naval seamen, would not object to merchant seamen.
The camp, he wrote London and Ottawa, was not visible from the
sea and approachable only by one road four miles long which for five
months could be kept passable only by a snow plough. "A raider

would have either to capture St. John's and use the railway to the road at Carbonear, some eight miles away, or enter Conception Bay and land forces at Carbonear," he said. The presence of Allied land and sea forces and the proximity of two airports "would make this venture so hazardous that we can hardly imagine Germany undertaking it for merchant seamen."[20]

If there was objection to sending merchant seamen, the Dominions Secretary reminded Ottawa and St. John's on 29 October, the camp "on which expenditure of £40,000 has already been incurred would not be utilized" and the money would have been wasted. The Home Office ruled out the transfer to Newfoundland from Canada of civilian internees other than merchant seamen sent from the United Kingdom. From a list of 1,697 merchant seamen sent from Britain to Canada and held in "R Camp,"[21] 1,000 should be selected, the Dominions Secretary proposed on 2 November 1940. Transferees should not include men who by reason of age, health, or other paramount reason appeared unsuitable for transfer. Colonel O.M. Biggar, the Canadian chairman of the PJDB, confided to the Department of External Affairs in Ottawa his belief that no great expense had been incurred for Victoria camp. No more than a small portion of the £40,000, he argued, was spent on the POW camp and the £40,000 included the cost of construction begun for other purposes. "If it was a bad idea at £10 it is no better at £10,000," Biggar was quoted as saying. However, he did not think the PJDB needed this information to veto the merchant seamen proposal.[22]

External Affairs in Ottawa referred the final decision about the transfer of enemy merchant seamen from Canada to Newfoundland to the PJDB and instructed Governor Walwyn to attach the same weight to the opinion of this Board as Ottawa intended to do. Walwyn feared that Ottawa might be unwilling to consider Newfoundland's commitments and Britain's investment, and requested that the Board also consider the purely military aspects from the American point of view. "The camp will be ready for occupation on 15 November," Walwyn angrily wrote External Affairs in Ottawa on 8 November 1940. "We are naturally most anxious not to withdraw our offer of assistance to Great Britain if we can possibly avoid doing so. Having studied matter from all angles, we do not ourselves attach the same importance to the practical difficulties which seem to disturb your mind." On 15 November the Canadian government relayed to London the opinion of PJDB "that establishment of internment camps in Newfoundland would create an unnecessary and dangerous hazard." To help solve Britain's problem, Canada would be prepared to receive an additional 1,000 airmen on the same financial conditions as those pertaining to POWs and internees already transferred to Canada. Since the Canadian government did not bother to inform Newfoundland of its decision, Governor Walwyn had to obtain the eagerly awaited news by way of a despatch from London on 25 November.[23]

In bilateral discussions of defense questions with representatives of the Canadian government in St. John's at the end of November 1940, the Commission of Government reiterated its wish to put Victoria Camp to use for internees. In what appeared to be more an empty gesture than a viable proposal, the Cabinet War Committee in Ottawa on 13 December 1940 agreed that as far as the Canadian government was concerned, "the camp at Carbonear, of which Newfoundland was anxious to make use, might be utilized for civilian internees." The Committee was aware that the British government, so far, had not been prepared to intern civilians at Victoria. On 14 December 1940, the Dominions Office ruled out all possibility of asking Newfoundland to receive civilian internees because the British government began to release the refugees it had hastily interned. Until April 1942, the British government complained periodically about the depreciation of its assets near Carbonear. This caused the PJDB in April 1941, and August 1942, to reaffirm its opposition to an enemy POW camp as a "serious and unwanted menace to the security of Newfoundland, Canada and the United States of America."[24]

Occupying an enclosed area of 600 x 1,100 feet, Victoria Camp was completed on time at a cost of $200,000. It consisted of twenty bunk houses and latrines for internees, five kitchen mess house blocks, one officers' mess and quarters, three bunk houses and latrines for guards, a kitchen mess house for guards, a guard house, an administration building, a hospital building, a quartermaster's store and offices, an underground vegetable store, and six sentry posts. The camp had electric floodlights and electric wiring in all the buildings. A supply of blankets, drugs, cutlery, crockery, enamelware, and tinware was ready for use. According to a watchman's report of 12 January 1941, the camp contained 2,224 mattresses and pillows, "all placed in readiness." The report also lists "quite a lot of boxes containing soap, hardware, cooking utensils . . . in the original packages." Considering it "unwise not to obtain possession of the land, at least for a period commensurate with the life of the buildings," the government of Newfoundland offered to purchase the twenty-acre camp site from the British government for $3,100 in December 1940.[25]

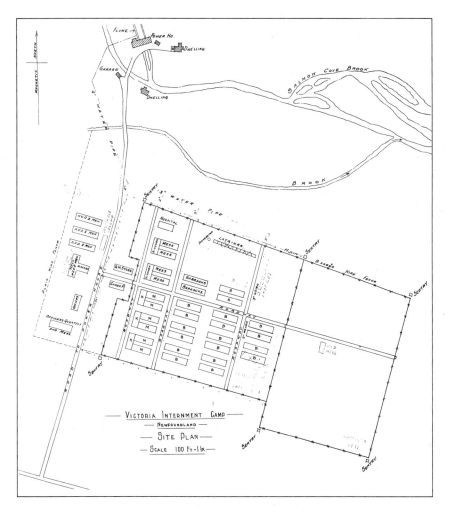

Victoria Internment Camp, Newfoundland. Site Plan, 1940. Credit: PANL.

In the spring of 1941, Commissioners Penson and Emerson, as well as the Dominions Office hoped in vain that Victoria Camp might be taken over by the U.S. or Canadian military forces stationed on the island.[26] The camp's location and inaccessibility made it undesirable to the Newfoundland government as training barracks for its militia. Throughout 1941 and early 1942, the Commissioners toyed with the idea of using the camp or some of its buildings either as a sanatorium or convalescent home or as a temporary accommodation for distressed and injured seamen, but were deterred by the cost of conversion and upkeep.[27] In June 1941, news was received that the Fleet had orders to capture four or five French bankers fishing on the Grand Banks. Suspected of sympathizing with France's pro-Nazi Vichy regime, the fishermen were to be interrogated and either be interned as enemy aliens or form a pool of free French merchant mariners. Faced with a lack of accommodation for up to 200 crew members of these French vessels, the Newfoundland government made their internment contingent on the use of Victoria Camp, the provision of military guards and the consideration of costs,[28] but nothing came of the scheme.

In August 1942, London finally decided to dispose of the camp for the benefit of army funds. The Commanding Officer of the Canadian Troops in Newfoundland, Major General L.F. Page, recommended purchase of the facilities, with all their contents and the barbed wire fence, for $50,000. His engineers had estimated that the structures were worth more than that amount. Since there was a shortage of building materials in Newfoundland, owing to the Allied military construction boom, the camp's ultimate worth turned out to be the materials with which it was built.

Never ever used for anything, the camp was sold to the Canadians and dismantled in the spring of 1943, with its recoverable assets credited to the British government. Unaware that the camp had been torn down by the end of July, the Secretary of State for External Affairs informed the Canadian High Commissioner in St. John's on 2 August 1943 of the possibility that "with the changing fortunes of war consideration may again be given to the use of this camp for Axis prisoners."[29]

The brief history of Victoria Camp contains more than one irony as far as Newfoundland's association with refugees from the Third Reich is concerned. Most obviously, Newfoundland had no meaningful input into the camp's use which was dictated by and entirely at the mercy of British and Canadian *ad hoc* needs. Britain determined its construction and Canada decided whether, when, and how it would be occupied. More noteworthy is the Commission's eagerness to fill it with interned refugees, a desire conflicting noticeably with the prewar aversion to admitting refugees. The contrast is made all the more conspicuous by the Commission's ostensible disregard for Canada's concerns over Newfoundland's wartime safety, concerns which loomed so much larger in the Commission's wartime treatment of local residents of non-British background and nationality (as will be related in the following chapter). Why did it not seem to matter in the least to the Commission whether refugees or enemy airmen would be the camp's occupants? What made the operation of a wartime facility like Victoria Camp such an appealing proposition to the Commission and why was the nature of its prospective inmates irrelevant? Apart from an unquestioned subservience to Britain's wartime needs born out of Newfoundland's intense sentiment of loyalty to the mother country, the promise of economic spinoffs from a camp to be guarded and maintained at no expense to Newfoundland appears to have been a compelling enticement to the Commission.

THE PATERSON SCHEME

The spring of 1941 confirmed that Newfoundland was just as eager to cooperate with Britain in facilitating the release of interned refugees as in keeping them interned. At that time yet another proposal for Victoria Camp as a possible accommodation for refugees came up for discussion. The refugees in question were to be released from Canadian internment on condition that they would be able to enter Newfoundland and immigrate from there to the United States. In February 1941 Alexander Paterson, H.M. Commissioner of Prisons in the United Kingdom, and S. Goldner of the newly formed Montreal Central Committee for Interned Refugees, visited St. John's to propose a scheme which envisaged 1,000 interned refugees to be moved over a period of some six months, in weekly groups of 50, from Halifax to St. John's. Various Newfoundland officials suggested that the refugees use Victoria Camp while awaiting their American visas. Paterson and Goldner, however, rejected the inaccessible camp in favor of the city's two fire halls which the Chief of Police offered as an alternative. For a number of reasons, local officials considered it expedient to restrict the refugees' freedom of movement. The Secretary for Justice was worried, despite assurances to the contrary, that the internees might be Nazis. There was concern that the internees might become involved in brawls or that they might congregate in large numbers speaking German. The Chief of Police insisted that the internees be kept together to facilitate supervision. In the end it was agreed to admit the refugees as tourists with minimal supervision.[30]

For some of the refugees the planned sojourn in St. John's would have been an ironic twist of fate. Less than one year earlier they had been deported to Canada on the *Sobieski* whose refugee passengers had originally been destined for internment at Victoria Camp. If they had remained in England, they would have been able to proceed with their plans to emigrate to the United States. Now they were to be released from Canadian internment by way of Newfoundland if they wanted to join relatives in the United States. The arrangement was devised by Paterson, who had been sent to Canada on a special mission in November 1940. After the British Home Office had begun to set free category B and C internees in Britain in late 1940, he was to work out the details of the release of the internees that Britain had deported earlier and who were not a security risk. Of the 2,284 B and C internees sent to Canada from Britain, 900 accepted the opportunity to return to Britain between December 1940 and June 1941. But the majority elected to stay in Canada. Of these about 1,000 had originally hoped to join relatives in the United States. They were mostly boys and young men: 45 percent were under the age of 25 and 87 percent under 30.[31]

In order to enable the latter to emigrate to America, geography suggested to Paterson the choice of Newfoundland as a way station. The need for a neutral stopover arose from the United States' refusal to accept immigrants direct from internment and the Canadian government's unwillingness to release interned refugees on Canadian soil. Newfoundland was the nearest and most accessible territory where, as Paterson explained, "they might be given their release by the British Government, and whence they might proceed as free agents and as ordinary civilian passengers to a port in the United States, having received an American visa in neutral territory." Internees proceeding to Central or South America would also pass through Newfoundland.[32] In order to avoid alerting the American press, which might distort the plan as an invasion by interned aliens, Paterson wanted the project to proceed as inconspicuously as possible. Having been warned in numerous instances that "nothing happens in St. John's without publicity," Paterson sought and obtained the cooperation of each of the editors of the three main papers published in St. John's.

S. Goldner of the Montreal Central Committee had worked out arrangements whereby refugee agencies agreed to maintain a hostel in the two St. John's fire halls. There successive batches of internees could stay while obtaining their official release from internment and their visas from the American consul. The fire halls were to be provided with cots, kitchen utensils, and a cook at the expense of the Central Committee. The Newfoundland government, at the insistence of Paterson, would supply bedding without charge. It had originally been purchased for the use of internees at Victoria Camp.

Since about 75 percent of the internees to arrive were Jewish and the rest mostly Roman Catholic, Goldner planned to form a local non-sectarian committee to look after their welfare and conduct. The St. John's Jewish community, numbering only twenty families, was too weak to billet or subsidize the refugees but offered its community hall as a club center. Although there were a number of members of Catholic orders among the refugees, Rev. Ronald McDonald Murphy, Secretary to the Archbishop and representing the city's large Roman Catholic community, was non-committal. Anglican Rector Canon Higham, by contrast, expressed keen interest in the plight of the internees and offered all his assistance. According to Paterson's and Goldner's assurances to local officials, Newfoundland "should not pay one cent in connection with the scheme," the British government and refugee agencies would foot the bill, and even some of the refugees were prepared to spend a portion of their own money if the Newfoundland Exchange Control Board would accept English currency. [33]

At the time he approached the Newfoundland government on 6 February 1941, Paterson had secured the support of the Department of External Affairs in Ottawa, the immigration and visa departments of the State Department in Washington, the American Attorney General, and other high officials. In Montreal the Central Committee of the refugee organizations was preparing a list of internees most likely to obtain visas rapidly. The list was to show at which American consulate the internee's papers had been filed, enabling the head of the visa department in Washington to have these papers transferred to the office of the American consul in St. John's. After the specified internees had been released by the Home Office in England, the Department of External Affairs in Ottawa would then issue identity certificates giving internees authority to proceed from Halifax to St. John's. The internees, according to Paterson's memorandum to the Commission of Government,

> will be taken under guard to the ship at Halifax, given their identity certificates which will act as travel documents, and on arrival in St. John's will be given their freedom on parole. They will be required to reside at such place or places as the Central Committee have prepared for them, and comply with such regulations as may be laid down by the representative of the Central Committee. Those

who have not yet registered for immigration can do so at St. John's.
Internees who do not obtain a visa will be returned to a camp in
Canada.[34]

The Acting Commissioner for Justice, J.C. Puddester, recommended the scheme to his colleagues after Paterson and Goldner
had agreed that (1) the number of internees proceeding to Newfoundland per steamer would not exceed fifty, (2) a guarantee or a
cash deposit would cover all expenditures incurred in Newfoundland, (3) they would produce evidence that the American and
Canadian governments concurred with the scheme, and 4) Canada
would take back any person not admitted to the United States. The
Commission of Government signified its approval of the project on
21 February 1941 subject to additional conditions. These provided
that Canada transport and maintain whatever police escort would
be necessary to ensure repatriation of internees refused admission
to the United States, and Canada bear all expenses incurred in such
repatriations. Governor Walwyn, who originally "expressed surprise
over the scheme," was sure it would go ahead.[35]

While Paterson awaited formal American confirmation of the
entire scheme, his assistant Chaim Raphael returned to St. John's
to prepare accommodations for the first one hundred young men.
These had either received American visas already or had parents or
first-degree relatives in the United States. Paterson waited in vain.
On 20 May 1941 the Newfoundland government was still expecting
word from Paterson that the scheme would go ahead. By that time,
however, Secretary of State Cordell Hull had referred the final
decision to his foreign policy advisor Assistant Secretary of State
Breckinridge Long who in April 1941 blamed opposition by the
American Legion for his veto. For a while hopes were kept alive by
the submission to Congress of the so-called Allen Bill which, while
seeking to ban all immigration, explicitly allowed for exceptions in
cases of family reunion. However, the Congressional Committee
misrepresented the Paterson plan and chose to omit "the all-impor-
tant fact that a number of these refugees are boys, with their parents
and all their families in the U.S.A." The unfortunate impression was
thus created that a "cast-iron scheme" was being "foisted on the
American public by a British Official."[36]

In reality, and unknown to Paterson, Long had advised the
American Minister in Ottawa, the U.S. Justice and Immigration
Departments, and the Under-Secretary of State against the scheme
as early as December 1940. "It would be very difficult to justify the
admission into the United States of individuals who have been
interned in England or Canada," Sumner Wells was reported having

quoted Attorney General Robert Jackson on 26 December 1940. It is therefore not surprising that, even after substituting Cuba for Newfoundland, Paterson was no more successful in his endeavors to obtain entry for released Canadian internees to the United States.[37] Paterson later believed it would have been wiser to send the released internees unofficially and in small batches quietly through Newfoundland or Bermuda to the States. He attributed his failure ultimately to expecting too much from the United States. Why should the U.S. State Department accept persons unwelcome in either in England or Canada? "Latent but potent was an anti-Semitic bias, rarely admitted, as rarely missing."[38]

MISSED OPPORTUNITIES?

The Victoria camp and the Paterson schemes constitute a noteworthy chapter in the fortuitous odyssey that in 1940–41 brought thousands of refugees as internees from the British Isles to Canada and eventually to the United States or back to Britain. In both cases Newfoundland offered to take refugees but was denied several opportunities to do so through the intervention, on different occasions, of Britain, Canada, and the United States. Both schemes would have cost Newfoundland nothing but, instead, would have produced revenue and instant economic spinoffs. The long-range social and economic consequences, however, especially of the Victoria Camp scheme, might have been immeasurable. As related earlier, the scheme failed to reach fruition in July 1940 when the torpedoing of the *Arandora Star* with its tents necessitated the diversion to Canada of the contingent of 1,000 refugee internees originally destined for Newfoundland.

The eminent effect a small number of the 1,000 refugees had on Canada after their release indicates how Newfoundland might have benefitted from these freed internees. As early as 1941, Paterson reported the discovery to Canadian authorities of 38 highly skilled draughtsmen and tool makers among the refugee internees. Recognized as invaluable in the munitions factories of Canada, they were released and offered trade-union wages. Other internees identified for release in 1941 included a research expert of value to the Central Film Board, a leather expert to be employed by a large commercial firm, as well as numerous distinguished professors and industrial chemists of value to Canada's war effort.[39] Consisting largely of German and Austrian Jews coming from all social and occupational strata of society, the internees included academics, artists and scientists who continued their careers in Canada or started them there.

The enormous potential of spiritual and creative energy this group represented is suggested by the following random listing of interned refugees who immigrated to Canada: geophysicist Ernst Deutsch; urbanist Peter Oberlander, theologian Gregory Baum, a leading member of the Ecumenical World Council; professor of English Studies F.D. Hoeninger; professor of Germanic Studies Ernst Reinhold; musicologist Helmut Kallmann, author of the *History of Music in Canada, 1534–1914* (Toronto, 1960); mathematician Walter Kohn; professor of philosophy Emil Fackenheim; Deans at McGill University Walter Hirschfeld (Graduate Faculty) and Helmut Blume (Music); Dean of the Faculty of Arts at the University of British Columbia Kaspar Naegele; Academic Vice President of the University of Alberta and author Henry Kreisel; famous pianist John Newmark; founder of the Montreal Dominion Gallery and well known promoter of Canadian art Max Stern; leading representative of the Toronto Group of Eleven Oscar Cahén; impresario Walter Homburger who launched pianist Glenn Gould; publicist Carl Weiselberger; journalist Ernst Wängler; authors Eric Koch, Franz Kramer, Ernst Bornemann, and Charles Wasserman; lyricist Anton Frisch; architect Henry Fliess.[40]

According to former refugee internee Eric Koch's autobiographical record, many of his fellow refugees had done well in business "and some have done very well." But more characteristic of the group was the large number of intellectuals who went into the professions, academic life, and the arts. "The universities were at the beginning of their great expansion, and so was Canada's cultural life. In 1940 only four fully professional orchestras existed."

> The war had transformed the country from a colonial backwater of the British Empire into a modern nation. We came in at just the right time, at the beginning of the cultural and economic postwar boom, and most of us were at just the right age. There we were, rejected by Europe and unwanted by the United States, anxious to adopt Canada as our new home and eager to do well in it. There had hardly been any immigration to Canada since the 1920s, and we did not have to compete with other groups, as the postwar immigrants have had to do. As immigrants we had, as it were, a monopoly.[41]

Koch's description of the experience of these refugee immigrants in Canada tantalizingly implies what their impact on Newfoundland might have been had they been allowed to enter.

"Intern or Deport"   9

Refugees as Fifth Column Suspects, 1939–1945

MEASURES AGAINST ENEMY ALIENS AND SUSPECTS

For a year after the outbreak of the war, European refugees continued to apply for admission to Newfoundland. Some were sponsored by Newfoundland residents, some were recommended by the Dominions Office, and some were encouraged by the Commission's late realization of the possibility of benefits accruing to Newfoundland from self-supporting refugee industries. A few of the economically promising applicants were permitted to visit Newfoundland briefly, but no permanent sanctuary was granted any of them. The outbreak of war in Europe and the subsequent climate of fear and suspicion of everything foreign that gripped the island, which from 1940 on bordered on paranoia, generated apprehensions that not only refugees of German birth but even refugees from countries allied with or occupied by Germany might be enemy agents. The experience of the six refugee doctors and nurses contracted for medical work in outports epitomized the fate awaiting European refugees in wartime Newfoundland.

As aliens, refugees in wartime Newfoundland were at the mercy of restrictive government measures and paranoid public attitudes. Restrictive measures affecting refugees were prompted by defence requirements, enemy alien regulations, British government communications, and public opinion. Responsible for applying and enforcing aliens restrictions was L.E. Emerson, now Commissioner for Justice and Defence. Wartime public attitudes towards aliens were influenced by the perception of danger to the community. The nature and degree of the danger perceived to be most imminent was, by and large, determined by media reports and comments. Depend-

ing on the kinds of news items and comments they chose to feature,
newspaper editors were able to trigger defensive reactions from the
public. For instance, focusing on the potential disloyalty of resident
aliens was tantamount to inciting anti-foreign responses. In wartime
the media must be credited with a large responsibility for public
perceptions and hence reactions.

The scope of enforceable restrictions was indicated by the
Defence Act and a series of Defence Regulations passed as early as
1 September 1939. Modelled on similar British and Canadian legislation, these statutes conferred upon the Governor in Commission
far-reaching powers to make regulations exceeding those of the War
Measures Act of 1914. They included the power to control the
landing, residence, movement, and deportation of aliens, as well as
measures to prevent "espionage, sabotage, signalling, etc.," and
enemy propaganda, to impose censorship, control firearms, imports
and exports, foodstuffs, and prices, etc. By exercising these powers,
mostly secretly, the Commissioners restricted civil liberties at their
discretion and residents were unable to appeal the violation of their
civil rights. The lack of a parliament, the local press noted, left the
Defence Act with no safeguards against dictatorial abuse.

> Parliament and the Governor in Council are one and the same.
> There could be no recourse from a decision—no matter what it
> might involve . . . An order under the present system of govern-
> ment may emanate from one member of the administration. Even
> to commissioners might be applied the observation that it is human
> to err.[1]

The Defence Act and Defence Regulations provided the legal
basis—often on the scantiest of evidence—for police registration,
expulsion, deportation, and relocation of aliens, and for virtually
indiscriminate arrest and confiscation of property of those suspected of being enemy agents.[2] The spirit of many of these provisions
directly encouraged fifth column hysteria.[3] According to regulations
72 and 73, Newfoundlanders were obliged to denounce suspects to
the police, and any act preparatory to the commission of a prohibited
act was punishable. Guilty of an offense might, in fact, be anyone
who "does any act of a nature which may be prejudicial to the public
safety or the defence of the Island and is not specifically provided
for in the foregoing Regulations" (Regulation 69).[4]

Newfoundland's wartime alien and refugee policy was also influenced by communications from the British government. This is
illustrated by developments in connection with the previously
described Victoria Camp and Paterson schemes, and in other ways.
In September 1939 the advice from London was "to avoid treating

as enemies those who are friendly to the country which has offered them asylum," such as citizens of the former republic of Czechoslovakia. One year later, however, London and Ottawa warned St. John's to beware of Czech-born sales representatives because the Canadian and American branches of the Czech Bata Shoe Company may have come under enemy influence.[5] In May 1940 the Dominions Office requested that all German refugees proceeding to neutral destinations on neutral ships be interrogated and suspected enemy agents be detained pending further inquiries.[6] In June 1940 Downing Street forwarded for information a confidential bulletin on *Fifth Column Activities*. It attributed German military successes in Poland, Scandinavia, and the Low Countries to the subversive activities of German fifth columnists and referred to refugees as potentially dangerous if they had relatives exposed to the Gestapo.[7] Throughout the war the Commission was apprised, and advised to apply the lessons, of Whitehall's alien and refugee policy.

In St. John's at the outbreak of the war, the public was reported to be much agitated over the possibility that enemy aliens who were professed Nazis were still at large.[8] Four of the fourteen local residents who held German citizenship[9] were thereupon interned in a specially erected "concentration camp" (as it was locally known), together with 25 merchant seamen. The seamen had been removed from the German freighter *Christoph von Doornum*, which was seized eight days before the outbreak of the war while loading lead-zinc concentrates in Botwood. No additional local Germans were interned because the police found most of the accusations against them to be without foundation and there were no facilities to accommodate a larger number of prisoners of war. The Department of Justice was confident that systematic police surveillance of the small number of aliens[10] would be able to detect any subversive activity.

In order to implement police surveillance, the Commission was faced with the awesome task of creating Newfoundland's first systematic register of all "alien" residents as provided for in Defence Regulation No. 20 of 1 September 1939. Alien registration took almost one year to complete and turned into a bureaucratic nightmare, partly because the notion of what constituted an alien, or even an enemy alien, expanded steadily and partly because it was found that no reliable data existed about Newfoundland's population of non-British origin. The lists of "aliens" compiled by the police and the Department of Justice identified not only 375 non-naturalized residents, but also 393 "aliens naturalized in Newfoundland from 1893 to date" (including 18 natives of Germany, 3 of Austria, 33 of Poland, 12 of Norway, 9 of Denmark, 3 of Lithuania, 2 of Latvia) and

14 "foreigners who appear to have adopted English names, natural-ized since 1919."[11]

The approach to registration proved to be a major drawback to establishing meaningful controls and in dealing equitably with a large spectrum of residents classified as "aliens." It revealed a tendency to question the allegiance of every Newfoundlander of non-British background, to confuse the retention of non-British cultural attributes with a lack of loyalty and to see an enemy alien in every native of a central or east European country. As a result, not only German nationals became the subject of police surveillance and preventive measures, but also all kinds of related "aliens," such as natives of neutral and annexed European countries and people who considered themselves to be Newfoundlanders. Seamen from various European countries, such as Finland, were detained, inter-ned, and deported, while Austrian and Czech refugees from Nazi persecution suffered from unwarranted suspicions and from the threat of internment. Even the "very Teutonic name" of Captain C.M.R. Schwerdt, private secretary to the Governor and English-born, became a matter of concern among the public.[12]

PUBLIC AND MEDIA ATTITUDES TOWARDS ALIENS

The signal for an uncompromising attitude in the public debate was given in several newspaper editorials and comments on European events warning of the danger posed by the infiltrations of refugees with fifth column activity such as spying and spreading the spirit of defeatism. The gist of the alarming message is contained in the *Evening Telegram's* column "Enemy Within" of 23 May 1940 in which an anonymous local "analyst" approvingly quotes a speech by the Rt. Hon. Lord Queensborough justifying mass internment of refugees in Britain:

> Let us remember that very large numbers of refugees from Ger-many, Austria and Czechoslovakia were men of strong left-wing and almost Communist sympathies; we cannot rely on their loyalty to the country which has given them shelter. In addition to this it is well known that the Gestapo has planted its agents among the refugees and that many self-styled exiles were and are, in fact, the paid secret agents of the Nazi power.
>
> Their work not only includes the obvious duties of espionage and sabotage, but the equally dangerous and infinitely less easily detectable work of spreading defeatism, preaching Nazi doctrines, and using revolutionary elements to weaken the Home Front . . .
> In their own interests and in the interests of our own Country and People, all aliens whose antecedents and character are not beyond

the slightest shadow of suspicion should be put under restraint or made subject to severe restrictions.

Comparing unfavorably Newfoundland's lack of preparedness against acts of enemy aliens with Canada's exemplary measures "against the enemy already within the gate," editorials in the *Evening Telegram* castigated the Newfoundland authorities for their lackadaisical attitude towards the dangers from within.[13] Jeffery's editorial stance provoked a flood of hysterical anonymous letters expressing the conviction that "there is no one who can vouch for any alien after an acquaintance of a few years, or even a life-time today." Why had the government "brought in so many aliens, especially during the past eighteen months?" was the recurring question, and the solution was wrapped up in the slogan: "Come along Newfoundlanders, see to it that your country gets rid of all Aliens by internment or deportation."[14]

For the *Evening Telegram*, in contrast to the *Daily News* and *Observer's Weekly*, it seems to have been editorial policy to feed readers a steady diet of news about the untrustworthiness of refugees. On their visit to St. John's in February 1941 the representatives of the Montreal Central Committee for Interned Refugees (see chapter 8) were warned of the difficulty of restraining this editor from exploiting and distorting refugee-related issues. They were told "in numerous instances" that "nothing happens in St. John's without publicity."[15] Throughout the summer and fall of 1940 the *Evening Telegram* kept stoking the fires of fifth column hysteria by its selection of news, xenophobic editorials, and headlines, such as "Refugees" (21 May), "Fifth Column" (10 June), "The Quisling Factory" (17 July), "Canada Smashes at Fifth Column" (8 August), "Check the Refugees" (23 August), and "Gestapo Mingles with Refugees" (29 August). After tainting the refugees' search for sanctuary as "nefarious work" of fifth columnists, the editorial entitled "The Stranger Within" (3 July) urged that the door should be "shut and bolted" against them. The *Daily News*, Newfoundland's only other main daily newspaper, attempted in vain to exert a moderating influence.

The media campaign for drastic measures against suspected fifth columnists triggered direct approaches to the governor from the public. The Commissioners devoted considerable attention to a letter of 15 May 1940 from a Mrs. F.R. Emerson [no relation to L.E. Emerson], speaking as an active member of the Red Cross Society, who felt so strongly on the subject of home defence that she did not wish to advertise her proposals "for the information of the enemy in our midst." In an obvious reference to the half dozen Jewish refugee doctors serving as nurses, Mrs. Emerson urged

> that every alien, male or female, no matter how long since he left his country, and all those, no matter what credentials they bring, who are arriving so easily and establishing themselves at such points of vantage, just before the Germans may make an aerial attack, be interned at once without exception, so that our efforts for defence may not be reported straight to Germany as they develop.[16]

The Commission, although not entirely immune to public pressures, resisted demands for the wholesale internment or deportation of aliens.

The surge of xenophobic rhetoric and behavior after the outbreak of the war was obviously fuelled by public alarm over the island's exposed and seemingly defenseless strategic location, and by the traditional intense loyalty to Britain. It was sustained by the islanders' bottomless fear of the submarine, its ubiquity and sur-reptitiousness. In 1942 the sinking in Cabot Strait of the passenger and freight ferry *Caribou*[17] with the loss of 136 lives, plus two submarine raids on four ore ships anchored at Bell Island with 69 lives lost, nurtured persistent rumors of sabotage and submarine landings. Newfoundlanders could not know that German naval strategies attached a relatively low priority to Newfoundland,[18] that the tragic Bell Island and *Caribou* sinkings were by U-boats whose destinations were the Strait of Belle Isle and Chesapeake Bay,[19] and that U-boats disliked operating in the waters around New-foundland.[20] Newfoundland's significance to Allied shipping obscured the fact that during the six years of World War II the island itself never did become a major target or theater of submarine warfare.

Newfoundlanders were no doubt aware that the construction and maintenance of seventy American bases[21] on the island and in Labrador, plus additional Canadian bases, brought not only pros-perity but also increased security.[22] The arrival of Canadian forces in June 1940 and of American troops in January 1941 significantly reduced the likelihood and potential severity of enemy attacks by sea or air. Canadian and American forces established complete defenses for the ports and airports of St. John's and Botwood, and an umbrella of RCN escorts; RCAF patrols and American fighter planes protected the coastline.[23] The local perception of having been in the eye of the storm[24] has largely obscured the equally eminent fact that the war gave respectability to existing prewar anti-foreign prejudices and with the help of the media allowed them to be directed against a widening spectrum of innocent aliens.

WARTIME IMMIGRATION CONTROLS AND REFUGEE IMMIGRATION

One of the tactics used by the *Evening Telegram* to stir up fifth column panic was to keep repeating the assertion that "immigration regulations are non-existent" and that "our immigration laws have for years remained wide open."[25] In reality, the outbreak of war restricted entry to four ports (St. John's, Botwood, Corner Brook, and Port aux Basques) where the Department of Customs had Aliens Officers. Nationals of any non-Empire country in Europe were prohibited from landing "for any purpose" without the prior permission of the Chief Commissioner of Immigration. Citizens of America, Canada, and some other countries were admissible with identity papers.

In August 1940 Penson recommended new rules governing the landing of six classes of aliens: (1) aliens of enemy nationality: to be excluded; (2) aliens of neutral nationality but born in enemy countries, or whose parents were either enemy aliens or born in enemy countries, and (3) aliens other than the foregoing and other than U.S. citizens: to obtain prior permit from Chief Commissioner of Immigration, plus voucher or credentials from reputable parties; (4) American citizens not falling within class (2), and (5) British subjects other than Canadians: to be admitted by Aliens Officer at port of entry, if the applicant can produce credentials and establish legitimate purpose of visit; (6) Canadians: to be admitted on similar terms as (4).

To administer these regulations all persons, including returning Newfoundlanders, had to fill out an Admissions Form prior to landing. It asked, among standard personal data, for such information as the immigrant's race, nationality, how and when that nationality was acquired, previous nationality, nationality of parents and how acquired, and parents' previous nationality. Penson admitted recommending these rules "with some reluctance" and in response to representations from the Department of Justice and recommendations of the Customs Department. These Departments, Penson claimed, considered the old controls "not sufficiently watertight" because they depended "more on the alertness and intelligence of these men [i.e., Aliens Officers] rather than on any prescribed rules." For Emerson, Penson's draft Regulations were a commendable "step forward in the right direction" but did not go far enough. Naturalized British subjects should be treated as aliens of neutral nationality by naturalization, he urged, and all tourist traffic

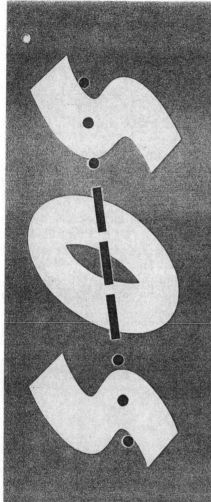

SOS

Never in the bar or barber's
Talk of ships or crews or harbours
Idle words – things heard or seen
Help the lurking submarine

Careless talk costs lives and ships

Official poster displayed in St. John's in 1942. It warned people of loose talk and enemy agents. By suggesting local contacts with enemy submarines, it contributed to fifth column fears. Credit: PANL.

east of and in Corner Brook should be prohibited to keep out the saboteur. He knew of no harbor more desirable for an enemy to enter than St. John's and it was time the Commission treated the question of enemy activities seriously. Newfoundland was about to be fortified from the sea, the air, and the land, and Emerson felt strongly "that the least we can do is to take strict precautions to see that these fortifications are not in any way jeopardized for the matter of a few dollars which would be spent by the cheapest kind of tourist." Penson's draft was published with Emerson's amendments[26] in the *Evening Telegram* on 31 August 1940.

The escalating fifth-column panic counteracted the late realization of the benefits which might accrue to Newfoundland from self-supporting refugee entrepreneurs, professionals, tradesmen with special skills and independent farmers. From September 1939 until April 1940 applications from eligible refugee immigrants had been officially solicited and "considered individually on their merits"[27] by the New Industries Committee, a voluntary association of business and professional representatives chaired by the Commissioner for Natural Resources. The committee's formal constitution was officially announced on 22 August 1939 and its chairman J.H. Gorvin prided himself on his initiatives to recruit refugee entrepreneurs and specialists.[28] He himself invited Paul B. Wallheimer, Maurice and Julio Metal (see below), and Bernhard Altmann.[29] But many other highly qualified refugee applicants were refused.

Among those rejected by the Commission were Tibor S. Vadnai (a 32-year old Hungarian Jew, educated in the U.K., fluent in English and four other languages, with capital of his own and experience in the fishing and timber trades), as well as three Hungarian physicians who had acquired their medical diplomas at the University of Pavia, Italy, which would have qualified them to register for medical practice in Britain without examination. In rejecting these Hungarians, the Commission repudiated its own decision with regard to foreign doctors.[30] In July 1940 a group consisting of one Newfoundland citizen, one Belgian (who had been residing in the U.K. for 30 years), and two Austrian refugee families applied for entry in order to develop some mining rights which they were about to purchase. The Commission decided that, while no objection would be raised to any Newfoundland citizen wishing to return, Austrians and Belgians could not be admitted "in the circumstances now obtaining."[31]

In July 1940 a community of 289 German Hutterites in Britain who had fled Germany between 1936 and 1938 (see chapter 2) asked the Dominions Office to convey their request to the Government of Newfoundland that they be permitted to send out two representatives to examine local conditions and to discuss possibilities of settling there. They stated that their well-to-do fellow groups in Canada and the United States would finance their settlement. Reputed to be a law-abiding and industrious religious community, they practiced agriculture and local industries and also did educational work. The British Ministry of Agriculture spoke of their farm work in laudatory terms. Exempted from internment in Britain owing to their Christian pacifism, and planning to settle in England, they were suffering from the hostility of their English neighbors.[32]

Although the Hutterites had planned to settle permanently in England—they had founded two communal farms in Wiltshire and earned their living by mixed farming, market gardening, wood turning, publishing and printing—in 1940 they were compelled to resettle overseas. What had happened? Hutterite leader Hans Meier recalled that the English neighbors were very friendly toward the community until the fall of France and the defeat and evacuation of the British forces from Dunkirk. From that moment on the Hutterites experienced "the mass psychosis of fear and mistrust toward any foreigner." Because they were conscientious objectors, their English brethren were despised as traitors. The sale of their products was stopped, they were harassed, big concrete blocks were put in their fields to "prevent German parachutists or gliders from landing," and they were accused of sending light signals to the German bombers. "Neighbors who in earlier times had greeted us and even invited us for a cup of tea now withdrew and shut their doors when we passed," Meier recalled.[33]

The Governor of Newfoundland did not recommend the visit of a Hutterite representative because "hostility to which community subjected in United Kingdom would almost certainly be experienced here probably in marked degree."[34] In the fall of 1940 the two Hutterite representatives who were to visit Newfoundland travelled through Canada and the United States in a vain search for sanctuary. Hans Meier, who was one of the two, remembered that in the United States they were unwanted because, among other reasons, they refused to salute the flag. In Ottawa they were informed "in no uncertain terms" that Canada "already had enough difficulties with Hutterites." Through the good offices of the Mennonite Central Committee, Paraguay finally offered them a haven in 1941. In 1974 they relocated to Woodcrest, New York.[35]

The case of Anna Elizabeth Givens indicated that the Commission could not afford to be inflexible in refusing refugees categorized as enemy aliens. As a Chilean citizen the German-born wife of R.C. Givens, Chief Electrical Engineer with the Buchans Mining Company, requested admission in Spring 1940. According to her testimony to the Newfoundland authorities, she had fled to Chile in 1935 after she had been jailed in Nazi Germany for refusing to join the Nazi Party as a school teacher. Marrying her husband in Chile and permitted to enter the United States in his company in 1939, she intended to follow him with their newborn baby to Buchans where he was transferred in April 1940. When she was refused permission to enter Newfoundland despite her credentials as an anti-Nazi refugee, her husband's employer protested strongly and Mr. Givens gave notice of his intention to resign from his post in Buchans. Because of the overriding necessity of maintaining unchecked the flow of concentrate exports the Commission now decided to reverse its decision. The Chief Commissioner of Immigration reasoned that, if the policy of refusing admission could be shown to react unfavorably upon production, "then we should have to depart from the narrow letter of the regulations whether we wished to do so or not."[36]

In the absence of circumstances forcing the hand of the Commission, however, exclusion and expulsion of aliens were the rule, as the case of Adam Swirsky illustrates. A 26-year old Jewish native of Poland, recent resident of New York and naturalized British citizen who had lived in Palestine, Swirsky came to visit his brothers in Corner Brook and his sister in St. John's, all merchants, in November 1939. After the expiry of his three-months' tourist permit, the Corner Brook Jewish Congregation asked him to remain for one year as a teacher of Hebrew. His request for an extension of his permit triggered the following note from Chief Commissioner of Immigration Hutchings to the Chief of Police:

> This man has made application through the Governor in 1938 from Palestine and was refused. On that application his occupation was shown as "Labourer"; today he classes himself as a Teacher. His request . . . has naturally been refused, and I would be grateful if you would be so good as to have your Police Officer at Corner Brook ascertain whether Mr. Swirsky has, in fact, left the country.[37]

REFUGEE SPECIALISTS AND ENTREPRENEURS

The first victim of malicious denunciations sanctioned by the government was Paul B. Wallheimer, a non-Jewish refugee married to a member of the well-known Jewish family in Hamburg named Warburg. After his release from three weeks of maltreatment in a German concentration camp in the wake of *Kristallnacht*, he was admitted to Canada in early 1939. In the summer of 1939 Newfoundland's New Industries Committee recruited Wallheimer from Canada as a peat technologist in order to develop a peat moss industry. His services were initially appreciated[38] and his contract was to be extended in February 1940 so that Wallheimer could be entrusted with the development of peat fuel. At that moment, however, Wallheimer was attacked in the *Evening Telegram* (20 February 1940) as a "foreign expert of whose nationality and abilities very little is known." At the same time a Canadian-born peat technologist, who had earlier unsuccessfully applied for Wallheimer's position in Newfoundland and subsequently found employment with the censorship authorities in Ottawa, denounced Wallheimer as a German spy. The Director of Immigration to Canada F.C. Blair, an avowed anti-Semite,[39] did little to dispel suspicions when he identified Wallheimer as a German Jew and an enemy alien whom Newfoundland might not wish to keep. In April 1940 the New Industries Committee recommended cancellation of Wallheimer's contract, an action which was tantamount to expulsion from Newfoundland.[40]

Typical of the treatment meted out to anti-Nazi refugees in wartime Newfoundland is the well-documented case of refugee entrepreneurs Julio and Maurice Metal. It exemplifies the basic pattern of the refugee experience: media denunciations fanning public rumors and culminating in punitive government action. Julio Metal and his secretary Walter E. Sondheimer arrived in St. John's from New York on 19 December 1939 at the invitation of Newfoundland Commissioner for Natural Resources J.H. Gorvin to discuss the launching of a small industry. The party intended to set up Julio's son Maurice Metal as director of a woodworking industry named Terra Nova Development Company. S.T. Wood, Commissioner of the Royal Canadian Mounted Police (RCMP), interviewed Julio Metal as the latter travelled through Canada to Newfoundland. Wood assured the Newfoundland government on 26 January 1940 that he was left "with no particular suspicions of Metal."[41]

Maurice Metal arrived from England on 11 January 1940. Before he had a chance to get down to business, an *Evening Telegram* editorial of 3 February 1940 under the title "Who−and Why?" alluded to the Metals as sympathizers with the Hitler regime. This allusion was followed by a request dated 7 February 1940 from RCMP Commissioner Wood that Newfoundland re-investigate the activities of the Metals. The Newfoundland government's censorship of the suspects' mail and inquiries into their assets and banking connections revealed that the Metals were Jews, conducted much

Julio Metal. Credit: PANL.

of their correspondence in German, claimed Polish nationality (Julio was born and married in Poland), held Liechtenstein passports, and had substantial investments in Germany, Austria, Switzerland, the United Kingdom, and the United States. Sondheimer held an American passport and spoke English with a pronounced foreign accent.

The Metals' extensive correspondence, their interest in a wide variety of possible ventures, and their lack of a definite business aroused suspicions. Particular alarm was caused by the discovery that in August 1939 the Metals had had indirect contacts with Count Henckel von Donnersmarck, a person authorized by the German government and rumored to be a Gestapo agent. The contact was ostensibly for the purpose of "Aryanizing," i.e., liquidating the Metals' German properties and transferring abroad as much of their assets as possible, a not unreasonable purpose for the contacts. After scrutinizing the available evidence the Newfoundland Commissioner L.E. Emerson concluded on 21 February 1940 that the Gestapo rumor and most of the other suspicions were unfounded.[42]

Nevertheless, the damage caused by false rumors could not be undone. When Maurice Metal's logging operations got underway, the local people were reported to be asking: "Who is Mr. Metal? . . . Is it true that he is a German? What does he intend doing at Salmonier?" The nature and purpose of the wood operation, known as "the Central European Plan," were a mystery. An *Evening Telegram* editorial considered the wages Metal paid to loggers too low and wondered whether his operations could not have been undertaken equally well by Newfoundlanders. Metal replied in an open letter that he realized Newfoundlanders were suspicious at this time and that "I am not now nor have I ever been a German. Neither has my father or Mr. Sondheimer." He explained that his company had brought in its own capital to pay for its experiments, he paid the going rates, no one was forced to work for him, and his operations had reduced government relief payments to the district.[43]

In a letter written to his father Maurice stated that from mid-February to mid-April he had cut 600 cords of wood and spent $2,000 of his own assets, $1,700 of it on wages and salaries. Of his 60 workers, all were doing well except for 10 who either disobeyed cutting instructions or had a very low work ethic.[44] Interviews in the Salmonier area 39 years later reveal that Metal is remembered there as a German. But they also confirm that Metal's logging operation gave work to all the available men in the nearby communities from Mount Carmel to St. Mary's, that he paid good wages from a fat chequebook which he used to carry on him, that he was the most

Maurice Metal. Credit: PANL.

efficient and progressive logging operator they had ever seen,[45] and that, if allowed to stay, he would have had the biggest sawmill in the area. Metal paid his workers according to what they cut which often amounted to more than the $7 rate per cord which local operators paid. The latter naturally did not like foreign entrepreneurs paying higher wages and had a vested interest in seeing Metal leave.[46]

The catalyst in the final act of Metal's drama was again the *Evening Telegram*. An editorial of 1 June 1940 entitled "Intern or Deport" was destined to raise the temperature of the spy fever and to force the hand of the government. In it the editor wondered "why, when the cause of suspicion can be removed, should the public be caused uneasiness by the presence of persons who come within such category?" He then advised that "the method of removal is simple. Intern those of whose sincerity there is doubt. Better still, give them notice to take themselves to the country from which they came within forty-eight hours." In May 1940, when Metal's permit came up for renewal, the government decided to heed the editor's advice and asked Metal to leave the country by 15 June. Apart from the fifth column hysteria which was sweeping Newfoundland following the fall of France, no new incriminating evidence against the Metals had come to light. Emerson, who disliked Gorvin, confided to Secretary for Justice L.B. Summers that he was suspicious of "the crowd" [i.e., the Metals] chiefly "because of their association with Gorvin!!"[47] Governor Walwyn echoed a widespread perception when he cabled to London that "their conduct well supports the theory of masquerade."[48]

Maurice Metal left for New York on 15 May, planning to resume his logging operations and believing the expulsion to be temporary. After his departure the Department of Justice ordered that the luggage Julio and Maurice Metal had stored in Hotel Newfoundland be opened and the voluminous correspondence contained in it be translated and analyzed in the hope "that some evidence might be found to substantiate certain suspicions which the conduct of these gentlemen had aroused." The correspondence was in several languages and its translation required more than three months by two faculty members from Memorial University College. It contained evidence revealing the Metals' hatred of Nazi Germany and its anti-Semitic policies and confirmed Emerson's findings of 21 February 1940. Despite these findings Metal was not invited to return to Newfoundland although he had forwarded funds to his local foreman in Salmonier to continue logging operations for another half year. One thousand cords of scaled timber was abandoned to rot in the woods and the local people were left to believe that Metal was expelled on account of his connections to a spy.[49]

REFUGEE DOCTORS, NURSES, AND RABBIS AS SPY SUSPECTS

The largest group of refugees, the six doctors and/or nurses recruited by the Department of Health in the summer of 1939, experienced almost insurmountable difficulties of adjustment from the day of their arrival in Newfoundland. Their first experiences were typical of what was in store for them. After the *Evening Telegram* welcomed them in July 1939 as undesirable, unqualified and suspicious foreigners (see chapter 6), the medical establishment questioned their competence as physicians, and officials of the Department of Health and the Constabulary frequently denied them their earned title of Doctor. One of the refugees recalled that the Chief of the Newfoundland Nursing Services, Miss Lilian Whiteside, who introduced them into their duties as district nurses for the outports, "never hid her conviction that we doctors were in many ways inferior to the regular nurses."[50]

Adjustment to substandard living and working conditions was difficult enough without unfair invectives. On making their first sick calls in St. John's, the refugees were overwhelmed by "such stark poverty" as they had "never seen before." The diary of Ilka Deutsch (published in 1981 under her married name, Dickman), affords unique insights into what awaited central European refugees arriving as nurses in Newfoundland. A 41-year-old Jewish physician who had been practicing medicine in her hometown of Prague for twelve years, Deutsch was assigned to a nursing station serving 1,200 souls in seven South Coast outports between Rencontre West and Cross Cove. Their only connection with each other and with the outside world was by boat. She was the only medical person along a 25-mile coastline—the next cottage hospital was 100 miles away—and served also as dentist, veterinarian, social worker, first-aid teacher, librarian and undertaker.

In none of the seven outports for which she was responsible "was there a tree, a road, running water, or electricity. Drinking water was fetched in pails from a running creek. There were no toilets, not even outhouses and no sewers." Of Rencontre West's population of 250, only seven could read and write. School lasted for three months a year, and the teacher had the only battery-powered radio. In the community of Francois with a population of 350 "the people sit and do not do anything. Sometimes a clock ticks and life goes by." The merchant determined who got the dole by making people sign blank receipts for goods which he then distributed. He filled out the blanks

Dr. Ilka Deutsch. Credit: PANL.

at a later date. There was "abject poverty" and boredom everywhere, and Deutsch found it hard to comprehend how people managed to live and even bring up their babies with everything lacking. In nine months, she relates, she went through three stages of adjustment. First, she was happy to learn that life was bearable, though hard. Then came the realization "of the truly tragic background of the people around her; the lack of a future for them; the narrowness of their outlook on life, their ignorance, their suspicion of anything outside their confines." She found this difficult to adapt to. But gradually she accepted things as they were.

An unforgettable part of Deutsch's 15-month experience in Newfoundland was "the vicious talk about the nurses from Europe being spies." Her refugee colleague Erika Mohr, stationed in the adjacent district of Pushthrough, was suspected of smuggling money to Germany and accused of siding with the Germans. She was warned of the consequences. When the three refugee nurses from the South Coast went to St. John's on a four-day holiday in July 1940, rumor had it that they were being taken to jail for spying. The *Evening Telegram* (3 and 5 July 1940) intimated that the refugees had been distributed "at strategic points" and wondered how long they would be allowed to continue. Harmless sketches that Deutsch had drawn of outport scenes were rumored to serve espionage purposes and were confiscated by the constabulary. They became the cause of an investigation by the Department of Justice and were not released to her until after the war, even though she managed to relocate to the United States in November 1940. Deutsch was grateful that she was able to leave Newfoundland.[51]

Austrian Jewish-born refugee physician Josephine Maiwald, aged 42 and stationed at the South Coast Cottage Hospital of Burgeo, described her experience as a district nurse in Rencontre West to an American lawyer in Texas who applied for an American visa on her behalf in October 1941:

> You cannot imagine under what conditions and how hard I am working here. I acquired a phobia of the sea when I happened to come into a very squally sea and found myself confronted with danger of life, seeing four men had to work hard in order to prevent our dory from being shattered at a rock to which the waves were driving it. I did not believe we might come out safely. Ever since I tremble when I see a dory coming in, it might be a call. I simply can't go out in such a small craft to the open sea. Everybody knows it is a rough bit of coast I have to cover in this district. I informed the Department and was expecting to be discharged. Instead I got an answer that they would not pay my wages as I stated my intention to neglect my duties and not to follow my professional

call. They ordered me to stay and do my duties. If I left I should quit
their service. Being an alien in the country I do not know whether
they may be able to bring me in trouble if I leave in conflict.

The letter was intercepted and the Newfoundland Constabulary
advised that its suspicious contents be referred to F.B.I. Director
Hoover "for his usual co-operation in this connection." Maiwald had
been transferred to St. Bride's, Cape Shore, in November 1940 where
her refusal to visit a patient after 11 p.m. on a very stormy night,
and her protestation that she "would not go for the King of England"
to visit persons after dark, became the subject of the next police
report.[52]

Maiwald was on the Chief Censor's special list of suspects
because she was corresponding with her husband, a retired professor living in Vienna, through an intermediary in Romania. She was
also erroneously suspected of sending uncensored mail through the
Red Cross boats. The Registry of Aliens was particularly upset when
in one of the censored letters to her husband she allegedly stated
that she was "being hounded by the Doctor and Nurses of the
Cottage Hospital, Burgeo, and spoke very unfavorably about the
treatment afforded her generally by the people of this country." She
apparently went on to say that the treatment she was receiving was
"something similar to the treatment handed out in the German
Concentration Camps." In connection with an intercepted letter of
January 1943 to her friend Ilka Deutsch in Philadelphia, in which
she characterized a German-American physician at the Twillingate
hospital as a Nazi for his attitude with regard to Jews, the censor
commented that Maiwald "has always found fault with the people
with whom she worked and lived." The German-American physician
appears to have taken the post in Newfoundland to escape U.S.
military service.

When in May 1942 Maiwald's three-year contract with the
Department of Health expired, she took up a position as an intern
in Twillingate. Having lost all her belongings in a fire there in the
summer of 1943, Maiwald considered it unreasonable to be refused
permission by the Department of Justice to visit Grand Falls, the
nearest town to Twillingate. "After a year everybody will need to go
to town to see a dentist, a hairdresser or to do some shopping for
the winter even if he was not burnt out as I was," she explained to
the Secretary for Justice. In December 1943 her request for a
transfer to Eastport, Bonavista Bay, where she hoped to share the
company of refugee physician L.H. Redlich, was similarly rejected.
The Chief of Police saw no necessity for two foreign lady doctors in
that district and remarked: "We have in the past met with consider-

able difficulty in controlling Aliens in this country including Dr.
Maiwald. They do not seem to be content at any place and wish to
be moving from time to time." As a last resort she pleaded gynecologi-
cal trouble requiring attention by a female doctor as the reason for
needing to visit Eastport. The Department of Justice decided that it
had no legal authority to forbid the visit. It even permitted her to
stay and take up the post of Redlich who was departing for England.
However, she was allowed to proceed to Grand Falls for dental
treatment only with prior approval from the Secretary for Justice
and on condition that she report to the police daily.

In July 1945 Maiwald was still waiting at Eastport for her
American visa, probably with the sense of indignant impatience
which her petition of June 1943 to Commissioner Emerson suggests:

> Austrians are regarded as friendly aliens in the U.S.A., in Great
> Britain and in Canada. From the U.S.A. I know they are enjoying
> the liberty of unrestricted free movement. Personally I am sure no
> sensible human being will really believe that I have any use for this
> country's enemies who are my enemies first and foremost, and by
> whose guilt I am running astray without my well beloved husband,
> without anybody of my family for more than four years.[53]

Austrian physician Lisbeth H. Redlich, 30-year-old adoptee of a
Jewish family that fled to England in 1938, was under continuous
investigation as a prime spy suspect throughout her four years of
service as a district nurse and then as an intern in six different
hospitals and stations in Newfoundland and Labrador. As early as
26 February 1940 an anonymous letter to the *Evening Telegram*
demanded Redlich's internment. The writer, who called himself or
herself "British," credited the editor with drawing attention to the
"importation of some Austrian doctors and nurses" and noted with
"some surprise" that

> one of those nurses has sailed for a hospital on the South Coast,
> and in one of our Water St. stores where she was purchasing some
> of her requirements she wasn't at all backward in stating "*I am a
> German.*" Can you beat this? . . . instead of this lady being sent to
> this hospital, if her words as to her nationality are correct, the
> proper place for her is down by the Lake Side. [The St. John's
> internment camp was by Quidi Vidi lake.]

During her first, brief service in the St. John's General Hospital
sixteen members of the hospital staff offered signed statements to
the Constabulary accusing Redlich of sending light signals from her
room in the Hotel Newfoundland. They accused her of defending
Hitler, admitting to being a spy, stealing official envelopes for her

personal correspondence, and being friendly to three hospitalized German civil internees by talking German to them and paying their cigarette bills. From every station where she was transferred, complaints of her flouting pro-Nazi sentiments reached St. John's. Even two of her fellow refugees who could not get along with her imputed her behavior to Nazi sympathies. The Registry of Aliens, however, noted in July 1942 that Redlich lived with a Jewish family in St. John's, that her contacts were mostly Jews, and that she could not be identified with any subversive activities.

In May 1943 Redlich was one of three foreign-born physicians who applied or intended to apply for naturalization in order to regain their full civil rights and find better protection against the never-ending aspersions of disloyalty. With reference to the application of Latvian-born Dr. Wolf Grobin (who entered Newfoundland in 1938 with U.K. certified qualifications)[54] and Redlich's known intention to apply, District Inspector M.P. Mahoney suggested that for the time being "no naturalization should be granted to Aliens of this kind." He apprised the Chief of Police that "these aliens arrived in this country on or about the time when Hitler was placing his agents throughout the world and with this in view I am of the opinion that no naturalization should be granted until after the war."[55]

Upon expiration of her three-year contract, Redlich was desperate to return to England and resume medical work there. She resented the restrictions imposed on her freedom of movement in Newfoundland. When she applied to the passport control officer in July 1942 for a visa, Commissioner Emerson approached the High Commissioner for Canada in St. John's with a request for her internment in Canada on account of her suspicious conduct. Her arrest and deportation were averted only because the Canadian authorities were in the process of releasing their last female internees at Kingston Penitentiary and declined to offer special accommodation for Redlich. The Canadian High Commissioner, furthermore, considered Redlich's internment to be undesirable. There was no provision in Canada for female refugee internees because none of this class of persons deported from the United Kingdom had been sent to Canada. Redlich's application to depart was refused until December 1943 when, due to the serious illness of her mother, a plea on compassionate grounds was granted.[56]

Austrian-born Eric G. Wermuth was the only refugee physician to serve as a "medical health officer." Awarded an M.D. by Vienna University in 1937, he had fled to London after his arrest by the Gestapo in 1938 at the age of 24. Recruited by the Department of Health in summer 1939, he arrived in St. John's on 21 February

1940. Like Redlich, he was received with the greatest suspicion at the various hospitals and public health stations to which he was assigned in Newfoundland. During his initial term as an intern in St. John's he was accused of the same transgressions as Redlich. After his transfers, first to St. Mary's Bay, and then to the Burin Peninsula, the people in these places viewed his mysterious trips into the country by day and night and the large pack of unknown contents he carried with him as suspicious. Among former patients in St. Joseph's, S.M.B., however, Wermuth is also remembered as an exceptionally dedicated doctor who would respond to calls from the remotest places in any weather. According to a memo by the Secretary for Public Health and Welfare, H.M. Mosdell, of June 1940, Wermuth was greatly concerned over the aspersions made against him, especially in the columns of the local press, but was advised by his superiors not to enter into a public controversy.

In February 1943 Wermuth asked for consideration of his 1941 application for a certificate of naturalization on the grounds that his case was an exceptional one since he had offered his services to the British Armed Forces and had a wife and a son, both native-born Newfoundlanders. By marrying him, his wife had lost her British nationality and had become a stateless person under British and Newfoundland law. "The moral and spiritual gain thus afforded me would . . . be invaluable and incalculable," he pleaded with Commissioner Harry A. Winter (who had been Rose Zuber's solicitor in 1939). Wermuth also reminded Winter that the Newfoundland government requested his services and took the initiative in arranging for his entry, and he felt therefore certain that his legal status would be well and favorably clarified.

Although Winter was aware that the Commission had decided against naturalization of aliens during the war, he counselled his colleagues not to "apply the rule inflexibly." However, the Commission ruled to defer Wermuth's application until the end of the war. Secretary Summers argued that action was undesirable for security reasons. "These arguments apply with particular strength in respect of Dr. Wermuth who is of enemy nationality." Lady Eileen Walwyn, the Governor's wife, whose good offices in support of his application Wermuth had requested, concurred instead with the rejection. "It always seemed to me a pity," she remarked to Winter, "that these Austrians were allowed to come out here in the first instance when war was so imminent."[57]

In the case of 31-year-old Austrian Jewish refugee physician Livia Rosenfeld, née Spiegler Halasz, the Commission did not hesitate to resort to expulsion. The pretext for expulsion was her

Dr. Livia Rosenfeld, née Spiegler Halasz. Credit: PANL.

Dr. Julius L. Rosenfeld. Credit: PANL.

marriage in March 1940 to American Jewish physician Julius L. Rosenfeld who had been stationed as a medical practitioner at Hare Bay, Newfoundland, since 1938. The marriage allegedly broke each of their contracts with the Department of Public Health. Seeking the advice of the Secretary for Justice on the options for restitution, Secretary for Public Health Mosdell reasoned:

> If we secured a court judgement against her for repayment of the expenses involved in bringing her to Newfoundland and in establishing her in our service, it is certain that we would not recover the amount involved as the doctor has no assets on which we could levy. Our only hope would be to collect from her husband. This you state we cannot do.[58]

The underlying reason for the expulsion, however, appears to have been the Commission's desire to accommodate "considerable adverse public comment on refugees being brought here to work . . . thinking that it is only a means of obtaining admission to the country, especially by foreigners of whom we know very little." Prior to her expulsion the Commission considered prosecuting Halasz for attempting to continue sending monthly remittances of $10 to her mother in Budapest. Although Hungary was not an enemy country in June 1940, the Chief Censor advised "that a prosecution in this instance, if the Justice Department considers it feasible, would act as a deterrent to others who might be tempted to try to evade the Defence, Exchange or Censorship Regulations."

The Rosenfelds were ordered to leave Newfoundland in September 1940. To the consternation of the Commission, Julius L. Rosenfeld returned legally to Newfoundland in May 1941. He was stationed at the U.S. Army Base in St. John's as a member of the U.S. Medical Corps and it was expected that his wife would follow him shortly. In a note to the Secretary for Justice, the Chief Commissioner of Immigration regretted that if the doctor was engaged by the Americans "we would not be able to interfere with his stay in this country; but if he was discharged . . . he would be returned to America."[59]

Even rabbis were not above the suspicion of collaborating with the country whose violent persecution had forced them to become refugees. In September 1941 a rabbi named Haler was refused permission to enter Newfoundland for the sole reason that he was of German origin.[60] St. John's police put Rabbi Max Katz under regular surveillance in August 1940 as an enemy alien. A weekly report of his activities went to the Department of Justice, although the police and the Secretary of Justice had a sworn statement from Katz that he and his family had to flee Germany because of their

Jewish descent and dedication to the Jewish cause (Katz had been a Jewish minister since 1919 and his father had been a rabbi). The Newfoundland authorities knew that Katz, as well as his family, had been stripped of their German nationality after their arrival in St. John's in 1938. The surveillance seems to have been triggered by a harmless personal letter—an acquaintance of Katz in the United States had written asking for a loan of $500 passage money to rescue a Jewish friend trapped in Holland. The letter was found by chance on a street in St. John's and turned over to the constabulary.[61]

Local residents associate Katz' difficulties in St. John's with other letters addressed to the editor of the *Evening Telegram* after the outbreak of the war. On 26 February 1940 the *Evening Telegram* published three anonymous letters criticizing the Newfoundland Jewish community. One wondered why, since this war started in Poland, "should Polish offsprings be the last to respond to British appeals for volunteers?" The other letter called the internment camp "the proper place" for the Austrian doctors and nurses imported in 1939, and a third one stated that "some" St. John's business firms were not doing their share to supplement the low military service pay of $1.10 (Canadian volunteers received $1.30) which their employees who had enlisted as volunteers were receiving. On 1 August 1940 another anonymous writer in the *Telegram* even demanded that all enemy aliens, "nurses or preachers" be "put under lock and key without further delay." This was an open call for the internment of Rabbi Katz.

An upset Katz reportedly visited the *Evening Telegram* editor to get to the bottom of the unwarranted attacks against Newfoundland's small and innocent Jewish community. Jeffery denied any anti-Semitic implications behind his questioning of the loyalty of Katz and other Jews. "I was as loyal a subject to the Kaiser as you are to George V, and as a conscript during 1915–18 I was decorated with the Iron Cross," Katz is remembered to have said in his defense. Jeffery allegedly retorted that "you can't put on patriotism like a cloak." After that incident the *Evening Telegram's* advertising business from local Jewish business firms declined and it took the *Telegram* years to regain their confidence.[62]

The World War I record of Katz is confirmed in his statement to the police. Not surprisingly, Rabbi Katz and his wife became the subjects of a special alien report by the Newfoundland Constabulary before they and their children were permitted to emigrate to the United States in December 1940. In the summer and fall of 1940 the Newfoundland Constabulary had observed Katz's every movement and had denied him contacts with members of his faith. One was the request of a 54-year old German Jewish refugee widow who claimed that she had been "treated very badly in Germany" and had been residing in St. Pierre since May 1939 with permission from the French Consul at Frankfurt am Main. In St. Pierre she was waiting to enter the United States.[63]

Typical for the ironic situation in which Newfoundland's few refugees from the Third Reich found themselves until the end of World War II was the experience of German Jewish refugee Franziska Mayer. In 1938 at age 23, she was invited on a three-year contract to work for the International Grenfell Association at isolated stations in Labrador in such different capacities as nurse, designer, weaver, and orphanage assistant. From 1940 on, the Secretary for Justice ordered Mayer as an "enemy alien" to remain in St. Anthony, where her movements could be watched by a member of the police or Ranger force. In Labrador, the Chief of Police contended, she would be able "to assist any German submarine that might try to establish a base or supply shelter." Mayer recognized the necessity for the orders given her and followed them conscientiously until seven weeks after the end of the war. On 26 June 1945 she wondered whether the Department of Justice would lift the restrictions on her movements to enable her to immigrate to the United States. She pleaded: "Please could the term 'enemy alien' be discontinued?" Seeing that I am stateless, I desire to be classified as a refugee." Mayer explained that

> in 1934 I left Germany because of Jewish persecution. Our people were opposed to Nazism from the beginning. In 1941 the Nazi Government separated all Jews from German citizenship . . . I would be truly grateful if Newfoundland would grant me full democratic equality and restore to me the right of unrestricted travel.

The Secretary for Justice signified his approval on 7 July 1945 with the words: "In this case, I am inclined to agree."[64]

In Newfoundland the mood was such that refugees, if they were not expelled, seized the first opportunity to leave the island. Although known to be fleeing victimization by the Third Reich, refugees encountered official mistrust and systematic petty harassment not only at the beginning of the war, as in Britain and Canada, but until 1945. Regardless of their loss of enemy nationality, they were placed under police surveillance, restricted in their movements, and subjected to possible internment and expulsion as if they were enemy agents. The censored personal correspondence of these suspects was circulated among and commented on by various government officials unsympathetic to the refugees' plight, and the suspects were judged, or rather misjudged, on the basis of harmless personal information intended for and fully understood only by the correspondents. The suspicious attitude of the public and the Commission of Government did not appear to have been ameliorated in the least by periodic reports in the Newfoundland press beginning in December 1942 that European Jews were being sent to gas chambers, that at least two million had perished, and that many more millions were being tortured in concentration camps and in danger of extermination.[65]

Public and official suspicions were never warranted by any concrete evidence of espionage or disloyalty. The government was fully aware of the identity of the refugees who landed, most of whom it had deliberately recruited. In November 1941 Commissioner Emerson stated at a security meeting that the small size of the Newfoundland community permitted an intimate check to be maintained upon people locally. "The number of aliens was limited and their movements and affairs known in considerable detail." By 1943 security arrangements with regard to all persons arriving in and leaving Newfoundland by sea or air were among the tightest in North America.[66] The punitive treatment of a handful of refugees, therefore, cannot be accounted for solely, or even primarily, in terms of security and defence requirements.

In reviewing the reaction of the government, the media, and the lobbies, it is impossible to ignore abundant evidence indicating that the perception of unfathomable danger to the island community from the mysterious fifth column in conjunction with the surreptitious submarine was enhanced by the equally irrational weapon of entrenched xenophobic prejudice. The media, especially the *Evening Telegram* as Newfoundland's opinion leader and opinion maker in times of crisis, did much to prepare a pointedly negative reception for the refugees by eagerly exploiting the fifth column panic and by insinuating that the refugees might be subversives. The appointed Commission of Government was not constitutionally accountable to the public and therefore would not have had to bow to public pressure. In trying to appease the local elite and media-inspired public opinion, the Commission consciously rejected the opportunities for turning the refugees' quests for sanctuary into a beneficial experience for both Newfoundland and the refugees.

Commission of Government of Newfoundland, December 1944. Left to Right: A.J. Walsh, Commissioner for Home Affairs and Education; P.D.H. Dunn, Commissioner for Natural Resources; J.C. Puddester, Commissioner for Public Health and Welfare; W.J. Carew, Secretary; Humphrey Thomas Walwyn, Governor; Ira Wild, Commissioner for Finance; H.A. Winter, Commissioner for Justice and Defence; George E. London, Commissioner for Public Utilities and Supply. Credit: PANL.

"What Price Immigration?" **10**

Epilogue 1945–1949, Synopsis, and Conclusions

POST-WORLD WAR II IMMIGRATION AND REFUGEE POLICY

Despite changing public attitudes towards immigration and despite the continuation of wartime prosperity, the period from the end of the war until Confederation with Canada in 1949 witnessed the resumption, with no significant alterations, of the restrictive immigration policy charted prior to 1940.

In August 1945 the Commission agreed that the chief immigration officer should continue to enforce the rules approved in August 1940. As described in chapter 9, these restricted eligibility to (a) specialists intending to engage in an occupation for which a qualified Newfoundlander was not available, (b) persons intending to set up a new industry, (c) the spouse or child of (a) or (b), and (d) "a person who has adequate means and does not intend to engage in any gainful occupation." The restrictions were explicitly extended to Canadian and American citizens intending to take up employment with branches of Canadian and American businesses in Newfoundland or who as ex-servicemen had married Newfoundlanders. "The fact that an ex-serviceman had married a Newfoundland girl would not in itself be sufficient justification for the grant of permission to him to settle in this country," Commissioner for Finance Ira Wild emphasized in November 1945. Thus, when a Newfoundland girl married a serviceman, she in effect relinquished her right to live in Newfoundland. Wild referred to difficulties immigration officials had with a number of "Newfoundland girls married to Canadians, etc. who have become homesick and desire to return with their husbands to this country," an immigration problem eliminated four years later by Confederation.[1]

A memorandum of January 1947 reveals that to the above-mentioned conditions for entry, the Customs Department added the requirement for immigrants to produce proof that they could be returned to their country of origin or some other country and that their maintenance and that of their dependents would be assured. In 1942 the Justice Department had been concerned that persons could not be "deported with despatch if need be if proved undesirable" and that "even upon return to peace it will undoubtedly be necessary to have some law whereby deportation can easily be effected." By the summer of 1945 the Commission had found ways to apply further powers taken under the old legislation "to deport persons who have been allowed to enter the country for a limited period and have failed to leave when such period expired." Wild stressed that "much more is required than this." The regulations for permanent residence in force until 1949 required application to the Chief Commissioner of Immigration in St. John's and receipt of an advance permit from him, as well as a visa from a British consular officer. Only Canadians were exempted from the visa but not from the permit requirement. Neither the exclusion of enemy aliens, nor the discriminatory distinction insisted on by Emerson in August 1940 between British subjects by birth and by naturalization were officially repealed.[2]

Far from loosening any of the existing restrictions, the Commission thus shut Newfoundland's gates even more tightly after 1945. Commissioner Wild justified this policy with the argument that "prospects of peace-time employment in Newfoundland are not so bright that we can allow with equanimity the immigration of persons of the labouring and unskilled classes." Having "regard to our normal surplus of labour we should in practice only allow the immigration of Specialists," he reaffirmed in November 1945. For the politicians and bureaucrats concerned with defining and enforcing immigration controls, very little seems to have changed since the 1920s. While not denying that "it would be a pity if no new blood were allowed to come into the island," Wild could only imagine "a number of energetic and thrifty Scottish farmers" to be advantageous and desirable as settlers.[3] The explicit reference to Scottish farmers harks back to the double standard of Newfoundland's pre-Depression policy of inviting British while excluding foreign settlers. The traditional assumptions governing entry to the country seemed to have become inviolable, self-evident truths, immune to revision, regardless of social and economic changes, and defying new visions of the future.

Indicative of the Commission's postwar frame of mind was its concern with improving deportation procedures at a time of prosperity. In May 1945 Wild submitted to his colleagues a memorandum on "Immigration Policy" which attempted to breathe new life into the highly discriminatory and exclusionist draft immigration act "on Dominion lines" proposed by L.E. Emerson and aborted by the Dominions office in 1938. Wild's memorandum concluded with the proposal "to remind the Dominions Office that we still await their further advice as we should like to proceed with the drafting of the legislation [agreed upon in 1938] as soon as an opportunity occurs."[4]

Nothing epitomizes the perpetuation of anachronistic discriminatory entry controls better than the continued exclusion of Chinese. In October 1945 Wild and Chief Commissioner of Immigration J.G. Howell decided to permit 11 Chinese to immigrate, thereby bringing the size of the local Chinese community back up to a total of 181. The eleven had to pay the head tax of $300 each and were admitted on the grounds that they were replacing those who had died since the official termination of immigration in 1940. By August 1946 another 21 applications from relatives of local Chinese had accumulated. Although conceding that "the Chinese nationals living in Newfoundland have, as a rule, been law-abiding citizens and have not caused very much trouble, neither have they been a charge to the community or the Government," Howell now urged that the Chinese Immigration Act be amended to provide for a legal quota of Chinese living in Newfoundland. For the time being, the existing limit for the size of the local Chinese community might be raised. He proposed that "an arbitrary figure of 250 be made and if this amount is likely to be exceeded that we amend the Act." The Commission dealt with the problem by deciding to apply existing policy regarding immigration of aliens. This meant, according to Wild, "strictly" limiting "the entry for permanent residence of persons of any nationality." For the instruction of Howell, Albert J. Walsh (Emerson's successor as Commissioner for Justice) noted on the margin of the Commission's minuted decision of 13 September 1946: "apply normal rules as strictly as may be desired."[5]

In the period from February 1947 to May 1948 the Chinese question was brought to a head when the Commission was first faced with the unique challenge of an application for entry from a Chinese female whose husband was both a local resident and a British subject, and then in July 1947 with several applications from local Chinese for naturalization as British subjects. In February 1947 the Commissioner for Home Affairs J.C. Puddester submitted that "Chinese women were not admittable" and the only exception ever made was the wife of the Chinese Consul.

> If Mr. Fong can obtain admission for his wife through the expedient of naturalization, other Chinese could, and probably would, claim the same right by becoming naturalized, and a substantial increase in the Chinese Colony would take place. This, in my opinion, would be most undesirable.

If Mrs. Davey Fong as the wife of a British subject could not be legally refused admission, Puddester proposed that "disabilities in the law should be corrected for 'necessary protection' when similar circumstances are presented in the future."

In order to clinch his argument, Puddester introduced another reason why a review of existing legislation to further restrict Chinese immigration would be justified. He contended that the original purpose of the 1906 legislation highlighted "the need to prevent immigration from a country reputedly full of loathsome diseases as was China." This objective, he believed, was more valid "at this time" than ever:

> I have looked at Hand Book (China Proper), No. 1 of the Naval Intelligence Division, published in 1944, which refers to China as being *rampant* with such diseases as Leprosy, Plague, Tuberculosis, Syphilis and other loathsome diseases. It is stated that probably every inhabitant of an endemic area harbours leprosy bacilli and the heaviest rate is in young children.[6]

Commissioner of Finance R.L.M. James concurred and noted that the immigration authorities "have been satisfied for some time that there are already sufficient Chinese here to take care of the Chinese laundries and restaurants in the country and they have therefore refused to allow additions to the numbers." For this reason, 116 applications on hand from Chinese seeking entry had been turned down. If naturalization applications were allowed on any scale, James contended in March 1948, they would conflict with the policy of stabilizing the local Chinese population. Commissioner H.L. Pottle added that it was "quite possible that if these applications are granted a number of others will follow from Chinese who are watching the outcome."[7]

The matter was further complicated by advice received from the Justice Department "that when a British subject naturalized in Newfoundland marries, his wife automatically acquires the status of a British subject and has the same right as her husband to enter Newfoundland and reside here." Although immigration policy was on the agenda, the more alarming issue to be resolved was now naturalization. The Commission's decision was a foregone conclusion. According to the minutes of the 2 April 1948 meeting "it was felt that, owing to possible repercussions on immigration, it would not be desirable to accede to any applications from Chinese nationals for naturalization as British subjects."[8]

The unequivocal tone of messages from Government House in St. John's to Whitehall left little doubt about Newfoundland's position with regard to Chinese immigration. "There are in Newfoundland some 150 resident male Chinese and it is not desired, at present, that any facilities should be granted which might result in their number being augmented," read a despatch to the Secretary of State for Dominion Affairs of 2 March 1938. And a communication to the Secretary of State for Dominion Relations of 6 May 1948 elaborated that only

> replacements are permitted, i.e., when a Chinese returns to his native land permanently a permit is issued for another Chinese to enter in his place. Applications to the number of 116 are on hand from Chinese anxious to enter but under the policy stated they have been refused.[9]

The documented cases of Olan Lee and Tom Yet Kun are typical of the determination with which the Commission to its very last day in office enforced the exclusionist provisions of the 1906 Act. Olan Lee was the son of Kim Lee who in 1904 acquired British citizenship as Newfoundland's first naturalized Chinese immigrant. Born in Honolulu en route to China in 1932 (Mrs. Lee was believed to have visited Newfoundland for a brief period some time during 1931), Olan arrived in Newfoundland in mid-March and erroneously assumed he would be exempted from the $300 head tax. In a memorandum dated 12 May 1949 the Deputy Secretary for Justice informed the Chief Commissioner of Immigration that, according to the Chinese Immigration Act of 1906 and its amendments, "every person of Chinese origin, irrespective of allegiance, shall pay the head tax" and, unless "this young man can be brought into any of the exemptions set out in Section 1, the head tax should be paid in respect of his entry into Newfoundland."[10] Tom Yet Kun, aged 15, who also had to pay the head tax when he arrived by air on 18 March 1949 to attend St. Bonaventure's College, applied for a refund in May 1951.[11] When Newfoundland entered Confederation on 31 March 1949, Lee and Kun became residents of Canada where the head tax had been abolished in 1923 and exclusionist legislation been repealed in May 1947.

The arguments on which Newfoundland's postwar immigration controls were based flew in the face of postwar economic reality. In addition to the handsome benefits accruing from the American bases, industrial production and employment remained high. In 1948 a Canadian observer rated the levels of Newfoundland's export and import trade to be the highest in the country's history.[12] These were good times in comparison with the 1930s, and prospective iron ore developments in Labrador made them appear even better. Looming ahead, rather than unemployment, seemed a labor shortage and the need to recruit Europeans anxious to leave their countries. Press comments raised the specter of legislation that would prevent Newfoundlanders from continuing the tradition of quitting their local employment in any given industry for "greener pastures." It would indeed be a "tragedy if we had too much work for the available labor and then had to import miners, foresters and others to fill the jobs," concluded the *Evening Telegram* (16 January 1948).

THE IMPACT OF THE "FRIENDLY INVASION"

Despite the continued exclusion of Chinese and other foreign immigrants, immigration on a scale never imagined had already become a fact by 1945 as a result of the friendly wartime invasion of some 16,000 Canadians and 11,000 Americans stationed on or near the island. Newfoundlanders were not given any choice in the matter: they had to live with them, acquaint themselves with their ways, and mix socially with them. Outside the military, "several thousand" Canadians were reported to have worked in paper mills, construction projects, banks, insurance companies, industrial firms, and professions ranging from physician to clergyman. Among the Allied servicemen, their dependents and civilian personnel, there were many of non-Anglo-Saxon background. As might be expected, during the war Newfoundland government officials were so paranoid about the threat of fifth columnism that they even suspected Allied personnel of Central European ancestry of being potential spies and demanded the right to investigate them.[13] But Allied servicemen were "not here as spies or fifth column," an editorial columnist in the *Evening Telegram* (28 January 1948) remarked pointedly. Their presence "forged many friendships with ever-growing respect for each other's cause and outlook on life."[14]

The large number of Allied forces gave Newfoundlanders a practical demonstration of the effect a large immigration would have on the isolated homogeneous island community. The profound extent to which Newfoundland was "stirred up" as an isolated community by this "invasion of outsiders,"[15] has become a well-established fact. One source claims that on the island and in Labrador 25,000 Newfoundland women have married U.S. servicemen since 1940.[16] Many Newfoundlanders were reported first learning about racism and about racial tolerance from the American visitors.[17] "Accepted values and modes of behavior were profoundly challenged"[18] and social, cultural, and economic alternatives became visible and accessible "which before had only been imagined . . . The people of Newfoundland and Labrador could never go back to what they had been."[19]

The wartime invasion of friendly outsiders opened up entirely new perspectives on immigration. On the occasion of the tenth anniversary of Commission of Government, journalist and editor Michael Harrington articulated under the title "What Price Immigration?" in the *Daily News* (16 February 1944) provocative new ideas that would have been unthinkable on this topic earlier. Not afraid of being the devil's advocate, Harrington expounded the startling thesis that the chief hindrance to Newfoundland's growth and progress was its small population and its closed society that disapproved of any mingling with "foreign" blood. He presented the following contradiction: if it were true, as some maintained, that there were not enough people in the country "to ever make a 'go' of anything," how come so few dared to advocate immigration to stimulate economic development? It was because of the wiseacre's objection that there wasn't even enough work for those who were here already. Harrington set out to refute this stance, in his opinion illogical and defeatist, on several grounds. First, there were enormous unutilized opportunities and potential avenues of employment for all of Newfoundland's people to live in comfort and happiness, if they had wise direction and encouragement. He implied that this could come from the government as well as from immigrants. Second, there was room for more people. Harrington never heard it said that there were too many people in Newfoundland, despite the unemployment of the prewar years, since this was "a practically undeveloped country of 42,000 square miles and her huge dependency of Labrador virgin country, begging for people to help open it, and develop these uninhabited areas." Third, from war-torn Europe hundreds of thousands of uprooted people with all their possessions destroyed would again be looking to North America. Canadian officials had already stressed the necessity of immigration and declared that Canada would lift its present restrictions. Harrington challenged, "what about Newfoundland?"

Would the impending mass exodus from a Europe in the throes of rehabilitation not "be the kind of shot in the arm that this country needs," Harrington wondered?

> What an opportunity for Newfoundland! New blood, new ideas, new enterprise, new visions, new faith. It was immigration that made

the United States one of the greatest nations in the modern world.
The immigrants from the old world flocked to her shores, coming
most of them with nothing but hope.

This was a challenge Harrington thought well worth considering,
regardless of opposition from the reactionaries who believed in the
"fetish" of "race" and "stock" and disapproved of any intermingling
with foreign blood. These "diehards" had already been overtaken by
history, for the coming of the Allied forces marked in effect the
beginning of a new era of immigration, albeit in a slightly different
way.

Harrington, claiming to know "many people" who supported this
idea, sketched his captivating vision of the promises which a selective and prudent immigration might hold for Newfoundland:

> Dutch and Polish farmers, French and Belgian textile workers,
> Italian and Czech machinists would all fit into the great pattern of
> a revitalized, expressive, energetic, growing, thriving, educated,
> self-governing Newfoundland. Becoming Newfoundlanders them-
> selves and their children in a generation or two, they and we would
> work together in the grand common cause of making Newfound-
> land for the first time in its history, begin to find her way towards
> that inevitable destiny, which God and nature from the very begin-
> ning of our discovered history intended her to attain.

THE RECORD OF REFUGEE SETTLEMENT 1945 TO 1949

Harrington's vision, like plans and aspirations associated with the
prewar settlement of refugees from Nazi persecution, remained a
pipedream. The option was never seriously entertained by the
government and the elite of Newfoundland. The post-World War II
European exodus of hundreds of thousands of displaced persons
included a very high percentage of skilled professionals, tradesmen,
and farmers. Desperate for sanctuary anywhere immediately after
the war, they had to bypass Newfoundland. Newfoundland could
have recruited a selected number to great advantage. After Canada
opened its doors in mid-1947, its postwar development benefited
greatly from the displaced Europeans who arrived.[20]

In the period from May 1945 to April 1949 only three refugee
families are known to have been admitted to Newfoundland. One of
them consisted of Betty and Andreas Barban with their nine-month-
old son Gregory. They were sponsored by Esther Wilansky and her
son Maurice, prominent members of the local Jewish community
who had been in contact with Betty's brother in Montreal. The
Barbans arrived in St. John's in 1947 from their enforced wartime
exile in Shanghai. On 26 August Andreas arrived, followed by Betty

and Gregory on 18 September, and Andreas's parents in 1950. A professional musician who had studied piano and conducting in Germany, Andreas had supported his family in Shanghai by giving both private piano lessons and recitals on the French radio network. He came to Newfoundland as a needed specialist in music. At the time of his arrival there were no private piano studios—the few trained music teachers were connected with schools—and, apart from the performances of school orchestras and Salvation Army bands, no professional orchestral concerts in St. John's. Welcomed by one of their sponsors with the remark: "you will be an asset to Newfoundland" the Barbans were overwhelmed by the hospitality, security, and opportunities that Newfoundland was able to offer to refugees with their type of background.

Qualities like dedication, experience, talent, scholarly expertise, fluency in four languages (English, German, Russian, and Latin), and social graces put Andreas Barban at the forefront of musical life in Newfoundland and made him an invaluable asset to the country of his resettlement. Besides opening the first private piano studio in St. John's, he initiated weekly music appreciation classes in his home, in the homes of many Newfoundlanders, and through the Memorial University Extension Department. His lecture recitals every Sunday on the local radio station VONF (precursor of CBC) from 1948 to 1951 under the title "Mastering the Classics with Andreas Barban" spread his reputation as the leading—and, for some time, the only—local promoter of classical music. Shortly after his arrival he was asked to be organist at Gower Street Church for one year. In addition to giving many solo piano performances he accompanied hundreds of singers and instrumentalists on radio and TV programs and published numerous music reviews in the local press. From the beginning of the Kiwanis Music Festival in 1951 he was involved in developing the piano section of the syllabus and adjudicating piano performances in St. John's and other places. He was one of the first conductors (1963–66) of the St. John's Symphony Orchestra (now the Newfoundland Symphony Orchestra) and, when Memorial University's School of Music opened, a part-time instructor there. After his arrival in St. John's, he continued his professional training at the Toronto Conservatory of Music and in 1958 was awarded the Associate Diploma in Piano Performance.[21]

As a teacher, performer, conductor, adjudicator, organizer, and commentator, Andreas Barban has made a major and consistent contribution to the cultural life of St. John's and Newfoundland for almost half a century. Most importantly, he has helped to develop the pianistic talent of thousands of Newfoundlanders, many of

Dr. Andreas Barban, awarded the Degree of Doctor of Law (*honoris causa*) in 1985. Left to Right: Mrs. Paula Berliavsky (sister-in-law of Betty Barban), Dr. Andreas Barban, Mrs. Betty Barban, and their son Dr. Gregory M. Barban, ophthalmic surgeon. Credit: Andreas Barban.

whom have distinguished themselves in the music profession. His eminent contribution was publicly recognized in 1985 when Memorial University of Newfoundland awarded him the Degree of Doctor of Law (*honoris causa*), and in 1988 when the Private Music Teachers' Association of Newfoundland bestowed honorary membership upon him and invited friends, colleagues, students, and teachers to a large dinner party in his honor. For the contribution he was able to make in Newfoundland, Andreas Barban credits in large part his wife Betty. Throughout their odyssey she brought the warmth of a family, and was a supportive companion and sounding board in all of his musical endeavors.

Considering this outstanding record of one of the few refugees from the Third Reich who are known to have received permission to settle in Newfoundland in the two years prior to Confederation with Canada, can one imagine what positive contributions more such refugees would have made to the economic, social, cultural, and intellectual life of Newfoundland? This is suggested by the meritorious record of refugees from the Third Reich who settled in the Province of Newfoundland after Confederation. A case for the benefits of refugee settlement might also be made with regard to Newfoundland's pre-World War I Jewish and Maronite refugee immigrants. Their socio-economic role and historical contributions still await detailed examination.

The impact of the refugees of the 1930s on the countries that offered them sanctuary was immediate. That was demonstrated to Newfoundlanders most clearly in the case of Andreas Barban. But the *Evening Telegram* disclosed to its readers as early as 22 April 1940 that in the Montreal region alone a record number of industries had been brought by refugees in 1939 — five originated in Czechoslovakia, eleven in Germany, one in Holland, three in Hungary, two in Poland, one in Romania, as well as others. Barely one year later these industries were found to "constitute an unusually important and significant asset to the business and economic life of the Dominion," the *Telegram* quoted the annual report of the Montreal Industrial and Economic Bureau, and went on to declare that "this is particularly true of the so-called industrial emigres from Europe. Among this group are merchants and industrialists with a long and successful record of continental business experience."

It is not an idle exercise to speculate on what influence refugees would have had on the fortunes and prospects of this island-country because available choices for growth and development were consciously rejected by those placed in positions of power and influence. Newfoundland's nearly successful quest for the restoration of political sovereignty in 1948 would have been sustainable, as the proponents of Responsible Government realized, only in conjunction with economic self-reliance. Their problem was, as perceived by Albert Perlin, that "we shall have to be an importing country, for a long time, because we have not enough population to be able to produce at home most of the things we need, at prices below the cost of imported articles."[22] According to Michael Harrington the solution to controlled resource development and the "consumer-at-home problem" was a larger population and a more dynamic society, both of which could be obtained only at the "price" of immigration. Had the Commission accepted the challenge of refugee settlement, perhaps the cause of a sovereign Newfoundland as Michael Harrington sketched it in 1944 would have been strengthened.

On the other hand, it is unlikely that Responsible Government, and the vested interests advocating its restoration, would have pursued a more enlightened immigration policy than the Commission. The available evidence leaves little doubt that the approach to immigration controls throughout the Commission's fifteen-year history precluded any serious possibility of large-scale refugee settlement.

Cut off from new blood—and the new ideas, initiatives, and connections it would have brought—what did the future hold for an independent, self-governing Newfoundland? Few, if any, of those who regretted Newfoundland's entry into Canada have asked themselves this question. The preoccupation with Newfoundland as a country of emigration was so pervasive that even for those despairing of economic, social, and cultural stagnation, the need to regenerate society along the lines suggested by Harrington never became a public issue. Not even caring any more to question the premises of entry controls that perpetuated the island's backwardness in an era of global revolutionary change, the Commission and the local power elite had become too fossilized to be capable of laying the social and demographic foundations for an economically more viable Newfoundland. From this perspective, Confederation may, indeed, have come as a blessing.

SYNOPSIS AND CONCLUSION

The story of Newfoundland's responses to the European refugee crisis draws attention to hitherto little known aspects of Newfoundland's economic, social, and cultural history. It encourages inquiry into the extent and kind of opportunities for economic development, social change, and cultural diversification that might have occurred and to whose absence some of Newfoundland's subsequent problems may be attributable.

Since the refugee crisis overlaps chronologically with the Depression and the beginnings of Commission of Government, it is tempting to explain Newfoundland's responses as unique and conditioned solely by the severe economic problems at the time and the Commission's efforts to cope with them. However, a glance at the history of Newfoundland's immigration policy reveals the inadequacies of that approach. Newfoundland's denial of sanctuary to refugees from the Third Reich was entirely in line with the direction in which immigration policy had been moving since 1906 and signified the victory of continuity over the possibility of change. A comparison, furthermore, of official attitudes towards the refugees of the 1930s with attitudes discernible towards the pre-World War I Syrian, Jewish, and Chinese newcomers reveals significant parallels and affords additional useful insights.

What made so many central Europeans look to Newfoundland had little to do with specific attractions the economically depressed and relatively backward island might have had to offer—its living conditions were unknown, there were virtually no settlers of central European origin to provide a support system, and few middle class European amenities were available. Newfoundland's appeal to German Jews, Catholics, Hutterites, Czechs, Hungarians, etc., was almost entirely the result of the push factors that created the refugees. Most subjects of the Third Reich who became targets of political, racial, or religious persecution were reluctant to emigrate and delayed their flight until after the violent repercussions of *Anschluss* and *Kristallnacht* in 1938. By 1939 the gates of the traditional refugee- and immigrant-receiving countries were closed and among the few havens left were Shanghai and the Dominican Republic. Newfoundland's appeal resulted from its potential function as an escape route for survival, a destination for permanent settlement, or transit station for further migration to the United States and Canada. As noted earlier, some international refugee relief organizations, like the ICA, were aware of Newfoundland's liberal refugee law of 1906 which, if enforced, would have permitted entry to the clamoring refugees.

Analysis of the circumstances under which Newfoundland introduced its refugee law of 1906 has revealed that the enactment of this law was not prompted by the simultaneous arrival on the island of refugees from Tsarist Russia and the Middle East. On the contrary, the 1906 Aliens Act with its refugee clause was adopted in almost identical form from a British Act intended to establish immigration controls and restrict the influx of undesirable aliens. The Aliens Act was a companion and supplement to the Chinese Immigration Act of 1906; the latter—modelled after Canada's Chinese Immigration Act of 1903—imposed a head tax of $300, introduced the practice of excluding Chinese females, and provided a way to freeze the local Chinese community at below 200 members until 1949. Newfoundland's 1906 immigration legislation was introduced against a background of relative prosperity and an explicit desire to recruit British immigrants. It legalized the elite's intention to entrench its traditional manipulative privileges with regard to the country's economic and political destiny by preserving the ethnic homogeneity and social stratification of the island's population.

The 1906 legislation raising barriers against undesirable aliens marked the beginning of Newfoundland's immigration policy. Though based on the contention that a substantial influx of settlers was needed, this policy was not characterized by any concrete initiatives to recruit desirable settlers. Instead, it brought to light a significant amount of anti-foreign sentiment among Newfoundland's small, urban, upper class of merchants, manufacturers, professional groups, newspaper editors, officials, etc. The elite's exploitation of the common man's natural suspicion of strangers appears to have had some impact only on St. John's dockworkers who feared for the security of their jobs. The available evidence does not support the official rhetoric that foreign immigrants constituted any concrete threats to local jobs. Far from competing with local labor, the few foreign newcomers actually created job opportunities and produced revenue. The rural population, because of its total economic dependence and despite its extreme geographical and cultural isolation, was no more suspicious of outsiders than it was of the motives of the St. John's elite. In fact, in view of the manifold deprivations of outport life, many outports welcomed foreigners who had anything to offer.

The period 1919–1933 witnessed the unfolding of a pattern whose seeds were sown in 1906. On the one hand, there was evidence of a demand for more skilled labor in the burgeoning newsprint industry as late as 1926 and settlers of Anglo-Saxon background continued to be solicited. On the other hand, unemployment created by the crisis in the fishery was one of the triggers for the 1924 and 1926 legislation, which legalized the deportation and exclusion of foreign immigrants. The control of foreign immigration served the elite, in the absence of any serious attempt at economic reform, as an instrument for perpetuating its hold over the island's restive population. While the driving force behind the country's anti-foreign immigration policy was the elite's economic self-interest, its practice of exclusion and deportation was triggered by and modeled on postwar Canadian and American immigration restrictions. Stung by the barring and expulsion of Newfoundlanders from their traditional North American employment opportunities, but unable to retaliate in kind, Newfoundland's response was the virtual exclusion of all foreign immigrants. Its upshot was the proclamation of 1932 that excluded all Asians, Africans, Latin Americans, and most Europeans. The refugee-welcoming provision of 1906, though still on the statute books, was simply ignored. During the period 1919–1933 no foreign immigrants were admitted under it, although some appear to have been eligible for refugee status.

During its first month in office the Commission of Government was confronted with a choice when it received Belkin's viable proposal for refugee settlement. It could either conform to Newfoundland's 26-year-old immigration policy tradition or break with it. Funded entirely with international Jewish funds, the proposal was specifically designed to improve the country's economic situation. Furthermore, it was endorsed by the strongest and most senior of the six Commissioners who, coincidentally, happened to be an international authority on the world refugee question. The 1934 ICA proposal was the test case and set the precedent for subsequent Newfoundland refugee policy. Although the Commission had a mandate to bring in drastic reforms and was widely expected to do so, it succumbed to the opposition of determined vested interests. The opposition was spearheaded in this instance by the Newfoundland Medical Board, and supported by the bureaucracy and merchant elite. In the cases of the 1934 and 1936 refugee settlement proposals John Hope Simpson appears to have been ready to fight local vested interests, but his colleagues "did not have the stomach," as Peter Neary put it succinctly, to "promote and pay for a social revolution. Their overall approach to governing Newfoundland was ameliorative."[23]

It has been maintained that with regard to a wide range of issues the Commission did, in practice, not divide along United Kingdom-Newfoundland lines.[24] But the tug-of-war over the course to adopt with regard to refugees frequently divided and paralyzed the Commission. The Newfoundland Commissioners led by Emerson foiled repeated endeavors by their British colleagues Penson, Gorvin, Ewbank, and Woods to reach agreement on schemes for economically productive refugee group settlement, preferably in a remote area and without any financial obligation to the Commission. Having pledged at the 1938 Evian Conference to find room for refugees in

the Colonial Empire, Whitehall cautiously encouraged Penson and
Gorvin, but not at the price of costly confrontations with Emerson
who was known to act on behalf of the traditional interests of the
local commercial and professional elite. The publicity given to the
benefits Canada derived from employment-generating and foreign-
funded refugee industries gained this idea increasing numbers of
adherents in St. John's by 1939, thereby enabling Penson to per-
suade the Commission to agree to a narrowly circumscribed strategy
for recruiting such industries. The strategy failed, seemingly because of the pettiness of the agreed-upon terms, the refugees' lack
of funds, and the outbreak of the war. But Penson's failure can
actually be traced to the local elite's uncompromising hostility to any
refugee immigration, as evidenced in L.E. Emerson's relentless
quest for "watertight" entry controls.

This became abundantly clear in the treatment accorded to
individual requests for sanctuary. Of the estimated 4,000–5,000
applications for sanctuary, the Commission accepted none. It did
not matter whether the applicant was a needed professional, a highly
qualified specialist, an experienced farmer, a person financially
sponsored by a local resident, or even the parent or brother of a
naturalized Newfoundland citizen. The inability of a prosperous
local businesswoman and naturalized resident, despite the efforts
of the foremost St. John's law firm on her behalf, to rescue her
parents or brother from Poland on the eve of World War II, epitomizes
the relentlessly inflexible attitude of the ruling elite towards the
refugees, as well as the precarious position of Newfoundland's small
community of Polish Jews. Cases were not judged on the basis of
law, reason, usefulness, or compassion. Each applicant was rejected
on different grounds at the arbitrary discretion of the Chief Commissioner of Immigration or the Commissioner for Justice.

To keep refugees out, the Commission successfully devised a
"watertight" procedure of requiring permits in conjunction with a
visaed passport. This effectively perpetuated the rigorously exclusionist 1932 Proclamation past its expiration in 1934. It was the
compromise price the Dominions Office was prepared to pay for
refusing to ratify Emerson's highly discriminatory blueprint of a new
Immigration Act. The permit system effectively shut out all refugees
in complete defiance of the spirit of the 1906 refugee-welcoming law.
This law, ironically, retained its *de jure* validity until Confederation
with Canada in 1949. Canada, to be sure, also virtually closed its
gates to Jewish refugees in the 1930s. But in doing so, Canada did
not defy the letter or spirit of any statutory commitments to welcome
refugees.[25] The United Kingdom, on the other hand, in 1905 had

legislated a refugee clause identical to Newfoundland's and did not disavow it when the need to honor it was greatest, especially in 1938–39.[26]

In the public debate over the admission of central European refugees, the overwhelming majority of the documented comments were opposed. Their authors were predominantly representatives of business and professional groups who feared the refugees as competitors. Yet not all anti-refugee sentiment was economically motivated. Some of the manifestations of hostility were clearly inspired by anti-Semitism. Interestingly, government records and the daily press do not feature any conspicuously hostile reaction from labor. Also, the outports did not seem to share the urban prejudices against refugees, but rather, in some instances, even welcomed the services and employment opportunities refugees could have provided. Opposition to refugees appeared largely confined to the capital city's educated, professional, and commercial elite who formed the enduring driving force for Newfoundland's immigration and refugee policy.

In St. John's, a vociferous segment of the public expressed fears that immigration laws and officials imposed insufficient restrictions on the entry of foreigners. This outspoken segment pressured the Commission to maintain a policy of unqualified exclusion. Their mouthpiece and frequent opinion maker was the *Evening Telegram*, Newfoundland's oldest and most widely read daily newspaper. In spite of massive unemployment and a severe shortage of medical and social services, it reinforced existing prejudices and played on uninformed readers' suspicions of foreigners. Its editorial policy seemed aimed at deflecting public frustration over the protection of privileged commercial and professional interests. Only productive refugees not interfering with any sacred vested interest would be acceptable for admission. This, in reality, meant no refugees would be acceptable in view of the control vested interests exerted over virtually every aspect of organized life.

The wartime experience of the dozen refugees temporarily admitted to Newfoundland—despite, not because of, their refugee status—underscores the impact of anti-alienism fostered and articulated by the press. Their experiences were characterized by the basic pattern of media denunciations fanning public rumors and culminating in punitive government action. The surge of xenophobic sentiment after the outbreak of the war was fuelled by a number of factors, such as the islanders' traditionally intense loyalty to Britain and public alarm over the strategically located island's seemingly vulnerable condition. But these factors have tended to obscure the equally eminent fact that existing anti-foreign prejudices were encouraged as a legitimate behavior against a deliberately broad and ill-defined category of residents of non-British background who were labelled "enemy aliens" and treated officially as suspect. For innocent suspects such as the anti-Nazi refugees, the demoralizing experience of being constantly suspected of collaboration with the very regime whose persecution they had fled rendered adjustment to the unanticipated social environment and living conditions impossible. Each of them, if not actually expelled, seized the first opportunity to leave Newfoundland.

In a comparison of wartime refugee experiences with Britain and Canada, Newfoundland stands out not only for the minute number of fugitives from Nazi persecution who gained entry, but also for their harassment as suspects until well after the end of the war. Subjected to the pattern of stigmatization and treatment endured by a broad spectrum of innocent aliens, the refugees' wartime experience makes for interesting contrast with the much celebrated cordiality with which the American "friendly invaders" were allegedly welcomed. Paradoxically, the appearance of thousands of uniformed American and Canadian troops on the island, although they provided increasing protection and reduced the likelihood of enemy attacks, may have actually intensified the stigmatization of local aliens as suspects until 1945 by contributing to rising awareness of the imminent dangers of war. It is arguable, at any rate, whether in view of this negative wartime experience any attempt to settle and integrate refugees would have succeeded or whether they would not all have been interned and expelled. Refugees like Metal, who had the means and ability to make economic contributions, were not given the opportunity to do so. The only kind of refugees acceptable to Newfoundland during the war years seems to have been those confined to a guarded internment camp and those guaranteed to depart for the United States.

The Canadian precedent, on the other hand, demonstrates that refugees were able to adjust to their country of ultimate resettlement, despite negative wartime experiences. It is ironic that although refugee settlement was available as a unique option throughout the entire history of Commission of Government, the erection of insurmountable barriers to immigration precluded this option. The accommodation of 12,000 refugees would undoubtedly have been a herculean task and responsibility that the Commission might have been unable to undertake, but a smaller number—Penson suggested 1,000 families—would have been manageable. Having come close to bankruptcy in 1933, furthermore, Newfoundland was understandably preoccupied with its own survival during this critical period. Yet the evidence is clear—and was so to leading government officials at the time—that the European refugee crisis of the 1930s was rife with significant opportunities for Newfoundland's recovery and development. These officials rejected every opportunity—and their decisions were based on no compelling reasons.

When everything is said and done, the perception of the "foreign" immigrant as an undesirable, unwanted intruder in a closed, ethnically homogeneous society, emerges as *the* leitmotif of Newfoundland's pre-Confederation immigration and refugee policy. Cultivated and propagated since 1906 by the educated, professional, and commercial elite in St. John's for the protection of their privileged position in society and the economy, this perception projected a decidedly negative image of the refugees in the 1930s. Despite the widely publicized contemporary evidence of the refugees' ability to make economic contributions, Newfoundland continued to perceive refugees as taking rather than creating jobs. Once the negative image had been reinforced sufficiently so as to no longer be questioned, it was easy to justify the denial of sanctuary on the grounds of high local unemployment.

To be sure, the pervasiveness of anti-alien sentiment between the world wars was not unique to Newfoundland. It was equally prevalent in other dominions, such as Canada and Australia, as well as in most western countries. But while Canada and Australia continued to admit at least a token number of refugees between the wars, Newfoundland practiced what Canadian Immigration Director F.C. Blair preached: "None is too many." It was not afraid to renege on its legal commitments to provide sanctuary to refugees from religious and political persecution. Adoption of the British definition of asylum in its Aliens Act of 1906 would have obligated Newfoundland to adjudicate requests for protection on the grounds specified by law.

The legal default had equally serious humanitarian, demographic, sociological, ethnocultural, and economic ramifications. From a humanitarian standpoint, the relentless denial of sanctuary put Newfoundland in the same category as Canada—a country that cared little and did less. Not a single one of thousands appealing for rescue from persecution and destruction, including sponsored parents and brothers of naturalized Newfoundlanders, was saved. Demographically speaking, Newfoundland rejected an unprecedented windfall of human capital. The tide of refugee immigrants from the Third Reich knocking futilely on the door called the bluff of successive Newfoundland governments that had decried Newfoundland's small population, bemoaned its inability to attract settlers, and ceaselessly advertised the country's manifold challenges of development for immigrants. Ironically, the refugees' occupational, age, and class structure would have made them settlers ideally suited to Newfoundland's needs.

From the ethnocultural point of view, the extraordinary homogeneity of Newfoundland society encouraged a "British only" policy of immigration. Discernible in the 1906 legislation, this endeavor manifested itself increasingly in Newfoundland immigration policy to 1949. The World War I experience and postwar economic problems fostered the spreading of a fortress mentality, particularly among the small middle class population of the capital city, in defense of allegedly threatened British values and traditions. Today Newfoundlanders emphasize the prevalence of their characteristics of English and Irish descent. Students in school are taught to ascribe Newfoundland's present-day "distinctive homogeneous cultural entity" to its eighteenth- and early nineteenth-century English and Irish settlers.[27] That is true, but only half the story. There is no awareness that a methodical, exclusionary pre-Confederation policy artificially preserved this "distinct" cultural homogeneity. Had Newfoundland lived up to the spirit of its generous refugee legislation of 1906, it might have entered Canada culturally more diverse and economically richer.

The economic loss poses the greatest puzzle in view of Newfoundland's dire need for economic development. While the denial of sanctuary on humanitarian grounds might not be considered extraordinary in view of the western world's negative attitude toward the plight of Jewish refugees, the failure to maximize options for the benefit of the country seems inexplicable. This was not a case of failure attributable to outside powers or forces beyond the control of Newfoundland, or a course of action dictated by economic exigencies, but a calculated rejection of the known benefits refugee settlement would have entailed. Economically beneficial refugee settlement would have been in accordance with the economic recovery strategy adopted by the Commission of Government. Indeed, Commissioners Hope Simpson, Penson, and Gorvin recognized in refugee settlement a unique possibility to move toward a self-reliant, albeit pluralistic and multicultural society and away from those fatal dependencies long decried by local analysts as Newfoundland's seemingly inescapable destiny. The 1906 refugee legislation could have enabled the realization of this possibility, and the Commission's detachment from the local electorate and mandate for reform would have facilitated it.

The evidence points to the historic responsibility of the elite in charge of Newfoundland's affairs—a tiny privileged minority of merchants in association with the small urban middle class of manufacturers, lawyers, doctors, educators, and church leaders. Control over immigration and refugee policy gave them an important instrument to shape—or to petrify—social and economic change. The choices they made ensured that the safeguarding of traditional privilege remained the touchstone of the national interest. Foreigners would only spell change, they feared correctly, and their advent in large numbers or as competitors was to be avoided at all cost. Foreigners have therefore traditionally been stereotyped as pushy, unscrupulous, bent on undermining local values, and motivated by contempt for the people. Not surprisingly, apologists for the elite have frequently cast "foreigners" and "outsiders" in the role of scapegoats for the—regrettable but often predictable—plundering of local resources which resulted from the government's development deals with outside investors and corporations.

The record of Newfoundland's immigration policy demonstrates that cultural pluralism and the possible disturbance of entrenched privilege and unchallenged social and economic control was not a price the elite were prepared to pay for the well-being of the resident population. Despite the constant stream of official advertisements featuring the challenges awaiting skilled and productive settlers, the government excluded the only newcomers eager to come and take up those challenges. In fact, the government and the elite made no discernible concrete efforts to promote even "desirable" immigration, and it is arguable whether they really wanted any. This perspective may make intelligible the reason Newfoundland refused to offer protection to *bona fide* refugees and instead excluded and expelled refugees during the 43-year lifespan of its refugee law. It also becomes clear why Newfoundland's immigration policy has helped to retard the impoverished island instead of serving as an instrument of socio-economic change and development, and why this policy has fostered a legacy of attitudes inimical to growth and progress.

How, wondered a disheartened Simon Belkin in 1934, "can one interpret the refusal of proposals which would have been so beneficial to the country?"[28] A little known local journalist and organizer of a small Fishermen's Co-operative union believed in 1935 that he had the answer. The journalist was Joseph R. Smallwood who, inspired by this realization, subsequently launched Newfoundland's successful campaign for confederation. Every previous Newfoundland government had been "a false face for the real Government," namely "the Government on Water Street," he told a protest rally of sealers in St. John's. As recorded by a police detective at the rally, Smallwood voiced his concerns that the strong and independent Commission of Government was squandering its marvelous opportunity to change all that:

> I saw Sir John Hope Simpson three or four times and when I met him I said to myself, if ever a man was sent from God to help the poor people of the country, it was Sir John Hope Simpson. That was my opinion of Sir John Hope Simpson, and I kept on believing that, but I say tonight and I say it in all charity, I don't want to hurt his feelings, I say in all charity that in my opinion Sir John Hope Simpson would like to come to the rescue and assistance of the poor people. But the trouble with him and Mr. Lodge, they are the only two that count, is that they lack the courage and determination and backbone. Every time they look down through the windows of their offices they get frightened. Sir John Hope Simpson said to me in my last interview: "Mr. Smallwood, the merchants think we have the whip hand over them, I think it is the other way about, they have the whip hand over us." When the biggest man in the land has that feeling we cannot hope to expect anything from them.[29]

Notes

Chapter 1

1. Lisa Gilad, *The Northern Route: An Ethnography of Refugee Experiences* (St. John's, 1990), 6, 12, 227, 255, 261, 266, 278, 293f.

2. See Jacques Vernant, *The Refugee in the Post-War World* (New Haven, 1953), 3ff.

3. J.H. Simpson, *The Refugee Problem* (London, 1938), 3.

4. See Gerald E. Dirks, "The Plight of the Homeless: the Refugee Phenomenon," *Behind the Headlines*, XXXVIII:3 (August 1980), 3.

5. For a definition of the term "multiculturalism" see Jean Burnet, in *The Canadian Encyclopedia* (Edmonton, 1988), vol. 3, 1401.

6. Gilad, 300.

7. See Gerhard P. Bassler, "Auswanderungsfreiheit und Auswandererfürsorge in Württemberg 1815-1855: Zur Geschichte der südwestdeutschen Massenwanderung nach Nordamerika," *Zeitschrift für württembergische Landesgeschichte*, XXXIII (1976), 117-160.

8. Alan Dowty, *Closed Borders: The Contemporary Assault on the Freedom of Movement* (New Haven and London, 1987), 54, 89.

9. It asserted that "everyone has the right to seek and enjoy another country's asylum from persecution."

10. Louise W. Holborn, *Refugees: A Problem of Our Time. The Work of the UN High Commissioner for Refugees, 1951-1972* (Metuchen, N.J., 1975), 17.

11. Richard Breitman and Alan M. Kraut, *American Refugee Policy and European Jewry, 1933-1945* (Bloomington and Indianapolis, 1987), 10.

12. See Gerald E. Dirks, *Canada's Refugee Policy: Indifference or Opportunism?* (Montreal and London, 1977), *passim*.

13. See, e.g., Dirks, *Canada's Refugee Policy*, and Irving Abella and Harold Troper, *None Is Too Many: Canada and the Jews of Europe, 1933-1948* (Toronto, 1983).

14. Gilad, 167f.

15. Following Howard Palmer, *Patterns of Prejudice: A History of Nativism in Alberta* (Toronto, 1982), 7, nativism is defined as "opposition to an internal minority on the grounds that it posed a threat to national life."

16. Xenophobia, following *Webster's New Collegiate Dictionary* (Springfield, 1981), denotes "fear and hatred of strangers or foreigners or of anything that is strange or foreign."

17. Gerhard P. Bassler, "Newfoundland and Refugees from the Third Reich, 1934-1941," *Newfoundland Studies*, III:1 (1987), 37-70; "Attempts to Settle Jewish Refugees in Newfoundland and Labrador, 1934-1939," *Simon Wiesenthal Center Annual*, V (1988), 121-144; "Newfoundland's 'Dangerous' Internees Who Never Were: The History of Victoria Camp," *Newfoundland Studies*, V:1 (1989), 39-51.

18. Gerald E. Dirks, *Canada's Refugee Policy*. Michael R. Marrus, *The Unwanted: European Refugees in the Twentieth Century* (Oxford, 1985).

19. Simon Belkin, *Through Narrow Gates: A Review of Jewish Immigration, Colonization and Immigrant Aid Work in Canada, 1840-1940* (Montreal, 1966). Abella and Troper, *None Is Too Many*.

20. Eric Koch, *Deemed Suspect: A Wartime Blunder* (Toronto, 1980). Miriam Kochan, *Britain's Internees in the Second World War* (London, 1983). Bernard Wasserstein, *Britain and the Jews of Europe 1939-1945* (Oxford, 1979). Peter and Leni Gillman, *"Collar the Lot!" How Britain Interned and Expelled its Wartime Refugees* (London, 1980). Ted Jones, *Both Sides of the Wire: The Fredericton Internment Camp*, vol. I (Fredericton, 1988). Paula Jean Draper, "The Accidental Immigrants: Canada and the Interned Refugees," *Canadian Jewish Historical Society Journal*, II:1-2 (1978), 1-38, 80-112.

21. Paul Bartrop, ed., *The Dunera Affair: A Documentary Resource Book* (South Yarra and Melbourne, 1990); and "Enemy Aliens or Stateless Persons? The Legal Status of Refugees from Germany in Wartime Australia," *Journal of the Australian Jewish Historical Society*, X:4 (November 1988), 270-280.

22. G.W.L. Nicholson, *More Fighting Newfoundlanders: A History of Newfoundland's Fighting Forces in the Second World War* (St. John's, 1969); Herb Wells, *Under the White Ensign: A History of Newfoundland Naval Seamen in the Second World War* (Hull, 1977); Tony Murphy and Paul Kennedy, *The War at Our Doorstep: St. John's During World War Two. An Album* (St. John's, 1989). Numerous articles in the local press, especially the *Evening Telegram*, feature the uniqueness and significance of Newfoundland's World War II experience. On aspects of the Depression see Jim Overton, "Economic Crisis and the End of

Democracy: Politics in Newfoundland During the Great Depression," *Labour/Le Travail*, 26 (1990), 85–124; and "Public Relief and Social Unrest in Newfoundland in the 1930s: An Evaluation of the Ideas of Pliven and Cloward," in Greg Kealey, ed., *Class, Gender and Regions: Essays in Canadian Historical Sociology* (St. John's, 1988), 153–166.

23. See, e.g., Karl Baedeker, *The Dominion of Canada with Newfoundland and an Excursion to Alaska: Handbook for Travellers* (Leipzig: Karl Baedeker, 1907), 100–101. The section on Newfoundland was written by the Rev. Dr. Moses Harvey for the 1894 edition. D.W. Prowse, *The Newfoundland Guide Book*, Third Edition, (London, 1911). H.M. Mosdell, comp., *Newfoundland: Its Manifold Attractions for the Capitalist, the Settler and the Tourist* (St. John's. Published by the Direction of the Executive Government of Newfoundland, 1920), 15.

24. Melvin M. Firestone, "Mummers and Strangers in Northern Newfoundland," in Herbert Halpert and G.M. Story, eds., *Christmas Mumming in Newfoundland* (Toronto, 1969). John Widdowson, *If You Don't Be Good: Verbal Social Control in Newfoundland* (St. John's, 1977).

25. Alison Kahn, *Listen While I Tell You: The Story of the Jews of St. John's, Newfoundland* (St. John's, 1987).

26. Palmer, *Patterns of Prejudice*. Donald Avery, *"Dangerous Foreigners:" European Immigrant Workers and Labour Radicalism in Canada, 1896–1932* (Toronto, 1979). Robert England, *The Central European Immigrant in Canada* (Toronto, 1929).

27. See Jane Perry Clark, *The Deportation of Aliens from the United States to Europe* (New York, 1931), and Barbara Roberts, *Whence They Came: Deportation from Canada, 1900-1935* (Ottawa, 1988).

28. William E. Nawyn, *American Protestantism's Response to Germany's Jews and Refugees, 1933-1941* (Ann Arbor, 1980); Henry L. Feingold, *The Politics of Rescue: The Roosevelt Administration and the Holocaust, 1938-1945* (New Brunswick, N.J., 1970); David S. Wyman, *Paper Walls: America and the Refugee Crisis, 1938-1941* (New York, 1967), and *The Abandonment of the Jews: America and the Holocaust, 1941-1945* (New York, 1984).

29. Apart from Abella and Troper, *None Is Too Many*, see Cyril H. Levitt and William Shaffir, *The Riot at Christie Pits* (Toronto, 1987); David Rome, *Clouds in the Thirties: On Antisemitism in Canada, 1929-1939* (Montreal, 1977–1981); Lita-Rose Betcherman, *The Swastika and the Maple Leaf: Fascist Movements in Canada During the Thirties* (Toronto, 1975).

30. Paul R. Bartrop, "'Good Jews' and 'bad Jews': Australian perceptions of Jewish migrants and refugees, 1919-1939," in *Jews in the Sixth Continent* (Sydney, 1987), 169–184; M. Blakeney, *Australia and Jewish Refugees, 1933-1948* (Sydney, 1985).

31. See Ron Crawley, "Off to Sydney: Newfoundlanders Emigrate to Industrial Cape Breton, 1890–1914," *Acadiensis*, XVII:2 (1988), 27–51. Patricia A. Thornton, "The Problem of Out-Migration from Atlantic Canada, 1871–1921: A New Look," *Acadiensis*, XV:1 (1985), 3–34. Peter Neary, "Canadian Immigration Policy and the Newfoundlanders, 1912–1939," *Acadiensis*, XI:2 (1982), 69–83. Edward-Vincent Chafe, "A New Life on 'Uncle Sam's Farm:' Newfoundlanders in Massachusetts, 1846–1859," M.A. thesis, Memorial University of Newfoundland, 1982.

32. See, e.g., Robert Chambers, "Hidden Losers? The Impact of Rural Refugees and Refugee Programs on Poorer Hosts," and Barry N. Stein, "Durable Solutions for Developing Country Refugees," in the special issue on "Refugees: Issues and Directions" of *International Migration Review*, 20 (1986), 245–282, as well as the special issue on "International Migration: An Assessment for the '90s" of *International Migration Review*, 23 (1989).

33. Dowty, 241f, quotes a Canadian study which found that 5 percent of all adult immigrants started businesses within three years, which in themselves provided more than enough jobs to compensate for the displacement of native Canadians. See also Stephen L. Keller, *Uprooting and Social Change: The Role of Refugees in Development* (New Delhi, 1975); and Roland Tichy, *Ausländer rein! Warum es kein "Ausländerproblem" gibt* (second edition, Munich 1990).

34. David Alexander, "Development and Dependence in Newfoundland, 1880–1970," in *Atlantic Canada and Confederation: Essays in Canadian Political Economy* (Toronto, 1983), 6.

35. David Alexander, "Newfoundland's Traditional Economy and Development to 1934," in James Hiller and Peter Neary, eds., *Newfoundland in the Nineteenth and Twentieth Centuries: Essays in Interpretation* (Toronto, 1980), 17–39.

36. W.G. Reeves, "Our Yankee Cousins: Modernization and the Newfoundland-American Relationship, 1898–1910," Ph.D. thesis, University of Maine at Orono, 1987; and "Alexander's Conundrum Reconsidered: The American Dimension in Newfoundland Resource Development, 1898–1910," *Newfoundland Studies*, V:1·(1989), 1–37.

37. Peter Neary, *Newfoundland in the North Atlantic World, 1929–1949* (Kingston and Montreal, 1988), 354.

38. Ian D.H. McDonald, *"To Each His Own:" William Coaker and the Fishermen's Protective Union, 1908–1925* (St. John's, 1987), 145.

39. David Alexander, "Literacy and Economic Development in Nineteenth Century Newfoundland," in *Atlantic Canada and Confederation*, 111.

40. Breitman and Kraut, 2.

41. S.J.R. Noel, *Politics in Newfoundland* (Toronto, 1971). Ian D.H. McDonald, *"To Each His Own."* David Alexander, *Atlantic Canada and Confederation* (Toronto, 1983), Peter Neary, *Newfoundland.*

42. Stefi Jersch-Wenzel, "Ein importiertes Ersatzbürgertum? Die Bedeutung der Hugenotten für die Wirtschaft Brandenburg-Preussens," in R. von Thadden and M. Magdelaine, eds., *Die Hugenotten, 1685–1985* (Munich, 1985), 160–171. Werner Sombart, *Der moderne Kapitalismus: Historisch-systematische Darstellung des gesamteuropäischen Wirtschaftslebens von seinen Anfängen bis zur Gegenwart* (Munich and Leipzig, 1916), vol. I, 891. All translations from German language sources are my own unless otherwise indicated.

43. See Rudolf von Thadden and Michelle Magdelaine, eds., *Die Hugenotten, 1685–1985*. F.L. Carsten, *The Origins of Prussia* (London, 1954), 268f. Tichy, 112.

44. Gilbert Chinard, *Les Réfugiés Huguenots en Amerique* (Paris, 1925); Maldwyn Allen Jones, *American Immigration* (Chicago, 1960), 20.

45. Arthur A. Goren, "The Jews," in Stephan Thernstrom, ed., *Harvard Encyclopedia of American Ethnic Groups* (Cambridge, Mass., 1980), 591.

46. Anthony Heilbut, *Exiled in Paradise: German Refugee Artists and Intellectuals in America from the 1930s to the Present* (Boston, 1983), viii–ix.

47. Gustav Stolper, *The German Economy 1870 to the Present* (London, 1967), 226.

48. Quoted in William Henry Chamberlin, *The German Phoenix* (London, 1964), 70f.

49. Henry C. Wallich, *Mainsprings of the German Revival* (New Haven, 1955), 272–287.

50. Sombart, 883–919.

51. Keller, *Uprooting and Social Change*, 270–272.

52. *Ibid.*, 253–257.

53. *Ibid.*, 252.

Chapter 2

1. Michael R. Marrus, *The Unwanted: European Refugees in the Twentieth Century* (Oxford, 1985), 122–128, 132.

2. Raul Hilberg, *The Destruction of the European Jews* (Chicago, 1961), 45, 56.

3. *Deutsche Justiz*, October 1938, p. 1660.

4. See Dorothy Thompson, "Escape in a Frozen World," *Survey Geographic*, XXVIII:2 (February 1939), 94.

5. See, e.g., Wolfgang Benz, ed., *Das Tagebuch der Helga Nathorff. Berlin-New York: Aufzeichnungen 1933–1945* (Munich, 1987), 35–212.

6. Marvin Lowenthal, "Plight of a People," *Survey Graphic*, XXVIII:1 (January 1939), 73.

238 Sanctuary Denied

7. Hermann von Freeden, "Ein Beitrag zur Geschichte der Judenauswanderung aus Deutschland," (December 1945), 1–14, Bundesarchiv Koblenz (BA), Bestand Z 1, Band 882.

8. Wolfgang Zadek, ed., *Sie flohen vor dem Hakenkreuz. Selbstzeugnisse der Emigranten. Ein Lesebuch für Deutsche* (Reinbek, 1981), 101.

9. Emmy Arnold, *Gegen den Strom: Das Werden der Bruderhöfe* (Moers, 1983), 8–146.

10. Emmy Arnold, *Torches Together* (Rifton, N.Y., 1964), 185f. N.a., "Confrontation: Adolf Hitler/Bruderhof: Eberhard Arnold's Letters. Documentation," *The Plough* (publication of the Bruderhof communities, Ulster Park, N.Y.) 21 (April/May 1989), 7–18. Arnold, *Gegen den Strom*, 147–159.

11. Hans Meier, personal interview (New Harmony, Indiana), 30 September 1989. Hans Meier, *Hans Meier Tells His Story to a Friend* (Ulster Park, N.Y., 1979), 8–13. Arnold, *Gegen den Strom*, 159–181.

12. Meier, 14–19.

13. Wolfgang Benz, ed., *Die Juden in Deutschland, 1933–1945: Ein Leben unter nationalsozialistischer Herrschaft* (Munich, 1988), 412–417. Friedrich Battenberg, *Das europäische Zeitalter der Juden: Zur Entwicklung einer Minderheit in der nichtjüdischen Umwelt Europas* (Darmstadt, 1990), 264–268.

14. Dieter Marc Schneider, "Saarpolitik und Exil 1933–1955," *Vierteljahrshefte für Zeitgeschichte*, 25:4 (1977), 500.

15. Provincial Archives of Newfoundland and Labrador (PANL), GN 13, Box 38, File 88.

16. Juliane Wetzel, "Auswanderung aus Deutschland," in Wolfgang Benz, ed., *Die Juden in Deutschland, 1933–1945*, 414–418.

17. Werner Rosenstock, "Exodus 1933–1939: A Survey of Jewish Emigration from Germany," *Leo Baeck Year Book*, I (1956), 384.

18. See census data of Jewish population in Germany, reprinted in Wolfgang Benz, ed., *Die Juden*, 733–737. Sarah Gordon, *Hitler, Germans and the "Jewish" Question* (Princeton, 1984), 8–15.

19. Lucy S. Dawidowicz, *The War Against the Jews 1933–1945* (New York, 1975), 171.

20. Goebbels triggered the pogrom ostensibly to avenge the assassination of a secretary at the German Embassy in Paris by a Polish Jewish student. *Kristallnacht* (Crystal Night) got its name from the shattered glass of 7,000 Jewish businesses destroyed, the fire set to synagogues all over Germany and the killing of nearly a hundred Jews and tormenting of many more by the SA in the night of 9 to 10 November 1938. The police were ordered to arrest as many male German Jews, "especially rich ones," as the concentration camps Buchenwald, Dachau, Sachsenhausen and Mauthausen could accommodate and to release

only those who emigrated immediately. The Jews who stayed behind were ordered to repair the damages to their property, to transfer their businesses to non-Jews, to keep out of certain public places, such as theatres, movies, beaches, resorts and sleeping cars, to remove their children from German schools, and to pay a penalty of one million marks. By the end of December 1938, Jews had been effectively eliminated from German economic and public life. See Dawidowicz, 99–106; Hans-Jürgen Döscher, *"Reichskristallnacht:" Die November-pogrome 1938* (Frankfurt/M, 1990); Heinz Lauber, *Judenpogrom: "Reichskristallnacht" November 1938 in Grossdeutschland* (Gerlingen, 1981); Rita Thalmann and Emanuel Feinermann, *Crystal Night 9-10 November 1938* (London, 1974); Wolfgang Benz, "Der November-pogrom 1938," in Wolfgang Benz, ed., *Die Juden*, 499–544; and Helmut Krausnick, *et al.*, *Anatomy of the SS State* (New York, 1968), 38–43.

21. Carl J. Burckhardt, *Meine Danziger Mission 1937-1939* (Munich, 1960), 179–198.

22. Joseph Marcus, *Social and Political History of the Jews in Poland, 1919-1939* (Berlin, 1983), 378f. Harry M. Rabinowicz, *The Legacy of Polish Jewry: A History of Polish Jews in the Inter-War Years 1919-1939* (New York, 1965), 174.

23. Saul Rubinek, *So Many Miracles* (Markham, Ont., 1988), 44–48, 58, 79.

24. Dawidowicz, 377f, 396.

25. Dawidowicz, 379–385. Marrus, 144f.

26. PANL, GN 1/3 A, No. 5–17, File 9/39.

27. John Hope Simpson, *Refugees: A Review of the Situation Since September 1939* (London, July 1939), 24.

28. Norman Bentwich, "The Destruction of the Jewish Community in Austria 1938–1942," in Josef Fraenkel, ed., *The Jews of Austria: Essays on their Life, History and Destruction* (London, 1967), 467, 474.

29. John Hope Simpson, *Refugees*, 36f. Marrus, 174ff.

30. Kurt R. Grossmann, *Emigration: Geschichte der Hitler Flüchtlinge 1933-1945* (Frankfurt am Main, 1969), 114f.

31. Inge Deutschkron, *Ich trug den gelben Stern* (Cologne, 1978), 45f.

32. Hans Herlin, *"Kein gelobtes Land:" Die Irrfahrt der St. Louis* (Hamburg, 1961), 15ff.

33. Krausnick, 45–48. Jochen von Lang, ed., *Eichmann Interrogated: Transcripts from the Archives of the Israeli Police* (New York, 1984), 51–57.

34. PANL, GN 1/3/A, 1939, No. 5-17, File "Immigration into Newfoundland."

35. Ernst Deutsch, personal interviews (St. John's, Nfld.), 25 November 1983, 29 September 1990, and 11 September 1991.

36. Andreas Barban, personal interview (St. John's, Nfld.), 3 February 1986.

37. Quoted in Abella and Troper, *None Is Too Many*, 30f.

38. Grossmann, 188–232. For the deportation of German Jews from the Netherlands to Germany, see Dick de Mildt, "Kollaboration und Deportation in Holland," in Jörg Wollenberg, ed., "*Niemand war dabei und keiner hat's gewußt*": *Die deutsche Öffentlichkeit und die Judenverfolgung 1933–1945* (Munich, 1989), 226f.

39. A.J. Sherman, *Island Refuge: Britain and Refugees from the Third Reich 1933–1939* (Berkeley and Los Angeles, 1973), 204f. Herbert Rosenkranz, *Verfolgung und Selbstbehauptung: Die Juden in Oesterreich 1938–1945* (Vienna, 1978), 270, states that England took 30,850 of Austria's 128,500 Jewish refugees by 10 November 1941. The figures for Britain's Jewish refugees from the Third Reich vary from not more than 65,000 between 1933 and 1945, according to Andrew Sharf, *The British Press and Jews under Nazi Rule* (London, 1964), 155, to at least 73,000 by September 1939 according to Koch, *Deemed Suspect*, 8, and as many as 80,000 during World War II, according to Marion Berghahn, *German-Jewish Refugees in England: The Ambiguities of Assimilation* (London, 1984), 74.

40. Personal interviews with Andreas and Betty Barban (St. John's), 20 December 1983, 3 February 1986, 17 and 24 September 1990.

41. H. von Freeden, 5–10. Theodore Norman, *An Outstretched Arm: A History of the Jewish Colonization Association* (London, 1985), 217–225.

42. Figures as quoted in Wetzel, 438–444. Norman, 117–132, 204–217.

43. *Survey Graphic*, XXIX:11 (November 1940), 591f.

44. Yehuda Bauer, *American Jewry and the Holocaust: The American Jewish Joint Distribution Committee, 1939–1945* (Detroit, 1981), 24–34.

45. Marrus, 165f.

46. Hope Simpson, *Refugees*, 18–22.

47. John F. Rich, "Why, Where, Who—the Refugees?" *Survey Graphic*, XXIX:11 (November 1940), 572ff.

48. Gerhart Saenger, "The Refugees Here," *Survey Graphic*, XXIX:11 (November 1940), 578f.

49. Bruno Lasker, "An Atlas of Hope," *Survey Graphic*, XXIX:11 (November 1940), 584, 590f.

Chapter 3

1. The only noteworthy immigration was a small number of Highland Scots—one researcher counted 79 households by 1880—from Cape

Breton to the Codroy Valley in western Newfoundland between 1841 and 1860. See Rosemary E. Ommer, "Highland Scots Migration to Western Newfoundland: A Study of Kinship," in John J. Mannion, ed., *The Peopling of Newfoundland*, 215f; Margaret Bennett, *The Last Stronghold: Scottish Gaelic Traditions in Newfoundland* (St. John's, 1988).

2. S.J.R. Noel, *Politics in Newfoundland* (Toronto, 1971), 8.

3. McDonald, "*To Each His Own*," 11. Patricia Ruth O'Brien, 'The Newfoundland Patriotic Association: The Administration of the War Effort, 1914–1918," unpublished M.A. thesis, Memorial University of Newfoundland, 1981, 5, calculated the following occupational breakdown for the urban business and professional class: 35 clergymen, 225 teachers, 46 lawyers, 37 doctors, 344 merchants and traders.

4. Kenneth J. Kerr, "A Social Analysis of the Members of the Newfoundland House of Assembly, Executive Council, and Legislative Council for the Period, 1855–1914," M.A. thesis, Memorial University of Newfoundland, 1973, 509. Noel, 9.

5. Rev. P.W. Browne, *Where the Fishers Go: The Story of Labrador* (New York, 1909), 71f. Browne, who lived from 1864 to 1937, was educated at Harvard, Munich, and Oxford universities, and taught as a professor of history at the University of Ottawa and the Catholic University of America, Washington, D.C.

6. McDonald, 19.

7. *Ibid.*, 22.

8. Noel, 25.

9. Rev. Philip Tocque, *Newfoundland: As it was, and as it is in 1877* (Toronto, 1878), 86.

10. Alfred Bishop Morine, "A History of Newfoundland," unpublished book manuscript (about 1935), chapter XI, 15, deposited in PANL, P 4/3, Box 1, File 11.

11. Quoted in O'Brien, 2–3.

12. David Alexander, "Literacy and Economic Development in Nineteenth Century Newfoundland," *Acadiensis*, X:3 (1980), 8.

13. McDonald, 18.

14. Reeves, "Our Yankee Cousins," 449–502.

15. For instance, the *Evening Telegram* of 25 May 1907 reported that "the Dominion Steel Company has about 700 men now employed at Bell Island and there is room for 500 more, but they are not to be had." In 1914 Deputy Minister of Customs Henry William LeMessurier testified that during the period 1903–1913 a number of mechanics, artists and skilled labourers "have been brought in to fill the wants of the mines and the pulp and paper mills and a few other local industries." See Great Britain, Dominions Royal Commission, *Royal Commission on the*

Natural Resources, Trade and Legislation of Certain Portions of His Majesty's Dominions, Minutes of Evidence Taken in Newfoundland in 1914 (London, 1915), 1.

16. Thornton, "The Problem of Out-Migration," 10ff. The lure of Boston, for instance, was largely determined by the opportunities which that region's economic growth afforded as well as by a network of personal contacts with a colony of Newfoundlanders which grew steadily as a result of chain migration since the 1840s. See Edward Vincent Chafe, "A New Life on 'Uncle Sam's Farm.'"

17. Crawley, "Off to Sydney," 27–51.

18. Reeves, "Our Yankee Cousins," 456.

19. See Peter F. Neary and Sidney J.R. Noel, "Continuity and Change in Newfoundland Politics," in Ian McDonald, ed., *Newfoundland Since 1815: Selected Readings*, vol. 2 (St. John's, 1976), 284f.

20. Neary, "Canadian Immigration Policy," 39.

21. Alexander, "Literacy," 14.

22. Thomas Lodge, "Newfoundland Today," *International Affairs*, XIV:5 (1935), 637.

23. Thornton, "The Problem of Out-Migration," 12.

24. The rapid economic growth of late nineteenth century Britain, France, and Germany has in part been credited to a mass influx of East Europeans taking up work in agricultural, mining, and service industries. These immigrants from the East were replacing large numbers of skilled, educated, and often relatively prosperous native-born lost through emigration to North America. See Werner Sombart, *Das Wirtschaftsleben im Zeitalter des Hochkapitalismus. Erster Halbband* (Munich and Leipzig, 1927), 392–399.

25. As quoted in Patrick O'Flaherty, *The Rock Observed: Studies in the Literature of Newfoundland* (Toronto, 1979), 111f.

26. *Evening Herald*, 28 February, 2 and 9 March, 17 August and 3 September 1907.

27. Areas opened up were along the route of the transinsular railway which was completed in 1897 and along the so-called French Shore on the west coast of the island where French rights were terminated in 1904. On the official promotion of British immigration see PANL, GN 1/3A, 1904, Files 39–50, No. 45. Emigrants' Information Office, *Newfoundland, With Map: Information for Intending Emigrants* (London: H.M. Stationary Office, 1904), 3–10. Regarding the dashed expectations of Finnish immigration, see the *Daily News*, 25 May and 19 August 1899, 2 January 1901; *Evening Herald*, 10 and 21 August, 1899. On the importation of Swedish lumbermen see Province of Newfoundland, *Report of the Royal Commission on Forestry, 1955* (St. John's, 1955). The plans for a Salvation Army colony for bringing boys from England

are mentioned in evidence of Arthur Mews, Deputy Colonial Secretary, in Great Britain, Dominions Royal Commission, 3–4.

28. This is corroborated by various newspaper articles reporting arrivals at Bay of Islands on American schooners and from Lunenburg, N.S. See, e.g., *Western Star*, 15 May 1900; *Daily News*, 24 July 1914.

29. A. Mews in Great Britain, Dominions Royal Commission, 3.

30. Great Britain, Dominions Royal Commission, 6–10.

31. *Ibid.*, 5.

32. *Ibid.*, 4.

33. D.W. Prowse, *The Newfoundland Guide Book*, Third Edition, (London, 1911), 145–148.

34. Karl Baedeker, *The Dominion of Canada with Newfoundland and an Excursion to Alaska: Handbook for Travellers* (Leipzig: Karl Baedeker, 1907), 100–101.

35. *Evening Telegram*, 29 June 1906, 26 July 1906. *Evening Herald*, 9 May 1906. *Daily News*, 21 February 1906, 18 April and 9 May 1906. In 1911 government records identified by national origin 86 Syrians, 44 Turks, 26 Chinese and 25 Russians. See Dominions Royal Commission, 3.

36. In December 1914, the police count of adult alien males (naturalized and non-naturalized) was 77 Turkish nationals, 44 Chinese and 42 Russian Jews. See PANL, GN 1/1/7, 1914.

37. *Evening Herald*, 4 March and 16 January 1899. Thanks to Bill Reeves for drawing my attention to these articles.

38. *Evening Herald*, 2 January 1906. According to Margaret Chang, *Chinese Handbook, Newfoundland 1978* (St. John's, 1978), 39, the *Evening Telegram* advocated the exclusion of Chinese, Japanese, Poles, and Italians shortly after the first five Chinese arrived in St. John's in 1895.

39. *Evening Telegram*, 21 April 1906. *Evening Herald*, 18 April 1906.

40. *Evening Herald*, 1 and 3 May 1906.

41. *Evening Herald*, 9 May 1906, and *Daily News*, 10 May 1906.

42. *Evening Herald*, 11 May 1906.

43. *Evening Telegram*, 14 November 1906.

44. *Evening Herald*, 7 January 1907.

45. *Ibid.*, 30 October, 21 November, 4 December 1906 and 7 January 1907. *Evening Telegram*, 1 December 1906.

46. See *Evening Herald*, 29 April, 20 August and 3 December 1907.

47. In the *Evening Herald* of 21 November 1906 the Halifax Immigration Agent was quoted as complaining "that undesirable people and even some who had been refused entry at other points were taken to St.

John's, then to Port-aux-Basques and from there by the *Bruce* to North Sydney thus avoiding the immigration examination. It is known that certain foreigners have been carrying on this work and evading the immigration laws."

48. See, e.g., *Evening Herald*, 5 May and 22 November 1906.

49. The act, entitled since 1892 "Of the Disembarking of Paupers," is first traceable in the *Consolidated Statutes of Newfoundland 1872* (St. John's, 1874), 511, under the title "Of Mendicant and Infirm Immigrants." (Courtesy of Joan Ritcey, Centre for Newfoundland Studies, and Norma Jean Richards, Legislative Library of Newfoundland, St. John's).

50. House of Assembly proceedings of 27 April 1906, as quoted in *Evening Telegram*, 29 May 1906.

51. *Ibid.* The full text of the 1905 British Aliens Act is reprinted in C.F. Fraser, *Control of Aliens in the British Commonwealth of Nations* (London, 1940), 219–226.

52. Marrus, 37f. For the genesis of the British Aliens Act see Bernard Gainer, *The Alien Invasion: The Origins of the Aliens Act of 1905* (London, 1972), 166–198. David Saunder, "Aliens in Britain and the Empire During the First World War," *Immigrants and Minorities*, IV:1 (March 1985), 6f.

53. PANL, GN 1/1/17, 1911 (15/3/2); GN 1/3/A, 1911, Des. #52.

54. In Canada a 1902 Royal Commission Report characterized Chinese and Japanese as "obnoxious to a free community and dangerous to the state," and Canada's 1903 Chinese Immigration Act raised the head tax from $100 to $500. See Jin Tan and Patricia E. Roy, *The Chinese in Canada* (Ottawa, 1985), 8.

55. *Evening Telegram*, 18 April, 1906.

56. *Evening Herald*, 15 and 16 February, 1 May, 6 August 1906.

57. During 1905–1907 the media reported three cases of Chinese being smuggled to Canada from Newfoundland: 1. the *Bonita* case (*Evening Herald*, 8 October 1906); 2. the *Frolic* case (*Evening Herald*, 22, 24 and 29 September, 8 and 13 October, 17 December 1906); 3. the *Clorus* case (*Evening Herald*, 31 August 1907).

58. *Daily News*, 3 March 1906. *Evening Herald*, 16 February and 6 August 1906.

59. See, e.g., *Daily News*, 18 June 1906; *Evening Herald*, 10 July 1905. The pattern of physical attacks against Chinese was apparently still prevalent in the mid-1930s. A local Chinese resident recalled that he was regularly the subject of physical abuse on his way home from school and, suffering from bruises and filth thrown at him, frequently had to be carried home by a policeman. H. Fong, personal interview, 26 September 1991.

60. See Robert G. Hong, "'To take action without delay': Newfoundland's Chinese Immigration Act of 1906," Honours thesis, Memorial University of Newfoundland, 1987.

61. *Evening Telegram*, 4 August 1906. *Evening Herald*, 6 August 1906. As late as 1950 the unconfirmed tale was repeated that, when iron ore mining began on Bell Island, "some 300 Chinese were imported for the open pit operations as there was not sufficient labor supply in Newfoundland to meet the requirements." *Evening Telegram*, 18 March 1950.

62. *Evening Herald*, 1 May 1906.

63. The 1911 census showed only 731 residents, i.e., 0.3 percent of Newfoundland's population of 242,000, to be born outside the British Empire.

64. The Japanese, for instance, were frequently referred to as "Japs" and the standard characterization of French-born Newfoundlanders as "Jackatars" suggests that even they were viewed as undesirable outsiders. See, e.g., *Evening Herald*, 2 July 1906 and 15 February 1907.

65. Nativism is defined as opposition to an internal minority on the grounds that it poses a racial, religious, or enthnocultural threat to national life. Xenophobia denotes fear and hatred of strangers or foreigners, or anything that is strange or foreign.

66. See Palmer, *Patterns of Prejudice*, and John Higham, *Strangers in the Land* (New York, 1955).

67. See Firestone, 63–75.

68. Widdowson, 270.

69. G.M. Story, in Herbert Halpert and G.M. Story, eds., *Christmas Mumming in Newfoundland: Essays in Anthropology, Folklore, and History* (Toronto, 1969), 12, 30.

70. Mannion, 7.

71. J.R. Smallwood, "Life To-day in Newfoundland," in *Book of Newfoundland*, vol. I (St. John's, 1937), 27.

72. P.K. Devine, *In the Good Old Days* (St. John's, 1990), 6–8.

73. Melvin Baker, *et al.*, *The Illustrated History of Newfoundland Light and Power* (St. John's, 1990), 94.

74. George Earles, interviewed by Tonya Bassler, 11 April 1989.

75. Gerhard P. Bassler, "Central European Immigrants in St. John's, Newfoundland: Immigration and Adjustment," *Canadian Ethnic Studies*, XVIII:3 (1986), 45.

76. *Evening Telegram*, 9 and 16 August 1989. *Sunday Telegram*, 8 October 1989. *Globe and Mail*, 18 November 1989. *The Metro*, 1 December 1985.

77. Wilfred F. Butcher, "Inertia in Newfoundland," *Canadian Forum*, XX (November 1940), 246.

78. Letter to the Editor, *Evening Telegram*, 1 March 1990.

79. The term is probably derived from "Italy man." See G.M. Story, *et al.*, eds., *Dictionary of Newfoundland English* (Toronto, 1982), 556. *Evening Telegram*, 4 April 1989.

80. PANL, P 4/3, Box #1, File 17.

81. O'Brien, 227.

82. PANL, GN 1/10/0, (42/4/7), War Papers, July-November 1916. Augusta Mercer, born in 1901 as the daughter of a German immigrant (with no Jewish background) and attending school in St. John's in 1914–15, recalled that after the outbreak of the war people taunted her as a Jew which was meant (in her recollection) to be a greater put-down than being stigmatized as a German. Personal interview (St. John's), 1 May 1984.

83. See G.P. Bassler, "The Enemy Alien Experience in Newfoundland 1914–1918," *Canadian Ethnic Studies*, XX:3 (1988), 42–62. For the most recent undocumented reaffirmation of this legend of local Germans having acted as spies see Jack Fitzgerald, *Strange but True Newfoundland Stories* (St. John's, 1989), 75–77.

84. David G. Pitt, *Tales from the Outer Fringe* (St. John's, 1990), 3f.

Chapter 4

1. PANL, GN 1/3/A, 1919, Des.# 1308. Concerning the wartime deportation of Moravian missionary Karl Filschke, see Bassler, "The Enemy Alien Experience," 51–53.

2. *Ibid.*, 1921, Des. # 231.

3. PANL, GN 2/5, File 383(1), Minutes of the Meeting of the High Commissioners and Agents General Held at the Colonial Office, 5 March 1919.

4. PANL, GN 2/5, File 383 (1).

5. Great Britain, Oversea Settlement Office, *Official Statement for the Use of Women Who May Wish to Settle in the Oversea Dominions* (London, 1919), 8.

6. PANL, GN 2/5, File 383(2)–(3).

7. *Ibid.*, File 382, and GN 1/3/A, 1922, Des. #239.

8. H.M. Mosdell, comp., *Newfoundland: Its Manifold Attractions for the Capitalist, the Settler and the Tourist* (St. John's. Published by the Direction of the Executive Government of Newfoundland, 1920), 15ff, 27f, 37f.

9. *Ibid.*, 42.

10. PANL, GN 1/3/A, 1922. Des. # 239.

11. *Ibid.*, Des. # 239.

12. John A.R. Marriott, *Empire Settlement* (London, 1927), 48f.

13. C.H. Palmer, *The Salmon Rivers of Newfoundland: A Descriptive Account of the Various Rivers of the Island* (St. John's, 1928), 10.

14. PANL, GN 13/2/A, Box 227, File "Immigration (1921–1926)." Belkin, 183.

15. Noel, 156.

16. Marriott, 48.

17. PANL, GN 13/2/A, Box 227, File "Immigration (1921–1926)."

18. *Ibid.*

19. *Evening Telegram*, 30 March 1926.

20. *Evening Telegram*, 13 March 1926.

21. *Daily News*, 9 December 1920.

22. See Neary, "Canadian Immigration Policy," 73.

23. PANL, GN 13/2/A, Box 227, File "Immigration (1921–1926)."

24. PANL, GN 1/3/A, 1907, Des. #101.

25. PANL, GN 2/5, File 525F.

26. Robert H. Tait, *Newfoundland: A Summary of the History and Development of Britain's Oldest Colony from 1497 to 1939* (New York, 1939), 36.

27. PANL, GN 13/2/A, Box 227, File "Re Immigration," unsigned Memo for Minister, 28 March 1929.

28. *Ibid.*, File "Immigration," Acting Deputy Minister of Justice to Colonial Secretary, 14 September 1929, and to R.A. Squires, 22 September 1930. In this context it may be interesting to note that in August 1930 the Deputy Minister of Customs and Chief Commissioner of Immigration H.V. Hutchings submitted to Prime Minister R.A. Squires a draft Proclamation which provided that "no immigration be permitted to Newfoundland on terms more favourable than those on which Newfoundland citizens are permitted entry into the country of which the applicant is a national and/or in which he last resided." The Acting Deputy Minister of Justice B.E.S. Dunfield, however, was able to convince Hutchings that this draft would not meet the case, "partly because the countries in respect of which it is particularly desired to exclude immigration are those in respect of which there would probably be no obstacle to the immigration of our citizens." See *Ibid.*, Deputy Minister of Justice (Actg.) to A. Barnes, Secretary of State, 19 June 1931.

29. *Ibid.*, File "Re Immigration," Acting Minister of Immigration and Colonisation to F.C. Alderdice, 5 June 1933.

30. PANL, GN 1/3/A, 1921, Des. #819.

31. PANL, GN 13/2/A, Box 227, File "Immigration (1921–1926)."

32. The 1935 census showed an increase in Newfoundland's foreign-born from 1,168 in 1921 to 1,601, in relation to a total population growth from 263,000 to 290,000.

33. See, e.g., PANL, GN 13/2/A, Box 227, File "Immigration," Acting Deputy Minister of Justice to Arthur Mews, 8 October 1930.

34. PANL, GN 13/2/A, Box 227, File "Immigration (1921–1926)."

35. Newfoundland, House of Assembly, *Proceedings 1926*, 748–752.

36. PANL, GN 13/2/A, Box 227, File "Immigration (1921–1926)."

37. *Ibid.*

38. *Ibid.*, LeMessurier to Bennett, 22 February 1926.

39. PANL, GN 13/2/A, Box 227, File "Immigration (1921–1926)."

40. *Ibid.*

41. PANL, GN 1/3/A, 1922, Des. #496 and #542.

42. *Ibid.*, 1918, Des. #1481.

43. PANL, GN 13/2/A, Box 227, File "Immigration."

44. Newfoundland, House of Assembly, *Proceedings 1926*, 651, 747–750.

45. PANL, GN 13/2/A, Box 227, File "Immigration (1921–1926)."

46. *Daily News*, 22 August 1930, and *Evening Telegram*, 5 March 1931.

47. PANL, GN 13/2/A, Box 227, File "Immigration."

48. GN 13/2/A, Box 227, File "Re: Immigration."

49. *Ibid.*, Acting Deputy Minister of Justice to Deputy Colonial Secretary, 8 October 1930, and Deputy Minister of Justice (Actg.) to Secretary of State, 15 December 1931.

50. John Dufferin Sutherland, "A Social History of Pulpwood Logging in Newfoundland During the Great Depression," M.A. thesis, Memorial University of Newfoundland, 1988, 78f.

51. McDonald, 'To Each His Own,' 145.

52. At the Amulree Commission hearings in June 1933, William White as the representative of the Associated Newfoundland Industries pointed out that "Newfoundland, on account of its small population, can only support one, or at most two, factories in each line. If it is once decided that an industry is advantageous to the country, that industry should as far as possible, have the whole benefit of the local market." National Archives of Canada (NAC), MG 38 E82, Vol. 17, File #95.

53. In the 1928 Session of the Newfoundland House of Assembly (*Proceedings*, 217) the Minister of Finance attributed the "labor trouble" in St. John's to "so many people coming in from the outports . . . I do say that the immigration of people from the outports has been the cause to a great extent of the dole situation in St. John's." In the *Daily News*

of 18 May 1933 one "economist" articulated the same perception of these local migrants: "At home they lived rent free, they could raise produce and secure fish enough to help stock the larder, they got fuel without cost and paid no taxes. They crowded into St. John's. Many of them had to live in the congested streets, they demoralized the local labor market and put many of the regular workmen on the dole, and eventually had to resort to the dole for existence."

54. See *Evening Telegram*, 3 November 1933, and NAC, MG 30, E 82, Vol. 18, File 97; "Newfoundland Royal Commission, 39th Day," 18ff, 31.

Chapter 5

1. Volkswirt Ben Smith, St. John's, "Ansiedlungspläne auf Neufundland," *Deutsche Siedlung*, No. 10, 5 February 1937, 4 pages. Typewritten copy in Zentralarchiv Potsdam (now: Bundesarchiv, Abteilungen Potsdam), Germany, Record Group 62 DAF 3, Vol. 13, No. 37181.

2. Noel, 224f.

3. Smith, "Ansiedlungspläne, 2-3.

4. PANL, GN 13/2/A, Box 227, File "Immigration (1921-1926)." Belkin, 172f. Norman, xiii, 217f.

5. *Ibid.*, 183f. Belkin assumed erroneously that the 1926 and 1932 regulations had temporarily suspended the liberal 1906 refugee provisions.

6. *Ibid.*, 184f.

7. *Ibid.*, 185.

8. PANL, GN 38, S 2-1-1, N.R. 19, undated memorandum by Commissioner Hope Simpson.

9. PANL, GN 38, S 2-1-12, File 7.

10. Belkin, 186. *Observer's Weekly*, 24 February 1934. *Evening Telegram*, 10 August 1939. Grossmann, 166. Walter Laqueur, *A History of Zionism* (New York, 1988), 491f.

11. The proposal was leaked in the *Evening Telegram* of 11 May 1934 by N.S. Fraser, member of the Newfoundland Medical Board.

12. PANL, GN 38, S 2-1-12, N.R. 39-36. Belkin, 186f.

13. Neary, *Newfoundland*, 104f.

14. PANL, GN 1/3/A, 1936, File #200, Humphrey Walwyn to Malcolm Macdonald, 25 March 1936.

15. *Observer's Weekly*, 14 July 1934.

16. *Ibid.*, 11 August 1934.

17. *Ibid.*, 18 August 1934.

18. PANL, GN 8/6, File 18, F.H. Borden to Fred Alderdice, 23 July 1932.

19. PANL, GN 8/2, File 96.2. Malcolm MacLeod, "Labrador For Sale – 27%

Off," *The Newfoundland Quarterly*, LXXV:2 (Fall 1979), 13–14.

20. Cyril Banikhin, personal interview, 19 October 1984. Cyril Banikhin is the son of Frank Banikhin.

21. PANL, GN 38, S 2-1-12, Memos 1936, F. Banikhin to Sir John Hope Simpson, 5 March 1936.

22. *Ibid.*

23. PANL, GN 38, S 2-1-12, Walwyn to MacDonald, 12 March 1936, and Memorandum by Commissioner for Natural Resources, 13 March 1936.

24. Public Record Office (PRO), DO 35/181, File 6652/126.

25. PANL, GN 38, S 2-1-12, Memos 1936, MacDonald to Walwyn, 10 July 1936.

26. Cyril Banikhin, personal interview, 19 November 1984.

27. Morine, "A History of Newfoundland," Chapter XI.

28. PRO, DO 35/500, File N1029/10, Hope Simpson to Harding, 24 September 1935.

29. Lady Hope Simpson shared her husband's judgement. The daughter of the head of a firm of Manchester cotton brokers, she wrote that she had never been able to witness before "what selfishness and greed in commerce mean to people. Here the merchants have exploited the fishermen . . . grown richer and richer and then [gone] away to spend and enjoy their wealth in England or America. The money made here is not, as a rule, spent here . . . The morale of the people has been undermined by all the conditions of their lives." Peter Neary, ed., "J.B. Hope Simpson's account of Sir John Hope Simpson's Newfoundland career, 1934–36," *Newfoundland Studies*, VI:1 (1990), 75, 82f. See also Neary, *Newfoundland*, 60.

30. PANL, GN 38, S 2-1-12, File 7.

31. PRO, DO 35/720, File M652/3.

32. *Evening Telegram*, 3 and 26 November 1938.

33. *Refugees: Preliminary Report of a Survey*, issued under the auspices of the Royal Institute of International Affairs, London (New York, 1938).

34. PRO, DO 35/706, File M529/39.

35. Saul Bernstein, "Report on Prospects for Jewish Colonization in Newfoundland," New York, 1 November 1938, typescript in American Jewish Archives, Hebrew Union College, Cincinnati.

36. *Observer's Weekly*, 14 February 1939.

37. *Daily News*, 2 March 1939. *Observer's Weekly*, 6 March 1939.

38. *Observer's Weekly*, 25 April, 9 May, 22 August 1939. Feingold, 193. Wyman, *Paper Walls*, 98–112.

39. PANL, GN 13/2/A, Box 233, File 106.

40. On 29 July 1939 the *Evening Telegram* reported that the president of the Santa Cruz Oil Company spoke to the St. John's Rotary of the need for new industries without mentioning the Labrador settlement project.

41. *Acts of the Honourable Commission of Government 1939*, 181–190.

42. *Evening Telegram*, 17 January 1939.

43. *Observer's Weekly*, 6 December 1938.

44. PANL, GN 38, S 1–2–5, File #8.

45. *Evening Telegram*, 28 and 29 November, and 2 December 1938.

46. PANL, GN 13/2/A, Box 336, File "Admission of European Immigrants to Nfld, 1939, Retain."

47. PRO, DO 35/706, File M529/91.

48. PANL, GN 13/2/A, Box 336, File "Admission of European Immigrants to Nfld., 1939, Retain," Secretary of State for Dominion Affairs to Governor of Newfoundland, 22 May 1939.

49. *Ibid.*, "Immigration of Refugees from Central Europe," Memorandum submitted by the Commissioner of Finance, 27 May 1939.

50. PANL, GN 1/3/A, 1939, No. 5–17.

51. PRO, DO 35/706, File M529/116.

52. *Ibid.*, File M529/108.

53. PANL, GN 13/2/A, Box 336, File "Admission of European Immigrants to Newfoundland 1939, Retain," memorandum "Jewish Immigration," 24 July 1939.

54. PANL, GN 1/3/A, 1939, No. 5–17, Telegram to Secretary of State for Dominion Affairs, 27 July 1939.

55. PANL, GN 38, S–5–1–1, File No. 4.

56. PRO, DO 35/706, File M529/126.

57. The 1939–40 estimates for the reconstruction budget of $2,000,000 provided for $200,000 assistance to new industries, $179,000 for technical training, and $55,000 for rural industries. Industrial initiatives thus ranked, after road development ($1,000,000), as the second largest expense item. PANL, GN 38, S 1–2–5, File No. 8, Memorandum by Commissioner of Finance, 6 February 1939.

58. PANL, GN 13/2/A, Box 233, File 106 "Re Suspects (1939)." Their names were listed as Volfs Jacobowitz and Leizers Levims, formerly merchants in Germany. Nothing else is known about their visit.

59. Newfoundland House of Assembly, *Proceedings*, 28 March 1955.

Chapter 6

1. *Evening Telegram*, 8 January 1934.

2. *Ibid.*, 5 December 1939, editorial.

3. Tait went on to explain that "any person representing himself or herself to desire unoccupied Crown land for the purpose of agriculture may apply for a lease . . . and an area not exceeding fifteen acres may be leased to any one person. The lease extends for five years at a rental of one dollar per year and upon the condition that the lessee clears and puts into cultivation ten percent of the area within five years of the date of the lease. Upon proof . . . that these conditions have been complied with, a grant in fee simple of the land will be issued. So, too, a person may acquire by lease unoccupied Crown land for residential purposes. Five acres may be allotted to any one person for a period of five years at a rental of one dollar per year . . . " Tait, *Newfoundland*, 31f, 104ff, 136f.

4. Neary, *Newfoundland*, 65, 85. Noel, 242.

5. O'Brien, 21.

6. I am grateful to Jack Green, Michael Harrington, Gordon Pushie, and George Snelgrove for information about C.E.A. Jeffery. See also *Who's Who in and from Newfoundland 1937* (St. John's, 1937), 193.

7. Morine, "A History of Newfoundland," Chapter XXIII.

8. PANL, P 4/3, Box 1, File 18.

9. Harold Horwood, *Joey: The Life and Times of Joey Smallwood* (Toronto, 1989), 99f.

10. Alison Joanne Kahn, "The Jews of St. John's, Newfoundland: A Rhetorical Approach to a Community Autobiography," M.A. thesis, Memorial University of Newfoundland, 1983, 238ff.

11. NAC, MG 30, E 82, Vol. 18, File 97, "Newfoundland Royal Commission, 39th Day," 18ff, 31.

12. *Observer's Weekly*, 17 December 1935, 28 April and 9 June 1936.

13. *Evening Telegram*, 7 February 1934.

14. *Ibid.*, 27 September; 7, 13, 15, and 28 October 1938.

15. See *Ibid.*, 24 November 1938; *Observer's Weekly*, 29 November 1939.

16. *Daily News* and *Evening Telegram*, 14 July 1939.

17. *Daily News*, 29 September 1939.

18. *Daily News* and *Evening Telegram*, 23 June 1939.

19. *Evening Telegram*, 30 November 1938, 27 February 1939; 23, 26 June, and 25 August 1939. *Observer's Weekly*, 29 November 1938; 20, 27 December 1938.

20. *Evening Telegram*, 2,5,7 and 14 June, 1939.

21. *Daily News*, 3, 6, 7, and 29 June 1939.

22. Herlin, 177.

23. Belkin, 183.

24. *Daily News*, 15 November 1938.

25. Newfoundland, House of Assembly, *Proceedings 1929*, 48–50.

26. Malcolm MacLeod, *A Bridge Built Halfway: A History of Memorial University College, 1925-1950* (Montreal and Kingston, 1990), 89f.

27. PANL, P8/B/11, Box 36, File 35, Hazen A. Russell to C.J. Fox, 28 January 1939.

28. PANL, GN 13/2/A, Box 336, File "Admission of European Immigrants, 1939, Retain," 12 April 1938.

Chapter 7

1. PANL, GN 1/3/A, 1934, No. 303–323, F. 316/34.

2. PANL, GN 13/2/A, Box 227, File "Re: Immigration," Howley to Trentham, 14 May 1934.

3. PANL, GN 13/2/A, Box 227, File "Immigration."

4. Editorial, "Mr. Justice Dunfield," *Evening Telegram*, 2 November 1939.

5. *Ibid.*, Memorandum for Hon. Sir John Hope Simpson, 1 April 1935.

6. For this and Thomas Lodge's characterization of Dunfield see Neary, *Newfoundland*, 69, 80, 95, 120.

7. Personal interview. Interviewee's name withheld by request.

8. PANL, GN 13/2/A, Box 227, File "Re: Immigration." It could not be ascertained whether these two fiancées were allowed to enter.

9. PANL, P8/B/11, Box 30, File 7 and Box 32, File 38.

10. *Ibid.*, Box 36, File 35.

11. Neary, *Newfoundland*, 45, 66, 354.

12. PANL, GN 38, S 4-1-5, No. J.24-'38, confidential memorandum "Immigration and Deportation," 11 April 1938.

13. PANL, GN 13/2/A, Box 336, File "Admission of European Immigrants, 1939, Retain.," memorandum submitted by the Commissioner for Finance, 12 April 1938.

14. PANL, GN 38, S 1-1-2, No. 199-'39 J.24-'38.

15. PRO, DO 35/720, File M651/2.

16. The proposed substitution for Section 12 of the 1926 Act reads: "The Governor in Commission may by Proclamation or order whenever he deems it necessary or expedient . . . prohibit or limit in number for a stated period or permanently the landing in Newfoundland . . . of immigrants belonging to any nationality or race or of immigrants of any specified class or occupation, by reason of any economic, industrial or other condition temporarily existing in Newfoundland or because such immigrants are deemed unsuitable having regard to the climatic, industrial, social, educational, labour or other conditions or requirements of Newfoundland or because such immigrants are

deemed undesirable owing to their peculiar customs, habits, modes of life and methods of holding property, or because of their probable inability to become readily assimilated or to assume the duties and responsibilities of Newfoundland citizenship within a reasonable time after their entry." PANL, GN 13/2/A, Box 336, File "Admission of European Immigrants to Nfld, 1939, Retain."

17. PANL, GN 1/3/A, 1934, No. 316.

18. PRO, DO 35/720, File M651/5.

19. PANL, GN 1/3/A, 1938, Nos. 111–302A, File "Passports – Abolition of Visas, Austria." GN 13/2/A, Box 336, File "Admission of European Immigrants . . ."

20. PANL, GN 1/3/A, 1939, No. 316, and GN 1/3/A, 1938, Nos. 11–302A. According to a German decree of 7 October 1938 all German passports belonging to Jews of German nationality who resided in the British Empire became invalid. Holders of such passports were required to hand in their passports to the local German passport authority in the district where they were staying. Failure to comply with this decree within a specified time was declared a punishable offence.

21. PRO, DO 35/720/M651/5.

22. PANL, P8/B/11, Box 36, File 35, Secretary [Renouf] to Penson, 22 April 1939.

23. *Ibid.*, Price to Renouf, 29 April 1939.

24. *Evening Telegram*, 6 May 1939. *Observer's Weekly*, 9 May 1939.

25. PANL, GN 13/2/A, Box 336, File "Admission of European Immigrants . . . ," memorandum "Immigration from Europe," 26 October 1938.

26. PANL, P8/B/11, Box 36, File 35, "Immigration," undated.

27. GN 13/2/A, Box 413, File "Aliens No. 1." *Evening Telegram*, 16 August 1938. *Daily News*, 16 and 18 August 1938.

28. PANL, GN 1/3/A, 1934, Nos. 303–323.

29. PRO, DO 35/706, File M529/132. PANL, GN 1/3/A, 1939, Nos. 5–17, File "Immigration into Newfoundland." GN 38, S 1-1-2, No. 250 '39.

30. PANL, GN 1/3/A, 1939, Nos. 5–17, 9/39. GN 2/5, File 731.

31. Bauer, 200, 295. Wyman, *Paper Walls*, 61.

32. PANL, GN 2/5, File 731.

33. PANL, GN 13/2/A, Box 233, File 118.

34. PANL, GN 1/3/A, 1939, Nos. 5–17, File "Immigration into Newfoundland."

35. PANL, GN 13/2/A, Box 233, File 118.

36. *Ibid.*, Penson to Winter & Higgins, 23 June 1938.

37   *Ibid.*, Winter & Higgins to Carew, 25 October 1938.

38   *Ibid.*, Assistant Secretary for Justice to Chairman Board of Customes, 17 November 1938.

39. PRO, DO 35/720, File M 652/7.

40. PANL, GN 1/3/A, 1939, Nos. 5–7, Chief Commissioner of Immigration to Mrs. R.R. Zuber, 8 July 1939.

41. PRO, DO 35/720, File M 652/7, comment signed "PAC," 26 July 1939.

42. PANL, GN 13/2/A, Box 134, File 9.

43. PANL, GN 38, S 7–1–2, memorandum "Application of Refugees from Central Europe," 2 May 1939. PRO, DO35/706, File M529/132.

44. PANL, GN 13, Box 38, File 88. David S. Zlatin, "The Administrative History of the Jewish Community in St. John's: Synagogue and Education," Special Project Report, Memorial University of New-foundland, 1978, 11.

45. PANL, GN 13/2/A, Box 193, File 69, and Box 337, File 40. GN 38, S 1–1–2: Meeting of 23 March 1939. GN 38, S 6–1–2, File 12. Ilka D. Dickman, *Appointment to Newfoundland* (Manhattan, Kansas, 1981), 15.

46. On 30 December 1938 the Secretary for Public Health and Welfare H.D. Mosdell wrote to Commissioner J.C. Puddester that "for the past four months the Overseas Nursing Association, London, have been endeavouring to recruit fifteen nurses for our service. During that period they have been able to secure only three nurses and of these one had already spent the usual contractual term in this country. It appears obvious that the organisation is finding it very difficult to supply our needs in this respect . . . Several nursing districts have had to be left unfilled although the people concerned were organised for the support of the service. We have not been able to supply the requisite nurses." PANL, GN 13/2/A, Box 337, File 40.

47. PANL, GN 1/3/A, 1939, File 9/39, Nos. 5–17, Governor to H.M. British Consul General, 17 August 1939.

48. Bauer, 202. Grossmann, 156–161. *Evening Telegram*, 4 April 1939; 18 June 1987.

49. Abella and Troper, vi.

Chapter 8

1.   PANL, GN 1/3/A, 1938, No. 694 (2), File "German Internees." NAC, RG 25, Vol. 2761, File 621-K-40C. PRO, DO 35/996, File 19/11, undated memorandum "Internees."

2.   *Ibid.*, No. 694, File "Aliens—Treatment of." GN 13/2/A, Box 413, File "Aliens No. 1."

3. Ernst R. Deutsch, personal interview (St. John's), 25 November 1983.

4. The phenomenon of the fifth column scare, its foundations and ubiquity, are analyzed in Louis de Jong, *The German Fifth Column in the Second World War* (Chicago, 1956). The term "fifth column" originated during the Spanish Civil War and is usually ascribed to the Falangist General Emilio Mola. Asked which of the four columns converging on Madrid he expected to capture the city, he is supposed to have replied "the fifth column," meaning organized sympathizers within the Spanish capital. During World War II the "fifth column" became the standard designation for alleged Nazi sympathizers acting as agents and saboteurs for the cause of the Third Reich.

5. Eric Koch, *Deemed Suspect: A Wartime Blunder* (Toronto, 1980). Miriam Kochan, *Britain's Internees in the Second World War* (London, 1983). Bernard Wasserstein, *Britain and the Jews of Europe 1939–1945* (Oxford, 1979). Peter and Leni Gillman, *"Collar the Lot!" How Britain Interned and Expelled its Wartime Refugees* (London, 1980).

6. Winston S. Churchill, *The Second World War*, vol. II (London, 1949), 561, as quoted by Wasserstein, 96; Koch, 27 and Gillman, 63.

7. PANL, GN 1/3/A, 1938, No. 694 (2), File "German Internees." NAC, Rg 25, G 2, Vol. 2397, File 698–40C.

8. Deutsch interview. He was able to read the *Sobieski's* Morse signal to the convoy: "We are going to St. John's."

9. See Karin Gürttler, "Henry Kreisel: A Canadian Exile Writer?" in Walter E. Riedel, ed., *The Old World and the New: Literary Perspectives of German-speaking Canadians* (Toronto, 1984), 94–106.

10. Jones, 19–21.

11. PANL, GN 13/2/A, Box 413, File "Aliens No.2."

12. *Ibid.*, File "Aliens No.1."

13. On conditions on the *Sobieski* and the anti-Semitism of its crew, see Kochan, 93ff; Ted Jones, *Both Sides of the Wire: The Fredericton Internment Camp*, vol. I (Fredericton, 1988), 21.

14. Koch, 75f, 95f. Gillman, 204ff, 238ff. Paula Jean Draper, "The Accidental Immigrants: Canada and the Interned Refugees," *Canadian Jewish Historical Society Journal*, II:1–2 (1978), 1–38, 80–112.

15. PRO, DO 35/996, File PW19/1/82, Report by Alexander Paterson, July 1941, p. 4.

16. Wasserstein, 96ff.

17. NAC, RG 25, Vol. 2761, File 621–K–40 C, Massey to "my dear Secretary of State," 22 July 1940. PANL, GN 1/3/A, 1938, Nr. 694 (2), File "German Internees."

18. PRO, DO 35/996, File PW19/82, Memorandum 5 October 1940.

19. David MacKenzie, *Inside the Atlantic Triangle: Canada and the Entrance of Newfoundland into Confederation* (Toronto, 1986), 44ff, 51ff.

20. PRO, DO 35/996, File PW19/84; Paul Bridle, ed., *Documents on Relations Between Canada and Newfoundland*, vol. 1, 1935–1949 (Ottawa, 1974), 216–37, 1388. PANL, GN 1/3/A, No. 694 (2), File "German Internees."

21. A code name for Red Rock Camp, near Nipigon, Ontario.

22. NAC, RG 25, G 2, Vol. 2397, File 698–40 C, ANR to Skelton, 9 November 1940. PRO, DO 35/996, File PW19/84.

23. PANL, GN 1/3/A, 1938, No. 694(2), File "German Internees."

24. Bridle, 171, 174, 182. PANL, GN 1/3/A, 1938, No. 694(2), File "German Internees."

25. PANL, GN 1/3/A, 1938, No. 694(2). GN 1/3/A, 1941, 1/41, File "Internees." GN 13, Vol. 1, File 34.

26. Bridle, 182. PRO, DO 35/996, File PW 19/3/7.

27. PANL, GN 1/3/A, 1941, 1/41, File "Internees."

28. PRO, DO 35/996, File PW19/3/7.

29. NAC, RG 25, G 2, Vol. 2397, File 698–40 C.

30. Canadian Jewish Congress Archives, Montreal (CJC/M), Internee Files, Memorandum by S. Goldner, 12 March 1941. I am grateful to Paula J. Draper, Toronto, for making these files available to me.

31. CJC/M, Internee Files, Coordinating Officer [Raphael] to Paterson, 12 June 1941, and undated memorandum "Immigration into the U.S.A. of Refugees Interned in Canada."

32. PRO, DO 35/996, File PW19/1/82. PANL, GN 38, S4-2-1, File 1.

33. CJC/M, Internee Files, Memorandum by S. Goldner, 12 March 1941.

34. PANL, GN 38, S4-2-1, File 1.

35. *Ibid.*

36. CJC/M, Internee Files, Raphael to Razovsky, 28 June 1941; Raphael to Lewis, 23 September 1941. PRO, DO 35/996, File PW 19/1/82, Paterson Report, 9.

37. PANL, GN 38, S 4-2-1, File 1. GN 13/2/A, Box 26, File 5. Gillman, 271–274.

38. PRO, DO 35/996, File PW19/1/82, Paterson Report, 10.

39. *Ibid.*, 18.

40. Karin R. Gürttler, "Exilschriftsteller in Kanada," in John M. Spalek and Joseph Strelka, eds., *Deutschsprachige Exilliteratur seit 1933*, vol. II (Bern, 1989), 1206.

41. Koch, 257f.

Chapter 9

1. *Evening Telegram*, 23 September 1940, editorial.

2. Defence Regulation 33 of 1 September 1939, for instance, declared taking a picture, sketch or other representation of any military work, or any dock or harbor work (defined as including "lights, buoys, beacons, marks and other things for the purpose of facilitating navigation in or into a harbour") without lawful authority, a punishable offence. Regulation 35 declared anyone guilty of an offence who "is upon any railway, or on, under or near any pier, wharf, bridge, viaduct or culvert, or loiters on or in any road or path or other place near a railway, pier, wharf, bridge, viaduct or culvert, with intent to do injury thereof [sic]." If a question arose as to whether a person affected by any such Regulation was an alien or not, article 4 of the Defence Act provided that "the onus of proving that person is not an alien . . . shall be upon that person." *Acts of the Honourable Commission of Government of Newfoundland 1939* (St. John's, 1939), 201.

3. Regulation 31, for example, made it an offence to "display any light or ignite or otherwise make use of any fireworks or other similar device or any fire in such a manner as could serve as a signal, guide, or landmark." Regulation 43 authorized the Governor or the Commissioner of Justice to "arrest without warrant any person whose behaviour is of such a nature as to give reasonable grounds for suspecting that he has acted, or is acting, or is about to act in a manner prejudicial to the public safety or the defence of the Island, or upon whom may be found any article, book, letter or other document, the possession which gives ground for such a suspicion, or who is suspected of having committed an offence against these Regulations."

4. *Regulations*, XIV, XXVIII, XXIX

5. It was feared that Czechoslovak employees of these branch firms might be used through pressure on their relatives in Nazi-controlled Czechoslovakia.

6. PANL, GN 1/3/A, 1939, No. 5–17, File "Fifth Column Activities." GN 1/3/A, 1938, Nos. 694(2) and (3).

7. PANL, GN 13/2/A, Box 42, File "Fifth Column."

8. *Ibid.*, 12 September 1939.

9. The 1935 Census counted 16 German nationals, but after the outbreak of the war the police found only 8 German nationals, plus 5 Austrians and one Czech.

10. According to the 1935 census these numbered 649, 420 of them were Americans and 117 Chinese nationals.

11. PANL, GN 13/2/A, Box 413, Files "Aliens No.1" and "Aliens No.2."

12. Letter from Rev. Clifford Knowles, 12 July 1989.

13. *Evening Telegram*, 10, 21, 22, 23, 31 May, 3 July 1940.

14. *Ibid.*, 4 June, 4, 5, 6, 8 July, 1 August 1940.

15. CJC/M, Internee Files, S. Goldner to Central Committee for Interned Refugees, 12 March 1941.

16. PANL. GN 13/2/A, Box 413, File "Aliens No.2."

17. See Douglas How, *Night of the Caribou* (Hantsport, N.S., 1988). Harold Horwood, *A History of the Newfoundland Ranger Force* (St. John's, 1986), 107, suggests that "the *Caribou* was a legitimate target for submarine attack, because she was used as a troop carrier."

18. German naval strategists assigned higher priorities to objectives in mid-Atlantic and along the Canadian and American coasts. See Great Britain, Ministry of Defence (Navy), *German Naval History: The U-Boat War in the Atlantic, 1939-1945*, compiled by Gunter Hessler, 3 vols. (London, 1989), vol. I, 75ff; vol. II, 2ff, 37, 51f, 56, 67, 105; vol. III, 7f, 32, 59, 81, 83. Michael L. Hadley, *U-Boats against Canada: German Submarines in Canadian Waters* (Kingston and Montreal, 1985). Dan van der Vat, *The Atlantic Campaign: World War II's Great Struggle at Sea* (New York, 1988). Jürgen Rohwer, *Axis Submarine Successes 1939-1945* (Annapolis, 1983).

19. Hadley, 112-143.

20. See, e.g., Wolfgang Hirschfeld, *Feindfahrten: Das Logbuch eines U-Boot Funkers* (Munich 1982), 191, 132-304.

21. According to the count by John C. Cardoulis, *Evening Telegram*, 27 July 1991.

22. Neary, *Newfoundland*, 126-168.

23. See Marc Milner, *North Atlantic Run: The Royal Canadian Navy and the Battle for the Convoys* (Toronto, 1985); James A. Boutilier, ed., *The RCN in Retrospect, 1910-1968* (Vancouver, 1982), chapters IX–XII. James Gerard Lynch, "Negotiations Leading Up to the Establishment of Canadian Bases in Newfoundland, 1936-1942," B.A. Honours thesis, Memorial University of Newfoundland, 1980, 31-44.

24. Hadley, 116, notes that the sinkings off Bell Island "kindled the same flames of unrest in Newfoundland as those in the St. Lawrence River and Gulf had done in Quebec . . . U-513's successful attacks, in the words of FONF's operations officer, had provoked 'a clamor for protection from outlying ports out of all proportion to their value in the strategic plan as a whole.'"

25. *Evening Telegram*, 14 February and 3 July 1940.

26. PANL, GN 38, S 4-2-1, File 1. Limited freedom of movement was restored to tourists in May 1941, when the Tourist Board feared the loss of Newfoundland's American tourist connections. Commissioner for Public Utilities W.W. Woods noted that a round-tripper tourist (i.e., one who departs on the same vessel on which he arrives) "who has to stay on board while the ship is in harbour because he has no passport

and visa is not likely to feel well disposed towards Newfoundland when he reaches home."

27. PANL, GN 13/2/A, Box 75, File "1940—Minutes of Meeting."

28. CJC/M, Internee Files, Memorandum by S. Goldner, 12 March 1941, p.7.

29. A world renowned Austrian knitting goods and textile manufacturer compelled to leave Austria, Bernhard Altmann applied for and was granted permission in February 1941 to enter Newfoundland with a number of his relatives to start a knitting industry. He never visited the island. See PANL, GN 13, Box 38, File 9.

30. In January 1939 Penson had cabled to the Dominions Office that "rule adopted here has been that qualifications necessary in case of Newfoundland should be similar to those required if immigrant in question would be allowed to practice in Great Britain." PANL, GN 1/3/A, 1939, Nos. 5–17, File "Immigration into Newfoundland," telegram by Governor to Secretary of State for Dominion Affairs, 11 January 1939.

31. PANL, GN 1/3/A, 1939, No. 5-17, File "Immigration into Newfoundland."

32. *Ibid.*

33. *Hans Meier Tells His Story to a Friend.* Printed in commemoration of the Golden Wedding of Hans and Margrit Meier, May 11, 1979 (Ulster Park, N.Y., 1979), 19–21.

34. PANL, GN 1/3/A, 1939, Nos. 5–17, File "Immigration into Newfoundland."

35. Hans Meier, personal interview (New Harmony, Indiana), 30 September 1989. *Hans Meier*, 21–36. See also Margot Granitsas, "Erst in Amerika fanden sie den Frieden: Der lange Weg der Hutterer von der Rhön bis nach Woodcrest im Staat New York," *Frankfurter Allgemeine Zeitung*, 13 June 1991.

36. PANL, GN 13/2/A, Box 38, File 58.

37. PANL, GN 13/2/A, Box 290, File "Swirsky, Abraham." A police inspector interviewed Swirsky in Corner Brook on 11 March 1940 and reported that on Swirsky's passport "his occupation is shown as a labourer, but he explained to me that labourer covers every trade in Palestine, he also produced a certificate which is written in Hebrew and which he claims is the certificate of a teacher."

38. "Mr. P.B. Wallheimer Reports on Peat Bogs," *Daily News*, 30 November 1939.

39. See Abella and Troper, 7–10, and *passim*.

40. PANL, GN 13/2/A, Box 39, File 59.

41. *Ibid.*, File 104.

42. *Ibid.*, File 105. Emerson revealed to Secretary for Justice L.B. Summers that he found out about Donnersmarck from Penson whose uncle nearly joined one of Donnersmarck's syndicates. About Graf Henckel von Donnersmarck see also Hermann von Freeden, "Ein Beitrag zur Geschichte der Judenauswanderung aus Deutschland," 9.

43. *Evening Telegram*, 19 December 1939, and 10, 17, 21 May 1940.

44. PANL, GN 13/2/A, Box 431, File: "Letters from Maurice Metal to his family."

45. For instance, Metal was observed cutting wood for a variety of purposes—pulpwood, firewood, sawlogs and pitprops—so he could use every crooked piece and avoid waste. He was the only logging operator known in the Salmonier area who burnt the twigs and scaled branches in the area to allow rapid reforestation. For starting fires in wet woods, Metal used little square sections of charcoal, a technique unknown in Newfoundland at the time.

46. Personal interviews in St. Joseph's, Salmonier, with Jack J. McCormack, 18 December 1988; Larry Daley, 17 December 1988, Charlie Daley, 28 December 1989; Peter Furey, 20 October 1990.

47. PANL, GN 13/2/A, Box 39, File 105, Emerson to Summers, 25 February 1940. Gorvin was relieved of his reponsibilities as a Commissioner in April 1941 at the request of Governor Walwyn. See Neary, *Newfoundland*, 124.

48. PANL, GN 1/3/A, 1938, No. 694 (2), File "Internees"

49. Jack J. McCormack, St. Joseph's, personal interview, 18 December 1988. PANL, GN 13/2/A, Box 38, Files 104 and 164. GN 13/2/A, Box 443, File "Metal, Julio & Maurice and Sondheimer, Walter E." GN 1/3/A, 1938, No. 694 (2). *Evening Telegram*, 23 May and 5 June 1940.

50. Dickman, *Appointment*, 15.

51. *Ibid.*, 11–49. William J. Dickman, *Stories We Lived* (Washington, D.C.: Corporate Press, 1985), 31–38, 106–110. PANL, GN 13/2/A, Box 38, File 34; and Box 262, File "Deutsch, Ilka."

52. *Ibid.*

53. PANL, GN 13/2/A, Box 404, File "Dr. Josephine Maiwald."

54. PANL, P8/A/34, Newfoundland Medical Board, Register 1894–1973, Vol. 2, No. 429.

55. PANL, GN 13/2/A, Box 227, File "Dr. Wolf Grobin."

56. PANL, GN 2/5/A, File 835. GN 13/2/A, Box 193, File 71; and Box 249, File "Redlich, Dr. Lisbeth Angela Henrietta."

57. PANL, GN 13/2/A, Box 193, File 76; Box 353 #2, File "Wermuth, Eric, George. GN 2/5/A, File 868. GN 38, S 3-1-1, Files 1 and 6. J.J. McCormack, Charlie Daley, and Peter Furey, St. Joseph's, personal interviews, 17, 18 December 1988 and 20 October 1990.

58. PANL, GN 13/2/A, Box 227, File "Health and Welfare Claim against Dr. S. Halasz."

59. PANL, GN 13/2/A, Box 38, File 73; Box 39, File 22; Box 400, File "Rosenfeld, Dr. J.L. & Mrs."

60. See PANL, GN 13/2/A, Box 36, File "Immigration Control 1941."

61. PANL, GN 13/2/A, Box 38, File 88.

62. Personal interview (St. John's), 11 November 1987. Name withheld by request.

63. In August 1940 Gertrud Sara Rawrawag had been advised to come to St. John's and apply to the American consul for the quota from Poland since she was a native of Bromberg which became Polish after World War I. The police report states that a St. John's constable "accompanied her while she was ashore and after her business was finished she was again placed on board ship and will not be allowed ashore." The constable reported to his Chief: "I had some conversation with this woman and she told me that she was treated very badly in Germany, this was prior to the present war, and she made application in 1938 to enter the U.S.A. She also made inquiries about one Max Katz, living on Henry St., St. John's. Upon questioning her as to how she knew this man she informed me that she had corresponded with him while in St. Pierre and would like to meet him, or if not, would I ask him to see her on the ship. I might say that I did neither, and she was conveyed on board ship immediately her business with the American Consul was finished." PANL, GN 13/2/A, Box 39, File 25.

64. *Ibid.*, Box 193, File 69.

65. See for instance *Daily News*, 4 December 1942, 13 August 1943, 8 July 1944, 14 March 1945.

66. According to a report by the Defence Security Officer in July 1943, control was so strict that it would have been "extremely difficult for the enemy to introduce an agent" even into the Portuguese fishing fleet. PANL, GN 38, S 4-1-2, Files 4 and 5, and GN 13/2/A, Box 50, File "Security 1941."

Chapter 10

1. PANL, GN 38, S 7-1-3, "Immigration Policy," memorandum by I. Wild, 8 November 1945.

2. PANL, GN 13/2/A, Box 336, File "Aliens," Howell to Secretary for Justice, 30 January 1947.

3. PANL, GN 38, S 7-1-3, File 1, memoranda "Immigration Policy" by Commissioner of Finance, 17 May and 9 November 1945.

4. PANL, GN 38, S 7-1-3, File 1, "Immigration Policy," by I. Wild, 17 May 1945.

5. PANL, GN 2/5, File 926, "Chinese Naturalization." GN 38, S 7-1-3, File 5, "Immigration of Chinese," memorandum by I. Wild, 9 September 1946.

6. PANL, GN 2/5, File 926, Commissioner for Finance to Commissioner for Home Affairs and Education, 12 February 1947.

7. PANL, GN 2/5, File 926, R.L.M. James to Commissioner for Home Affairs and Education, 19 March 1948; "Naturalization of Chinese," memorandum by H.L. Pottle, 29 March 1948.

8. See PANL, GN 2/5, File 926, memorandum "Naturalization of Chinese," 30 March 1948.

9. PANL, GN 1/3/A, 1938, File 86, "Passports for Chinese Nationals and Stateless Persons in China." GN 2/5, File 926, "Chinese Naturalization."

10. PANL, GN 13/2/A, Box 345, File 48.

11. PANL, GN 13/2/A, Box 345, File 47.

12. *Evening Telegram*, 27 and 28 February 1948.

13. See Gerhard P. Bassler, "Americans as Enemy Suspects in Twentieth-Century Wartime Newfoundland," paper presented to the 15th annual symposium of the Society for German-American Studies, Washington, D.C., 1991.

14. "Canadians in Newfoundland," *Evening Telegram*, 28 January 1948.

15. R.A. MacKay, ed., *Newfoundland: Economic, Diplomatic and Strategic Studies* (Toronto, 1946), 229f.

16. John N. Cardoulis, *A Friendly Invasion: The American Military in Newfoundland, 1940-1990* (St. John's, 1990), 166.

17. Malcolm MacLeod, *Peace of the Continent* (St. John's, 1986), 33.

18. Peter Neary, ed., *The Political Economy of Newfoundland, 1929-1972* (Toronto, 1973), 67.

19. P. Neary and P. O'Flaherty, *Part of the Main: An Illustrated History of Newfoundland and Labrador* (St. John's, 1983), 153.

20. See, e.g., Dirks, *Canada's Refugee Policy*, 122-175. Milda Danys, *DP Lithuanian Immigration to Canada After the Second World War* (Toronto, 1986). Gerhard P. Bassler, "Canadian Postwar Immigration Policy and the Admission of German Enemy Aliens, 1945-50," *Yearbook of German-American Studies*, 22 (1987), 183-197.

21. Personal interviews with Betty and Andreas Barban, St. John's, 20 December 1983, 4 August 1985, 3 February 1986, 24 September and 1 October 1990.

22. "The Wayfarer," *Daily News*, 14 February 1944.

23. Neary, *Newfoundland*, 354.

24. *Ibid.*, 351.

25. It had not assumed any commitments until after World War II. See Dirks, *Canada's Refugee Policy*, 35f, 228–230.

26. Kurt R. Grossmann, the former general secretary of the German League for Human Rights and himself a refugee from the Third Reich, states in his book *Emigration*, 15–16, 215–217, that after the Munich Conference of 1938 the British government authorized a few Jewish organizations to bring refugees into the country "without limiting their number," provided these organizations guaranteed the refugees' accommodation and ultimate resettlement. In 1938, and especially in 1939, thousands of refugees from Czechoslovakia, Austria, and Germany were admitted without much ado into the United Kingdom. In Richboro a transit camp was opened for 3,000 refugees who were received hospitably and assisted in every way possible. The Jewish community of Britain, supported by Christian (Quakers), trade union, pacifist, academic and other groups, have been credited for their extraordinary efforts through organizations such as the British "Inter-Aid Committee of the World Movement for the Care of Children coming from Germany," the "International Christian Committee," the "Society for the Protection of Science and Learning," and the "Emergency Committee for German Scientists." See also chapter II, note 39.

27. See, e.g., the widely used social studies school texts by Frank Cramm and Garfield Fizzard, *The Atlantic Edge: Living in Newfoundland and Labrador* (St. John's, 1986), 18–77; and Keith Matthews, *et al.*, *Our Newfoundland and Labrador Cultural Heritage* (Scarborough, 1984), 56–111.

28. Belkin, 187.

29. Quoted in Neary, *Newfoundland*, 353.

Bibliography

A. MANUSCRIPT SOURCES

American Jewish Archives, Hebrew Union College, Cincinnati. Saul Bernstein, "Report on Prospects for Jewish Colonization in Newfoundland," New York, 1 November 1938.

Bundesarchiv, Koblenz
Länderrat des amerikanischen Besatzungsgebiets (Bestand Z 1)
Committee on Emigration Questions, 1946–1948
Ausschuss für Auswanderungswesen 1945–1949
Aus- und Einwanderungsbestimmungen, Kanada 1947–1949
Auswanderung von Displaced Persons
Hermann von Freeden, "Ein Beitrag zur Geschichte der Judenauswanderung aus Deutschland" (Dec. 1945).

Canadian Jewish Congress Archives, Montreal
Internee Files.

National Archives of Canada, Ottawa
Newfoundland Royal Commission 1933, Evidence (MG 38 E82).
Department of External Affairs (RG 25)
Transfer to Canada of Enemy Internees from the U.K.
Files re Newfoundland (RG 25 G2)
Internment in Newfoundland of German POW

Provincial Archives of Newfoundland and Labrador, St. John's
Governor's Office, Despatches to Colonial Office, 1906–1914.
Governor's Office, Miscellaneous Despatches and Local Correspondence Received, 1904–1939.
Colonial Secretary, Special Subject Files, 1911–1948.
F.C. Alderdice Papers, 1932.
Department of Justice, Departmental files, 1916–1951.
Secretary to the Commission of Government, Minutes of meetings, 1939–1945.
Secretary to the Commission of Government, Papers re immigration, 1938–1939.
Commission of Government, Department of Natural Resources, papers and memoranda, 1934–1945.

Commission of Government, Department of Home Affairs and
Education, Government House correspondence and Private
Secretary's correspondence, 1946.
Commission of Government, Department of Justice and Defence,
memoranda, 1938–1943.
Commission of Government, Department of Justice and Defence,
Papers re defence schemes, 1941.
Commission of Government, Department of Public Utilities,
memoranda, 1939.
Commission of Government, Department of Health and Welfare,
memoranda, 1939.
Commission of Government, Department of Finance, memoranda,
1934–1945.
Commission of Government, Department of Finance, Papers re Customs reorganization, return, entries, and appointments, 1945.
Newfoundland Board of Trade, correspondence, letter books, and
minutes, 1934–39.
Newfoundland Medical Board, Register 1894–1973.
Alfred Bishop Morine, "A History of Newfoundland," unpublished
book manuscript, about 1935.

Public Record Office, London
Dominions Office
Jewish Refugees from Germany: proposed settlement in Labrador,
1936–1939 (DO 35/181).
Newfoundland affairs: quarterly reports, 1934–36 (DO 35/500).
Settlement of Jews in the Dominions: possibilities of Labrador as
a place of settlement, 1938 (DO 35/705).
Settlement of Refugees in the Dominions: settlement in
Newfoundland, 1938–1939 (DO 35/706).
Settlement of Refugees in the Dominions: Jewish immigration
into Newfoundland, 1939 (DO 35/706).
Emigration of political refugees (Jewish or other) from Austria and
Germany to the United Kingdom and Dominions, 1937–1942
(DO 35/716–718).
Newfoundland Immigration Regulations, 1938–1939 (DO 35/720).
Miscellaneous Migration Enquiries—Newfoundland (DO 35/720).
Internees and Prisoners of War in Canada, 1939–1941
(DO 35/996).

Zentrales Staatsarchiv, Potsdam (now: Bundesarchiv, Abteilungen
Potsdam)
Reichsministerium des Innern (15.01)
Auswanderungswesen
Auswanderung nach Kanada
Deutsche Arbeitsfront, Arbeitswissenschaftliches Institut (62 DAF 3)
Ein- und Auswanderung 1919–1939
Zeitungsausschnittsammlung Kanada, 1921–1944
Zeitungsausschnittsammlung Neufundland, 1933–1944

B. INTERVIEWS

Andreas and Betty Barban
Cyril Banikhin
William J. Browne
Pat Brownrigg
Margaret Chang
Charlie Daley
Larry Daley
Ernst Deutsch
George Earles
Hayford Fong
Robert S. Furlong
Peter Furey
Allan Gillingham
John J. Greene
Michael Harrington
Ferd Hayward
Rev. E. Clifford Knowles
Jack J. McCormack
Hans Meier
Augusta Mercer
Gerald Ottenheimer
Gordon F. Pushie
George Snelgrove

C. PUBLISHED PRIMARY SOURCES

Newspapers

Daily News (St. John's)
Deutsche Justiz (Berlin)
Evening Herald (St. John's)
Evening Telegram (St. John's)
Frankfurter Allgemeine Zeitung (Frankfurt am Main)
Metro (St. John's)
New York Times
Observer's Weekly (St. John's)
Survey Geographic (New York)
Times (London)
Western Star (Corner Brook)

Government documents and handbooks

Acts of the General Assembly of Newfoundland. St. John's, 1906, 1924, 1926.

Acts of the Honourable Commission of Government of Newfoundland, 1939

Baedeker, Karl. *The Dominion of Canada with Newfoundland and an Excursion to Alaska: Handbook for Travellers.* Leipzig: Karl Baedeker, 1907.

Bridle, Paul, ed. *Documents on Relations Between Canada and New-foundland*, vol. 1, 1935–1949. Ottawa, 1974.

Census of Newfoundland and Labrador, 1901–1949.

Great Britain, Dominions Royal Commission. *Royal Commission on the Natural Resources, Trade and Legislation of Certain Portions of His Majesty's Dominions, Minutes of Evidence Taken in Newfoundland in 1914*. London, 1915.

Great Britain, Ministry of Defence (Navy). *German Naval History: The U-Boat War in the Atlantic, 1939–1945*. Compiled by Gunter Hessler. Vols. I–III. London, 1989.

Great Britain, Oversea Settlement Office. *Official Statement for the Use of Women Who May Wish to Settle in the Oversea Dominions*. London, 1919.

Mosdell, H.M., comp. *Newfoundland: Its Manifold Attractions for the Capitalist, the Settler and the Tourist*. St. John's. Published by the Direction of the Executive Government of Newfoundland, 1920.

Newfoundland. *Building on Our Strengths: Report of the Royal Commission on Employment and Unemployment*. St. John's, 1986.

Newfoundland, House of Assembly. *Proceedings*, 1924–1929, 1955.

Province of Newfoundland. *Report of the Royal Commission on Forestry, 1955*. St. John's, 1955.

Prowse, D.W. *The Newfoundland Guide Book*, Third Edition. London, 1911.

Tait, Robert H. *Newfoundland: A Summary of the History and Development of Britain's Oldest Colony from 1497 to 1939*. New York, 1939.

Who's Who in and from Newfoundland 1937. St. John's, 1937.

Memoirs and autobiographic literature

Arnold, Emmy. *Gegen den Strom: Das Werden der Bruderhöfe*. Moers, 1983.

Arnold, Emmy. *Torches Together*. Rifton, N.Y., 1964.

Belkin, Simon. *Through Narrow Gates: A Review of Jewish Immigration, Colonization and Immigrant Aid Work in Canada, 1840–1940*. Montreal, 1966.

Bentwich, Norman. "The Destruction of the Jewish Community in Austria 1938–1942," in Josef Fraenkel, ed., *The Jews of Austria: Essays on their Life, History and Destruction*. London, 1967.

Benz, Wolfgang, ed., *Das Tagebuch der Helga Nathorff. Berlin-New York: Aufzeichnungen 1933–1945*. Munich, 1987.

Browne, Rev. P.W. *Where the Fishers Go: The Story of Labrador*. New York, 1909.

Burckhardt, Carl J. *Meine Danziger Mission 1937–1939*. Munich, 1960.

Butcher, Wilfred F. "Inertia in Newfoundland," *Canadian Forum*, XX (November 1940), 245–246.

Chang, Margaret. *Chinese Handbook, Newfoundland 1978.* St. John's, 1978.

Churchill, Winston S. *The Second World War,* vol. II. London, 1949.

Deutschkron, Inge. *Ich trug den gelben Stern.* Cologne, 1978.

Devine, P.K. *In the Good Old Days.* St. John's, 1990.

Dickman, Ilka D. *Appointment to Newfoundland.* Manhattan, Kansas, 1981.

Dickman, William J. *Stories We Lived.* Washington, D.C., 1985.

Grossmann, Kurt R. *Emigration: Geschichte der Hitler Flüchtlinge 1933-1945.* Frankfurt am Main, 1969.

Herlin, Hans. *"Kein gelobtes Land:" Die Irrfahrt der St. Louis.* Hamburg, 1961.

Hirschfeld, Wolfgang. *Feindfahrten: Das Logbuch eines U-Boot Funkers.* Munich 1982.

Koch, Eric. *Deemed Suspect: A Wartime Blunder.* Toronto, 1980.

Lodge, Thomas. "Newfoundland Today," *International Affairs,* XIV:5 (1935).

Meier, Hans. *Hans Meier Tells His Story to a Friend.* Ulster Park, N.Y., 1979.

Palmer, C.H. *The Salmon Rivers of Newfoundland: A Descriptive Account of the Various Rivers of the Island.* St. John's, 1928.

Rubinek, Saul. *So Many Miracles.* Markham, Ont., 1988.

Tocque, Rev. Philip. *Newfoundland: As it was, and as it is in 1877.* Toronto, 1878.

Von Lang, Jochen, ed. *Eichmann Interrogated: Transcripts from the Archives of the Israeli Police.* New York, 1984.

Zadek, Wolfgang, ed. *Sie flohen vor dem Hakenkreuz. Selbstzeugnisse der Emigranten. Ein Lesebuch für Deutsche.* Reinbek, 1981.

D. BOOKS, ARTICLES, AND THESES

Abella, Irving, and Harold Troper. *None Is Too Many: Canada and the Jews of Europe, 1933-1948.* Toronto, 1983.

Alexander, David. *Atlantic Canada and Confederation: Essays in Canadian Political Economy.* Toronto, 1983.

_____ "Newfoundland's Traditional Economy and Development to 1934," in James Hiller and Peter Neary, eds., *Newfoundland in the Nineteenth and Twentieth Centuries: Essays in Interpretation* (Toronto, 1980), 17-39.

_____ "Development and Dependence in Newfoundland, 1880-1970," *Acadiensis,* IV:1 (1974), 3-31.

_____ "Literacy and Economic Development in Nineteenth Century Newfoundland," in *ibid.,* 110-142.

Avery, Donald. *"Dangerous Foreigners:" European Immigrant Workers and Labour Radicalism in Canada, 1896-1932.* Toronto, 1979.

Baker, Melvin, et al. *The Illustrated History of Newfoundland Light and Power*. St. John's, 1990.

Bartrop, Paul, ed., *The Dunera Affair: A Documentary Resource Book*. South Yarra and Melbourne, 1990.

_____ "Enemy Aliens or Stateless Persons? The Legal Status of Refugees from Germany in Wartime Australia," *Journal of the Australian Jewish Historical Society*, X:4 (November 1988), 270–280.

_____ "'Good Jews' and 'bad Jews': Australian perceptions of Jewish migrants and refugees, 1919–1939," in *Jews in the Sixth Continent* (Sydney, 1987), 169–184.

Bassler, Gerhard P. "Americans as Enemy Suspects in Twentieth-Century Wartime Newfoundland," paper presented to the 15th annual symposium of the Society for German-American Studies, Washington, D.C., 1991.

_____ "Newfoundland's 'Dangerous' Internees Who Never Were: The History of Victoria Camp," *Newfoundland Studies*, V:1 (1989), 39–51.

_____ "Attempts to Settle Jewish Refugees in Newfoundland and Labrador, 1934–1939," *Simon Wiesenthal Center Annual*, V (1988), 121–144.

_____ "The Enemy Alien Experience in Newfoundland 1914–1918," *Canadian Ethnic Studies*, XX:3 (1988), 42–62.

_____ "Canadian Postwar Immigration Policy and the Admission of German Enemy Aliens, 1945–50," *Yearbook of German -American Studies*, 22 (1987), 183–197.

_____ "Newfoundland and Refugees from the Third Reich, 1934–1941," *Newfoundland Studies*, III:1 (1987), 37–70.

_____ "Central European Immigrants in St. John's, Newfoundland: Immigration and Adjustment," *Canadian Ethnic Studies*, XVIII:3 (1986).

_____ "Auswanderungsfreiheit und Auswandererfürsorge in Württemberg 1815–1855: Zur Geschichte der südwestdeutschen Massenwanderung nach Nordamerika," *Zeitschrift für württembergische Landesgeschichte*, XXXIII (1976), 117–160.

Battenberg, Friedrich. *Das europäische Zeitalter der Juden: Zur Entwicklung einer Minderheit in der nichtjüdischen Umwelt Europas*. Darmstadt, 1990.

Bauer, Yehuda. *American Jewry and the Holocaust: The American Jewish Joint Distribution Committee, 1939–1945*. Detroit, 1981.

Beach, Charles M., and Alan G. Green. *Policy Forum on the Role of Immigration in Canada's Future*. Kingston, 1988.

Bennett, Margaret. *The Last Stronghold: Scottish Gaelic Traditions in Newfoundland*. St. John's, 1988.

Benz, Wolfgang, ed. *Die Juden in Deutschland, 1933-1945: Ein Leben unter nationalsozialistischer Herrschaft*. Munich, 1988.

Berghahn, Marion. *German-Jewish Refugees in England: The Ambiguities of Assimilation*. London, 1984.

Betcherman, Lita-Rose. *The Swastika and the Maple Leaf: Fascist Movements in Canada During the Thirties*. Toronto, 1975.

Blakeney, M. *Australia and Jewish Refugees, 1933-1948*. Sydney, 1985.

Boutilier, James A., ed. *The RCN in Retrospect, 1910-1968*. Vancouver, 1982.

Breitman, Richard, and Alan M. Kraut. *American Refugee Policy and European Jewry, 1933-1945*. Bloomington and Indianapolis, 1987.

Cardoulis, John N. *A Friendly Invasion: The American Military in Newfoundland, 1940-1990*. St. John's, 1990.

Carsten, F.L. *The Origins of Prussia*. London, 1954.

Chafe, Edward-Vincent. "A New Life on 'Uncle Sam's Farm:' Newfoundlanders in Massachusetts, 1846-1859," M.A. thesis, Memorial University of Newfoundland, 1982.

Chamberlin, William Henry. *The German Phoenix*. London, 1964.

Chambers, Robert. "Hidden Losers? The Impact of Rural Refugees and Refugee Programs on Poorer Hosts," *International Migration Review*, 20 (1986), 245-263.

Chinard, Gilbert. *Les Réfugiés Huguenots en Amerique*. Paris, 1925.

Clark, Jane Perry. *The Deportation of Aliens from the United States to Europe*. New York, 1931.

Cramm, Frank, and Garfield Fizzard. *The Atlantic Edge: Living in Newfoundland and Labrador*. St. John's, 1986.

Crawley, Ron. "Off to Sydney: Newfoundlanders Emigrate to Industrial Cape Breton, 1890-1914," *Acadiensis*, XVII:2 (1988), 27-51.

Danys, Milda. *DP Lithuanian Immigration to Canada After the Second World War*. Toronto, 1986.

Dawidowicz, Lucy S. *The War Against the Jews 1933-1945*. New York, 1975.

de Jong, Louis. *The German Fifth Column in the Second World War*. Chicago, 1956.

de Mildt, Dick. "Kollaboration und Deportation in Holland," in Jörg Wollenberg, ed., *"Niemand war dabei und keiner hat's gewußt": Die deutsche Öffentlichkeit und die Judenverfolgung 1933-1945* (Munich, 1989), 224-233.

Dirks, Gerald E. "The Plight of the Homeless: the Refugee Phenomenon," *Behind the Headlines*, XXXVIII:3 (August 1980), 1-26.

_____ *Canada's Refugee Policy: Indifference or Opportunism?* Montreal and London, 1977.

Döscher, Hans-Jürgen. *"Reichskristallnacht:" Die Novemberpogrome 1938.* Frankfurt/M, 1990.

Dowry, Alan. *Closed Borders: The Contemporary Assault on the Freedom of Movement.* New Haven and London, 1987.

Draper, Paula Jean. "The Accidental Immigrants: Canada and the Interned Refugees," Ph.D. thesis, University of Toronto, 1983.

_____ "The Accidental Immigrants: Canada and the Interned Refugees," *Canadian Jewish Historical Society Journal,* II:1–2 (1978), 1–38, 80–112.

Economic Council of Canada. *New Faces in the Crowd: Economic and Social Impacts of Immigration.* Ottawa, 1991.

England, Robert. *The Central European Immigrant in Canada.* Toronto, 1929.

Feingold, Henry L. *The Politics of Rescue: The Roosevelt Administration and the Holocaust, 1938–1945.* New Brunswick, N.J., 1970.

Firestone, Melvin M. "Mummers and Strangers in Northern Newfoundland," in Herbert Halpert and G.M. Story, eds., *Christmas Mumming in Newfoundland* (Toronto, 1969), 62–75.

Fitzgerald, Jack. *Strange but True Newfoundland Stories.* St. John's, 1989.

Fraenkel, Josef, ed. *The Jews of Austria: Essays on their Life, History and Destruction.* London, 1967.

Fraser, C.F. *Control of Aliens in the British Commonwealth of Nations.* London, 1940.

Gainer, Bernard. *The Alien Invasion: The Origins of the Aliens Act of 1905.* London, 1972.

Gilad, Lisa. *The Northern Route: An Ethnography of Refugee Experiences.* St. John's, 1990.

Gillman, Peter and Leni. *"Collar the Lot!" How Britain Interned and Expelled its Wartime Refugees.* London, 1980.

Gordon, Sarah. *Hitler, Germans and the "Jewish" Question.* Princeton, 1984.

Granitsas, Margot. "Erst in Amerika fanden sie den Frieden: Der lange Weg der Hutterer von der Rhön bis nach Woodcrest im Staat New York," *Frankfurter Allgemeine Zeitung,* 13 June 1991.

Gürttler, Karin R. "Exilschriftsteller in Kanada," in John M. Spalek and Joseph Strelka, eds. *Deutschsprachige Exilliteratur seit 1933.* Vol. II (Bern, 1989), 1202–1256.

_____ "Henry Kreisel: A Canadian Exile Writer?" in Walter E. Riedel, ed., *The Old World and the New: Literary Perspectives of German-speaking Canadians* (Toronto, 1984), 94–106.

Hadley, Michael L. *U-Boats against Canada: German Submarines in Canadian Waters.* Kingston and Montreal, 1985.

Halpert, Herbert, and G.M. Story, eds. *Christmas Mumming in Newfoundland: Essays in Anthropology, Folklore, and History.* Toronto, 1969.

Heilbut, Anthony. *Exiled in Paradise: German Refugee Artists and Intellectuals in America from the 1930s to the Present.* Boston, 1983.

Higham, John. *Strangers in the Land.* New York, 1955.

Hilberg, Raul. *The Destruction of the European Jews.* Chicago, 1961.

Holborn, Louise W. *Refugees: A Problem of Our Time. The Work of the UN High Commissioner for Refugees, 1951-1972.* Metuchen, N.J., 1975.

Hong, Robert G. "'To take action without delay': Newfoundland's Chinese Immigration Act of 1906," Honours thesis, Memorial University of Newfoundland, 1987.

Horwood, Harold. *Joey: The Life and Times of Joey Smallwood.* Toronto, 1989.

_____ *A History of the Newfoundland Ranger Force.* St. John's, 1986.

How, Douglas. *Night of the Caribou.* Hantsport, N.S., 1988.

Jersch-Wenzel, Stefi. "Ein importiertes Ersatzbürgertum? Die Bedeutung der Hugenotten für die Wirtschaft Brandenburg-Preussens," in R. von Thadden and M. Magdelaine, eds., *Die Hugenotten, 1685-1985* (Munich, 1985), 160-171.

Jones, Maldwyn Allen. *American Immigration.* Chicago, 1960.

Jones, Ted. *Both Sides of the Wire: The Fredericton Internment Camp,* vol. I. Fredericton, 1988.

Kahn, Alison. *Listen While I Tell You: The Story of the Jews of St. John's, Newfoundland.* St. John's, 1987.

_____ "The Jews of St. John's, Newfoundland: A Rhetorical Approach to a Community Autobiography," M.A. thesis, Memorial University of Newfoundland, 1983,

Keller, Stephen L. *Uprooting and Social Change: The Role of Refugees in Development.* New Delhi, 1975.

Kerr, Kenneth J. "A Social Analysis of the Members of the Newfoundland House of Assembly, Executive Council, and Legislative Council for the Period, 1855-1914," M.A. thesis, Memorial University of Newfoundland, 1973,

Kochan, Miriam. *Britain's Internees in the Second World War.* London, 1983.

Krausnick, Helmut, *et al. Anatomy of the SS State.* New York, 1968.

Laqueur, Walter. *A History of Zionism.* New York, 1988.

Lauber, Heinz. *Judenpogrom: "Reichskristallnacht" November 1938 in Grossdeutschland.* Gerlingen, 1981.

Levitt, Cyril H., and William Shaffir. *The Riot at Christie Pits*. Toronto, 1987.

Lynch, James Gerard. "Negotiations Leading Up to the Establishment of Canadian Bases in Newfoundland, 1936-1942," B.A. Honours thesis, Memorial University of Newfoundland, 1980.

Mackay, R.A., ed. *Newfoundland: Economic, Diplomatic and Strategic Studies*. Toronto, 1946.

MacKenzie, David. *Inside the Atlantic Triangle: Canada and the Entrance of Newfoundland into Confederation*. Toronto, 1986.

MacLeod, Malcolm. *A Bridge Built Halfway: A History of Memorial University College, 1925-1950*. Montreal and Kingston, 1990.

_____ *Peace of the Continent*. St. John's, 1986.

_____ "Labrador For Sale—27% Off," *The Newfoundland Quarterly*, LXXV:2 (Fall 1979), 13-14.

Mannion, John J., ed. *The Peopling of Newfoundland: Essays in Historical Geography*. St. John's, 1977.

Marcus, Joseph. *Social and Political History of the Jews in Poland, 1919-1939*. Berlin, 1983.

Marriott, John A.R. *Empire Settlement*. London, 1927.

Marrus, Michael R. *The Unwanted: European Refugees in the Twentieth Century*. Oxford, 1985.

Matthews, Keith, *et al. Our Newfoundland and Labrador Cultural Heritage*. Scarborough, 1984.

McDonald, Ian D.H. *"To Each His Own:" William Coaker and the Fishermen's Protective Union in Newfoundland Politics, 1908-1925*. St. John's, 1987.

Milner, Marc. *North Atlantic Run: The Royal Canadian Navy and the Battle for the Convoys*. Toronto, 1985.

Murphy, Tony, and Paul Kennedy. *The War at Our Doorstep: St. John's During World War Two. An Album*. St. John's, 1989.

Nawyn, William E. *American Protestantism's Response to Germany's Jews and Refugees, 1933-1941*. Ann Arbor, 1980.

Neary, Peter, ed. "J.B. Hope Simpson's account of Sir John Hope Simpson's Newfoundland career, 1934-36," *Newfoundland Studies*, VI:1 (1990), 74-110.

_____ *Newfoundland in the North Atlantic World, 1929-1949*. Kingston and Montreal, 1988.

_____ "Canadian Immigration Policy and the Newfoundlanders, 1912-1939," *Acadiensis*, XI:2 (1982), 69-83.

_____ ed. *The Political Economy of Newfoundland, 1929-1972*. Toronto, 1973.

_____ and Sidney J.R. Noel. "Continuity and Change in Newfoundland

Politics," in Ian McDonald, ed., *Newfoundland Since 1815: Selected Readings*. Vol. 2. (St. John's, 1976), 277–295.

Neary, Peter, and P. O'Flaherty, *Part of the Main: An Illustrated History of Newfoundland and Labrador*. St. John's, 1983.

Nicholson, G.W.L. *More Fighting Newfoundlanders: A History of Newfoundland's Fighting Forces in the Second World War*. St. John's, 1969.

Noel, S.J.R. *Politics in Newfoundland*. Toronto, 1971.

Norman, Theodore. *An Outstretched Arm: A History of the Jewish Colonization Association*. London, 1985.

O'Flaherty, Patrick. "Voices Overheard in Newfoundland," *Newfoundland Lifestyle*, IX:2 (1991), 38–39.

_____ *The Rock Observed: Studies in the Literature of Newfoundland*. Toronto, 1979.

Ommer, Rosemary E. "Highland Scots Migration to Western Newfoundland: A Study of Kinship," in John J. Mannion, ed., *The Peopling of Newfoundland* (St. John's, 1977), 212–233.

Overton, Jim. "Economic Crisis and the End of Democracy: Politics in Newfoundland During the Great Depression," *Labour/Le Travail*, 26 (1990), 85–124.

_____ "Public Relief and Social Unrest in Newfoundland in the 1930s: An Evaluation of the Ideas of Pliven and Cloward," in Greg Kealey, ed., *Class, Gender and Regions: Essays in Canadian Historical Sociology* (St. John's, 1988), 143–169.

Palmer, Howard. *Patterns of Prejudice: A History of Nativism in Alberta*. Toronto, 1982.

Pitt, David G. *Tales from the Outer Fringe*. St. John's, 1990.

Rabinowicz, Harry M. *The Legacy of Polish Jewry: A History of Polish Jews in the Inter-War Years 1919-1939*. New York, 1965.

Reeves, W.G. "Alexander's Conundrum Reconsidered: The American Dimension in Newfoundland Resource Development, 1898–1910," *Newfoundland Studies*, V:1 (1989), 1–37.

_____ "Our Yankee Cousins: Modernization and the Newfoundland-American Relationship, 1898–1910," Ph.D. thesis, University of Maine at Orono, 1987.

Roberts, Barbara. *Whence They Came: Deportation from Canada, 1900-1935*. Ottawa, 1988.

Rohwer, Jürgen. *Axis Submarine Successes 1939-1945*. Annapolis, 1983.

Rome, David. *Clouds in the Thirties: On Antisemitism in Canada, 1929-1939*. Montreal, 1977–1981.

Rosenkranz, Herbert. *Verfolgung und Selbstbehauptung: Die Juden in Oesterreich 1938-1945*. Vienna, 1978.

Rosenstock, Werner. "Exodus 1933–1939: A Survey of Jewish Emigration from Germany," *Leo Baeck Year Book*, I (1956), 373–390.

Saunder, David. "Aliens in Britain and the Empire During the First World War," *Immigrants and Minorities*, IV:1 (March 1985), 5–27.

Schneider, Dieter Marc. "Saarpolitik und Exil 1933–1955," *Vierteljahrshefte für Zeitgeschichte*, 25:4 (1977), 467–545.

Sherman, A.J. *Island Refuge: Britain and Refugees from the Third Reich 1933–1939*. Berkeley and Los Angeles, 1973.

Sharf, Andrew. *The British Press and Jews under Nazi Rule*. London, 1964.

Simpson, J.H. *The Refugee Problem*. London, 1938.

_____ *Refugees: Preliminary Report of a Survey*. New York, 1938.

_____ *Refugees: A Review of the Situation Since September 1939*. London, 1939.

Smallwood, J.R. "Life To-day in Newfoundland," in *Book of Newfoundland*, vol. I (St. John's, 1937), 4–28.

Sombart, Werner. *Der moderne Kapitalismus: Historisch-systematische Darstellung des gesamteuropäischen Wirtschaftslebens von seinen Anfängen bis zur Gegenwart*. Vol. I. Munich and Leipzig, 1916.

_____ *Das Wirtschaftsleben im Zeitalter des Hochkapitalismus*. Erster Halbband. Munich and Leipzig, 1927.

Stein, Barry N. "Durable Solutions for Developing Country Refugees," *International Migration Review*, 20 (1986), 264–282.

Stolper, Gustav. *The German Economy 1870 to the Present*. London, 1967.

Story, G.M., et al., eds. *Dictionary of Newfoundland English*. Toronto, 1982.

Sutherland, John Dufferin. "A Social History of Pulpwood Logging in Newfoundland During the Great Depression," M.A. thesis, Memorial University of Newfoundland, 1988.

Tan, Jin, and Patricia E. Roy. *The Chinese in Canada*. Ottawa, 1985.

Thadden, R. von, and M. Magdelaine, eds. *Die Hugenotten, 1685–1985*. Munich, 1985.

Thalmann, Rita, and Emanuel Feinermann. *Crystal Night 9–10 November 1938*. London, 1974.

Thernstrom, Stephen, ed. *Harvard Encyclopedia of American Ethnic Groups*. Cambridge, Mass., 1980.

Thornton, Patricia A. "The Problem of Out-Migration from Atlantic Canada, 1871–1921: A New Look," *Acadiensis*, XV:1 (1985), 3–34.

Tichy, Roland. *Ausländer rein! Warum es kein "Ausländerproblem" gibt*. Second edition. Munich 1990.

van der Vat, Dan. *The Atlantic Campaign: World War II's Great Struggle at Sea*. New York, 1988.

Vernant,Jacques. *The Refugee in the Post-War World*. New Haven, 1953.

Wallich, Henry C. *Mainsprings of the German Revival*. New Haven, 1955.

Wasserstein, Bernard. *Britain and the Jews of Europe 1939-1945*. Oxford, 1979.

Wells, Herb. *Under the White Ensign: A History of Newfoundland Naval Seamen in the Second World War*. Hull, 1977.

Widdowson, John. *If You Don't Be Good: Verbal Social Control in Newfoundland*. St. John's, 1977.

Wollenberg, Jörg, ed. *"Niemand war dabei und keiner hat's gewußt": Die deutsche Öffentlichkeit und die Judenverfolgung 1933-1945*. Munich, 1989.

Wyman, David S. *The Abandonment of the Jews: America and the Holocaust, 1941-1945*. New York, 1984.

_____ *Paper Walls: America and the Refugee Crisis, 1938-1941*. New York, 1967.

Zlatin, David S. "The Administrative History of the Jewish Community in St. John's: Synagogue and Education," Special Project Report, Memorial University of Newfoundland, 1978.

Index

Abella, Irving, xiii, 10, 159
Alaska, 107, 109, 124
Alexander, David, 12f, 44
Alexis Bay, 107
Aliens Act
   Britain (1905), 55f, 223f, 229
   Newfoundland (1906), 1, 39,
     55f, 80, 84, 143, 154, 223f,
     229
Altmann, Bernhard, 189, 260(n29)
America; Americans (see United
   States)
American Jewish Joint
   Distribution Committee (JDC),
   35f, 150
Amulree Commission, 119,
   248(n52)
Anderson, Governor D.M., 98, 141
Anderson, John, 52
Angel, James, 52f
Anti-Semitism (see Jews)
Antwerp, 78, 125
Arandora Star, 166, 168, 179
Argentia, 163, 170
Argentina, 25, 35, 125, 158
Armenia; Armenians, 51, 87
Arnold, Eberhard, 23
Ashton Keynes, 24
Assyrian, 51, 53
Australia, 9ff, 34, 94, 109, 122,
   124, 152, 164, 169, 229
Austria; Austrians, 3, 7, 26, 28f,
   31, 33, 37, 87, 105, 120f, 124,

141, 145, 147, 151, 157, 164f,
   179, 183f, 189, 194, 199, 201f,
   203, 207
Austro-Hungarian, 67
Badger, 83
Baedeker, Karl, 51
Baltic, 80, 87
Banikhin, Cyril, 104
Banikhin, Frank, 101–104, 115
Barban, Andreas and Betty,
   31–34, 218–221
Barban, Gregory, 218ff
Bata, 37, 129, 183
Beirut, 83
Belgium, 31, 37, 85, 93ff, 120,
   125, 189, 218
Belkin, Simon, 10, 95ff, 99, 115f,
   126, 143, 225, 231
Bell Island, 43, 57, 63, 68, 79,
   147, 186
Belle Isle, Strait of, 186
Bennett, J.R., 80ff
Bentwich, Norman, 106
Bercovitz, Oscar, 82, 85
Berlin, 13, 24f, 26, 28, 35, 120f,
   124, 150,
Bermuda, 179
Bernstein, Saul, 107
Bessarabia, 83
Biggar, Colonel O.M., 171
Blair, F.C., 192, 229
Bolivia, 158
Bond Robert, 45

Boston, 43, 85, 242(n16)
Botwood, 79, 147, 170, 183, 186f
Boulos, Ed., 53
Bowring, Edgar R., 71f
Bradley, Gordon, 75, 80, 82
Britain (see England)
British Federation of University
    Women, 157
Browne, Rev. Patrick, 40
Buchans, 191
Budapest, 27, 149, 206
Burgeo, 100, 199f
Burin, 203
California, 109
Canada; Canadians, 1f, 34, 37f,
    42, 45, 51, 56, 68, 72, 101ff,
    124f, 129, 137, 164f, 169–172,
    174ff, 185, 187, 215, 221f, 226,
    228ff
    immigration, xi, xiii, 4, 8–11,
        31, 34, 39f, 43f, 48f, 53f,
        63, 70f, 75f, 78–83, 95,
        109, 117, 122, 129, 138,
        140f, 143f, 148, 158f, 167f,
        178ff, 190, 192, 201f, 208,
        211, 215–218, 223f, 226,
        228f
    military bases and personnel
        in Newfoundland, 170ff,
        174, 186f, 211
Cape Breton, 43, 76
Carbonear, 200f
Carew, W.J., 98, 152, 210
Caribou, 186
Chaisson, Charles E., 106f
Chamberlain, Arthur Neville, 106
Chesapeake Bay, 186
Chicago, 45
Chile, 158, 191
China, 11, 36, 63, 97, 214f
Chinese, 8, 51f, 55–63, 81, 152,
    213–216, 223f
Chinese Immigration Act
    Australia, 152
    Canada, 56, 215, 224
    Newfoundland, 52, 55f, 63,
        81, 213ff, 224
Christoph von Doornum, 183

Churchill, Winston, 74, 78f, 165
Churchill Falls, 102
Civil Re-Establishment
    Committee, 72
Clement, Lana M., 100
Clutterbuck, P.A., 103, 106, 111,
    113, 154f
Corner Brook, 75, 79, 82f, 88, 96,
    121, 147f, 187, 189, 191
Crefeld (Krefeld), 15
Cross, David, 83
Cross Cove, 197
Cuba, 28, 36, 82, 124f, 147, 150,
    158, 179
Curacao, 158
Curling, 82
Currie, John S., 119
Czechoslovakia, Czech, 3, 7, 23,
    26, 28f, 37, 87, 105, 107, 109,
    112, 121f, 124, 129, 147, 151,
    183f, 218, 221, 223
Daily News, 119–122, 125ff, 129,
    131, 165, 185, 217
Danzig, 26, 124, 147
Denmark, 34, 37, 85, 183
Deutsch, Ernst, 29f, 164, 166ff,
    180
Deutsch, Ilka, 197–200
Devine, P.K., 65
Disembarkation of Paupers Act,
    55, 244(n49)
    Amendment to, 82, 139
Dominican Republic, xiiif, 1, 37,
    124, 150, 158, 223,
Dominican Republic Settlement
    Association, 150
Doukhobors, 69
Downey, Joseph H., 49f
Druze, 51
Dunfield, Brian E.S., 139f, 152f,
    154, 157, 247f(n28)
Dunkirk, 165, 190
Dunn, P.D.H., 138f, 210
Dutch (see Netherlands)
Eastport, 200f
Egypt, 87
El-Joubbe, Hadet, 67f

Emergency Committee for German
   Scientists, 264f(n26)
Emerson, Mrs. F.R., 185f
Emerson, Sir Herbert, 36
Emerson, Lewis E., 134, 139–146,
   154, 163, 167, 170, 174, 181,
   187, 189, 194, 196, 201f, 209,
   212f, 225f
EMIGDIRECT, 35
England (Britain; United
   Kingdom), 3f, 9, 11f, 15, 24, 29,
   34, 36, 38, 42, 45, 51, 56, 65f,
   68, 70f, 73f, 82f, 85, 88, 93, 97,
   99, 101, 104ff, 109f, 112, 118,
   122, 124ff, 131, 137f, 141, 143–
   148, 151, 155, 157, 163–172,
   174–179, 181f, 190, 192, 194,
   201ff, 208, 212, 224–228, 230
Evening Herald, 45
Evening Telegram, xiiif, 38, 65, 67,
   80, 100, 109, 117ff, 121ff,
   125ff, 129–131, 133f, 165, 184f,
   187, 189, 192, 194, 196f, 199,
   207, 209, 216, 221, 227
Evian Conference, 36, 106, 122,
   225
Ewbank, Robert H., 110, 112,
   139, 225
Farnham, 168
Finland; Finnish, 45, 114, 124,
   184
Flanders, 15
Fong, Davey, 62, 214
Fong, Hayford, x, 61f, 244f(n59)
Fortune, 79
France; French, 13, 15f, 20, 31,
   37f, 85, 109, 120, 125, 165,
   167, 174, 190, 196, 208, 218f,
   242(n27)
   French Canadians, 168
   Newfoundlanders of French
      descent, 63, 66, 245(n64)
Francois, 197, 199
Frankfort, Ontario, 37f
Frankfurt am Main, 14, 29, 208
Fraser, Dr. N.S., 100
Fredericton, 168
French (see France)

Frolic, 56, 244(n57)
Furness Withy, 79f
Gander, xiii, 170
Garland, Charles F., 165f
Gaspé, 45
Genoa, 33f
German Jewish Aid Committee,
   114, 155
German League for Human
   Rights, 264(n26)
Germans, 13f, 20f, 23f, 25f, 31,
   33, 51, 67, 87, 100f, 121, 123,
   164–167, 170, 183f, 186, 194,
   201f, 206
   German Jews (see Jews)
   German refugees, 14, 26f, 28f,
      31, 36f, 95, 101, 105, 115,
      124, 147, 157, 180, 183f,
      191f, 207f
   immigrants of German-speak-
      ing background, 67, 82, 87,
      191, 200
Germany, 3f, 6f, 13ff, 20ff, 23,
   25ff, 29, 31, 33, 35–38, 87,
   93f,97, 100, 107, 109, 120–123,
   125, 134, 141, 145, 147, 150,
   155ff, 164f, 170f, 183, 186,
   189f, 194, 196, 199, 206ff, 219,
   221
Gervitz, Abe, 82
Gilad, Lisa, 1, 6, 10
Gillingham, Alan, 122f
Givens, Elisabeth and R.C., 190f
Glenwood, 53
Glover, Sir John, 45
Goebbels, Joseph, 26
Goldman, Nochau, 148f, 155
Goldner, S., 175–178
Goose Bay, 170
Gorvin, John H., 110, 112, 115,
   189, 192, 196, 225f, 230,
   261(n47)
Grand Banks, 174
Grand Falls, 43, 45, 88, 96, 102ff,
   200f
Great Britain (see England)
Greece; Greeks, 79f, 97
Green Bay, 45

Grobin, Dr. Wolf, 202
Gruenberg, Erich, 149f
Guyana, British, 35, 106, 124
Gypsies, 20
Haler, Rabbi, 206
Halfyard, W.W., 71
Halifax, 54, 175, 177
Hamburg, 28, 34, 125, 191
Hamilton River, 102ff
Hanseatisches Reisebüro, 29
Haranzy H. (see Rozany, H.)
Harrington, Michael, 217f, 222
Hare Bay, 206
Harris, C. Alexander, 73f
Harvey, Rev. Dr. Moses, 51
Hatcher, Professor A.G., 96
Heart's Content, 163
Hebrew Sheltering and Immigrant
   Aid Society of America (HIAS), 35
HIAS (see Hebrew Sheltering and
   Immigrant Aid Society of
   America)
HICEM, 35
Hickman, A.E., 122f
Hickman, E., 121
Higgins, W.J., 75, 80ff, 84f
Higham, Rector Canon, 177
Hilfsverein der deutschen Juden,
   35
Hitler, Adolf, 23f, 94, 120f, 123,
   192, 201f
Holland (see Netherlands)
Hoover, J. Edgar, 109, 200
Horwood, Harold, 119
Howell, J.G., 213
Howley, W.R., 83, 139f
Hudson Bay, 102
Huguenots, 13, 15f, 38, 109
Hull, Cordell, 178
Humber River, 74
Hungary; Hungarians, 7, 19, 26f,
   67, 87, 124, 147, 149, 189,
   206, 221, 223
Hutchings, H.V., 87, 139f, 191,
   247f(n28)
Hutterites, 7, 21–24, 189f, 223
ICA (see Jewish Colonization As-
   sociation)

IGCR (see Inter-Governmental
   Committee on Refugees)
Ile aux Noix, 168
Immigration Act of 1926, 81, 83ff,
   253f(n16)
Immigration Association of
   Lithuania, 80f
India, 16, 97
Inter-Aid Committee of the World
   Movement for the Care of
   Children Coming from
   Germany, 264(n26)
International Grenfell Association,
   156
Inter-Governmental Committee on
   Refugees (IGCR), 36, 106, 122,
   124
Ireland; Irish, 7, 39, 45, 65, 85,
   126, 166, 230
Italy; Italians, 19f, 31, 33f, 68,
   79f, 83ff, 124, 139, 164, 166,
   189, 218
Jackatar, 66, 245(n64)
Jamaica, 158
James, R.L.M., 214
Japanese, 56, 63, 243(n38),
   244(n54), 245(n64)
JDC (see American Joint Jewish
   Distribution Committee)
Jeffery, Charles E.A., 118f, 122ff,
   185, 207
Jewish Colonization Association
   (ICA), 39, 47, 95
Jews, 7, 10f, 16, 21, 24–29,
   31–38, 55, 67. 69, 73f, 95ff,
   99ff, 102–107, 109, 116,
   120–127, 131, 134, 140, 144,
   147, 149–159, 164f 168, 177,
   179, 189, 191ff, 223, 225f, 230
   anti-Semitism, 11, 21, 24–27,
   31, 38, 51, 97, 121f, 124,
   131, 149, 154, 167f, 179,
   196, 207, 227, 246(n82),
   256(n13)
   Canadian Jewish Congress, 4,
   95
   German Jews, 10, 20f, 24ff,
   28f, 33–38, 95ff, 100ff, 105,

109, 111, 120–125, 127,
141, 145, 150, 155, 157,
164f, 179, 191f, 208, 223
and Holocaust, 1, 11, 20, 26,
28, 125, 150, 209
Newfoundland Jewish community, 1, 6ff, 11, 51, 55,
83, 87f, 96f, 101f, 107, 119,
126f, 134, 140, 147f, 151–
157, 177, 191, 202, 206ff,
218–221, 223, 226
as non-Aryans (Nazi-defined),
20f, 24f, 29, 31, 145, 157,
194
as interned refugees, 2, 163–
180, 228
as refugee doctors and nurses, 96, 99f, 131, 157f, 181,
186, 189, 197–206, 208
Job Brothers & Company Ltd., 134
Kahn, Alison, 11
Kananaskis, 166
Katz, Max, 25, 156f, 206f
Keller, Stephen L., 16f
Kenya, 106
King, W.L. Mackenzie, 170
Kingston Penitentiary, 202
Klapisch, Henry, 105, 107, 109,
116
Kreisel, Henry, 167
Kristallnacht, 26, 28f, 31, 105,
122f, 125ff, 150, 191, 223
Kun, Tom Yet, 215
Kyle, 76
Kyte, Assad, 83
Labrador, 1, 3f, 6, 70, 76, 101ff,
106f, 109f, 113–116, 124, 127,
156, 170, 186, 201, 208, 216f
Lamaline, 79
Land Settlement Board, 72
Laski, Harold, 121
Latvia; Latvians, 80, 87, 183, 202
Lawrence, F.R., 80f
League of Nations, 7, 26, 31, 36,
97, 105f
Lebanon, 68
Lee, Kim, 56f, 215
Lee, Olan, 215

Leipzig, 31, 38, 109
LeMessurier, Henry William, 46,
49, 82, 84f, 241f(n15)
Lichtenstern, Dr. George, 149
Liechtenstein, 23, 85, 194
Lithuania; Lithuanians, 80ff, 140,
183
Liverpool, 80, 83
Lodge, Thomas, 44, 98, 103, 112,
139, 232
London, 4, 35, 38, 72f, 83, 103,
105f, 109, 112, 114f, 118, 122,
155, 157, 168, 202
Long, Breckinridge, 178f
Louis XIV, 13, 121
Luxembourg, 85
MacDonald, Malcolm, 103ff, 150
Machtig, Eric, 106, 112
MacPhail, Andrew, 73
Mahoney, Inspector M.P., 202
Maine, 44
Maiwald, Josephine, 199ff
Malcolm, Sir Neill, 106
Manitoba, 37
Maronite, 51ff, 221
Martin, Ronald, 129
Massey, Vincent, 169
Mayer, Franziska, 208
McDonald, Ian D.H., 12f
Meier, Hans, 21f, 24, 190
Mennonites, 15, 24, 69, 190
Metal, Maurice and Julio, 189,
192–197, 228
Mews, Arthur, 49f, 83
Mexico, 124, 158
Miami, 125
Miltzon, Johann, 147
Mohr, Erika, 199
Montreal, 4, 39, 74, 95, 105, 131,
156, 180, 218, 221
Montreal Central Committee for
Interned Refugees, 175ff, 185
Montreal Engineering Company,
65
Mount Carmel, 194
Moravian missionaries, 70
Morine, A.B., 42, 66f, 119
Morris, Edward, 44, 52, 73

Mosdell, Dr. H.M., 72f, 203, 206, 255(n46)
Mumming, 64
Munich, 263(n22)
Murphy, Rev. Ronald McDonald, 177
Musgrove vs. Chun Teong Toy, 152f
National Co-ordinating Commmittee for Aid to Refugees and Emigrants Coming from Germany, 155f
Neary, Peter, 12f, 141, 225
Netherlands (Holland, Dutch), 15, 24, 31, 37, 85, 93ff, 120, 124f, 137, 147, 207, 218, 221
New England, 43
New Industries Committee, 110, 115, 189, 192
New Zealand, 28, 94, 164
New York, 29, 35, 37, 85, 104f, 107, 109, 117, 150f, 155f, 158, 191ff, 196
Newfoundland Patriotic Association, 67
Niemoeller, Martin, 24
Noah, Kalleem, 53, 83
Norway, 50f, 85
Nuremberg Laws, 25
Observer's Weekly, 100, 119f, 122, 124, 185
Ottawa, 4, 37, 109, 157, 166, 169, 171f, 177f, 190, 192
Ottenheimer, Frederick William, 155
Ottoman Empire, 51
Page, Major General L.F., 174
Pakistan, 16
Palatinate, 15
Palestine; Palestinians, 25, 34, 38, 97, 99, 101–104, 109, 124, 191
Panama, 28, 125
Paraguay, 28, 125, 190
Paris, 35, 39, 95
Passfield Commission, 97
Paterson, Alexander, 163, 168, 175–179, 182
Paton, John L., 134

Penson, John H., 110–116, 129, 134, 143, 147, 149, 153, 167, 170, 174, 187, 189, 225f, 228, 230, 260f(n30,n42)
Perlin, Albert B., 88f, 119f, 222
Perlin, Israel F., 83, 119
Permanent Joint Defence Board (PJDB), 169–172
Petawawa, 166
Pittman, F.E., 72
PJDB (see Permanent Joint Defence Board)
Pogrom, 21, 26f, 105
Poland; Poles, 1, 3, 7f, 14f, 19, 26f, 37, 51, 82, 87, 101, 122, 140, 147f, 151–154, 166f, 183, 191, 194, 207, 218, 221, 226
Port au Port, 163
Port aux Basques, 79, 187, 244(n47)
Portugal, 19, 80, 85
Posen (Poznan), 15
Pottle, H.L., 214
Power and Paper Company of Corner Brook, 75
Prague, 28, 197
Price, C.R, 111ff, 143ff, 154f
Price, G.C., 146, 152f
Prince Edward Island, 73
Prowse, D.W., 72
Prussia, 13, 15
Puddester, J.C., 98, 178, 210, 213
Punjab, 16
Pushthrough, 199
Quebec, 37, 45, 73, 166, 168
Queensborough, Lord, 184f
Random Island, 163
Raphael, Chaim, 178
Rawrawag, Gertrud Sara, 262(n63)
*Reichsstelle für das Aus-
wanderungswesen*, 21, 34f
*Reichszentrale für die jüdische
Auswanderung*, 28
*Reichsvereinigung der Juden in
Deutschland*, 34f
*Reichsvertretung der deutschen
Juden*, 35

Reid; Reid Newfoundland Company, 65f, 72
Rencontre West, 197, 199
Riga, 80, 87
Roche, Archbishop E.P., 141
Romania; Romanians, 7, 19, 26f, 83, 122, 124, 147, 200f
Roosevelt, Franklin, 170
Rosenberg, James N., 149ff
Rosenfeld, Julius L., 205f
Rosenfeld, Livia, 203f, 205f
Rothermere, Lord, 121
Rozany, Hendrich, 147
Russia; Russians, 1, 6, 8, 14f, 35, 51, 67, 82, 87f, 97, 219, 223
Saar, 25
Sachem, 73
Sachsenhausen concentration camp, 31, 238(n20)
Saint John, N.B., 101
Salmonier, 194, 196f, 261(n45)
Salvation Army, 45, 219
Santa Cruz Oil Company, 107, 109, 251(n39)
Saskatchewan, 73
Schwerdt, Captain C.M.R., 184
Scott, ex-Magistrate of Curling, 82
Scotland; Scots, 13, 15, 65, 212, 240f(n1)
Seattle, 107
Shea, Ambrose, 45
Shanghai, 1, 28, 33f, 36, 138, 218f, 223
Sherbrooke, 168
Sherman, Abraham, 82
Sidel, Ida and Moses, 87
Silesia, 15
Simpson, Sir John Hope, 5, 36, 96–99, 101f, 104ff, 110, 139, 225, 230, 232
Simpson, Lady Hope, 250(n29)
Skoda, 37
Slovakia, 20, 26f, 147
Smallwood, Joseph R., xi, 65, 231f
Sobieski, 166ff, 176
Society for the Protection of Science and Learning, 264(n26)
Sombart, Werner, 15f,

Sondheimer, Walter E., 192, 194
Sorel, 37
Spain, 19, 36f, 80, 85
Sphyres, Thomas N., 53
Spiegler Halasz, Livia (see Rosenfeld, Livia)
St. Anthony, 156, 208
St. Bride's, 200
St. John's Longshoremen's Protective Union, 63
St. Joseph's, 194, 203
St. Lewis Bay, 107
St. Louis, 28, 125f
St. Mary's, 194
St. Mary's Bay, 194, 203
St. Pierre, 79, 208
St. Raphaelsverein, 34
Stockholm, 150
South Africa, 155
Sudetenland, 26, 105, 109, 124
Summers, L.B., 196, 203
Sweden; Swedes, 37, 45, 85,
Swirsky, Adam, 191
Swirsky, Ernest, 148
Switzerland; Swiss, 21, 23, 37, 85, 93ff, 194
Sydney, N.S., 45f, 85
Syria; Syrians, 1, 8, 51ff, 67f, 83, 87, 223, 243(n35)
Tait, Robert H., 117, 150
Tallies; Tallymen, 66, 68
Tanner, Väinö, 114f
Tanganyika, 106, 124
Thompson, Percy, 110
Tocque, Rev. Philip, 42
Tooton, A.M., 83
Tooton, Simon, 52f
Trentham, E.N.R., 98, 103, 138
Trois, Rivières, 168
Troper, Harold, ix, 10, 159
Troppau, 29
Truro, 72
Turkey; Turks, 51f, 87, 243(n35,n36)
Twillingate, 200
Ukraine, 101
United Kingdom (see England)
United Nations, 7, 56

United States of America;
Americans, 1–4, 9, 21, 29,
34–38, 51, 56, 72, 101f, 107,
109, 111, 127, 134, 170ff, 186f,
194, 207, 215
immigration, xi, 8, 11–14, 33,
37, 39f, 43f, 46, 48f, 51,
53f, 63, 68, 70, 75–85, 87f,
125, 129, 138, 147, 150f,
155f, 158, 163, 167, 175–
179, 190f, 199, 201, 208,
211, 217f, 223, 225
military bases and personnel
in Newfoundland, 170, 172,
186, 206, 211, 215ff, 228
Unruh, Benjamin, 24
Uruguay, 125, 158
Vadnai, Tibor S., 189
Vardy, O.L., 122f
Venezuela, 124, 158
Vichy France, 20, 37, 174
Victoria camp, 163, 167–179, 182
Vienna, 28f, 33, 122ff, 200, 202
Vladivostok, 33
von Donnersmarck, Henckel, 194,
262(n42)
von Freeden, Hermann, 21
Wallheimer, Paul B., 189, 191f
Walsh, Albert J., 210, 213
Walwyn, Governor Humphrey T.,
99, 137, 149, 158, 166, 170ff,
178, 196
Walwyn, Lady Eileen, 203
Weaver (Minerals) Ltd., 103
Wells, Sumner, 178f
Wermuth, Eric, 202f
Whitbourne, 163
Winter, Harry A., 152f, 203, 210
Wilanski, Esther and Maurice, 218
Wild, Ira, 210–213
Wiseman, R., 112, 115
Wood, S.T., 192
Woodcrest, 190
Woods, Wilfrid W., 112ff, 225,
259f(n26)
Wrong, Hume, 31
Wurfbain, A.L., 105
Yiddish, 51, 67

*Zentralausschuss für Hilfe und
Aufbau*, 35
*Zentralstelle für jüdische Aus-
wanderung*, 28
Zionism, 21, 28, 34, 99, 101, 103f
Zuber, Rose R., 149, 151–155,
203, 226

ISER BOOKS

Studies

49 **Port O' Call: Memories of the Portuguese White Fleet in St. John's, Newfoundland**—Priscilla Doel

48 **Sanctuary Denied: Refugees from the Third Reich and Newfoundland Immigration Policy, 1906–1949**—Gerhard P. Bassler

47 **Violence and Public Anxiety: A Canadian Case**—Elliott Leyton, William O'Grady and James Overton

46 **What is the Indian 'Problem': Tutelage and Resistance in Canadian Indian Administration**—Noel Dyck

45 **Strange Terrain: The Fairy World in Newfoundland**—Barbara Rieti

44 **Midwives in Passage: The Modernisation of Maternity Care**—Cecilia Benoit

43 **Dire Straits: The Dilemmas of a Fishery, The Case of Digby Neck and the Islands**—Anthony Davis

42 **Saying Isn't Believing: Conversation, Narrative and the Discourse of Belief in a French Newfoundland Community**—Gary R. Butler

41 **A Place in the Sun: Shetland and Oil—Myths and Realities**—Jonathan Wills

40 **The Native Game: Settler Perceptions of Indian/Settler Relations in Central Labrador**—Evelyn Plaice

39 **The Northern Route: An Ethnography of Refugee Experiences**—Lisa Gilad

38 **Hostage to Fortune: Bantry Bay and the Encounter with Gulf Oil**—Chris Eipper

37 **Language and Poverty: The Persistence of Scottish Gaelic in Eastern Canada**—Gilbert Foster

36 **A Public Nuisance: A History of the Mummers Troupe**—Chris Brookes

35 **Listen While I Tell You: A Story of the Jews of St. John's, Newfoundland**—Alison Kahn

34 **Talking Violence: An Anthropological Interpretation of Conversation in the City**—Nigel Rapport

33 **"To Each His Own": William Coaker and the Fishermen's Protective Union in Newfoundland Politics, 1908–1925**—Ian D.H. McDonald, edited by J.K Hiller

32 **Sea Change: A Shetland Society, 1970–79**—Reginald Byron

31 **From Traps to Draggers: Domestic Commodity Production in Northwest Newfoundland, 1850–1982**—Peter Sinclair

30 **The Challenge of Oil: Newfoundland's Quest for Controlled Development**—J.D. House

29 **Sons and Seals: A Voyage to the Ice**—Guy Wright

28 **Blood and Nerves: An Ethnographic Focus on Menopause**—Dona Lee Davis

27 **Holding the Line: Ethnic Boundaries in a Northern Labrador Community**—John Kennedy

26 'Power Begins at the Cod End': The Newfoundland Trawlermen's Strike, 1974–75 — David Macdonald

25 Terranova: The Ethos and Luck of Deep-Sea Fishermen — Joseba Zulaika (in Canada only)

24 "Bloody Decks and a Bumper Crop": The Rhetoric of Sealing Counter-Protest — Cynthia Lamson

23 Bringing Home Animals: Religious Ideology and Mode of Production of the Mistassini Cree Hunters — Adrian Tanner (in Canada only)

22 Bureaucracy and World View: Studies in the Logic of Official Interpretation — Don Handelman and Elliott Leyton

21 If You Don't Be Good: Verbal Social Control in Newfoundland — John Widdowson

20 You Never Know What They Might Do: Mental Illness in Outport Newfoundland — Paul S. Dinham

19 The Decay of Trade: An Economic History of the Newfoundland Saltfish Trade, 1935–1965 — David Alexander

18 Manpower and Educational Development in Newfoundland — S.S. Mensinkai and M.Q. Dalvi

17 Ancient People of Port au Choix: The Excavation of an Archaic Indian Cemetery in Newfoundland — James A. Tuck

16 Cain's Land Revisited: Culture Change in Central Labrador, 1775–1972 — David Zimmerly

15 The One Blood: Kinship and Class in an Irish Village — Elliott Leyton

14 The Management of Myths: The Politics of Legitimation in a Newfoundland Community — A.P. Cohen (in North America only)

13 Beluga Hunters: An Archaeological Reconstruction of the History and Culture of the Mackenzie Delta Kittegaryumiut — Robert McGhee

12 Hunters in the Barrens: The Naskapi on the Edge of the White Man's World — Georg Henriksen

11 Now, Whose Fault is That? The Struggle for Self-Esteem in the Face of Chronic Unemployment — Cato Wadel

10 Craftsman-Client Contracts: Interpersonal Relations in a Newfoundland Fishing Community — Louis Chiaramonte

9 Newfoundland Fishermen in the Age of Industry: A Sociology of Economic Dualism — Ottar Brox

8 Public Policy and Community Protest: The Fogo Case — Robert L. DeWitt

7 Marginal Adaptations and Modernization in Newfoundland: A Study of Strategies and Implications of Resettlement and Redevelopment of Outport Fishing Communities — Cato Wadel

6 Communities in Decline: An Examination of Household Resettlement in Newfoundland — N. Iverson and D. Ralph Matthews

5 Brothers and Rivals: Patrilocality in Savage Cove — Melvin Firestone

4 Makkovik: Eskimos and Settlers in a Labrador Community — Shmuel Ben-Dor

3 Cat Harbour: A Newfoundland Fishing Settlement — James C. Faris

2 Private Cultures and Public Imagery: Interpersonal Relations in a Newfoundland Peasant Society—John F.Szwed

1 Fisherman, Logger, Merchant, Miner: Social Change and Industrialism in Three Newfoundland Communities—Tom Philbrook

Papers

19 Living in a Material World: Canadian and American Approaches to Material Culture—Gerald L. Pocius (ed.)

18 To Work and to Weep: Women in Fishing Economies—Jane Nadel-Klein and Dona Lee Davis (eds.)

17 A Question of Survival: The Fisheries and Newfoundland Society —Peter R. Sinclair (ed.)

16 Fish Versus Oil: Resources and Rural Development in North Atlantic Societies—J.D. House (ed.)

15 Advocacy and Anthropology: First Encounters—Robert Paine (ed.)

14 Indigenous Peoples and the Nation-State: Fourth World Politics in Canada, Australia and Norway—Noel Dyck (ed.)

13 Minorities and Mother Country Imagery—Gerald Gold (ed.)

12 The Politics of Indianness: Case Studies of Native Ethnopolitics in Canada—Adrian Tanner (ed.)

11 Belonging: Identity and Social Organisation in British Rural Cultures—Anthony P. Cohen (ed.) (in North America only)

10 Politically Speaking: Cross-Cultural Studies of Rhetoric—Robert Paine (ed.)

9 A House Divided? Anthropological Studies of Factionalism—M. Silverman and R.F. Salisbury (eds.)

8 The Peopling of Newfoundland: Essays in Historical Geography— John J. Mannion (ed.)

7 The White Arctic: Anthropological Essays on Tutelage and Ethnicity—Robert Paine (ed.)

6 Consequences of Offshore Oil and Gas—Norway, Scotland and Newfoundland—M.J. Scarlett (ed.)

5 North Atlantic Fishermen: Anthropological Essays on Modern Fishing—Raoul Andersen and Cato Wadel (eds.)

4 Intermediate Adaptation in Newfoundland and the Arctic: A Strategy of Social and Economic Deveopment—Milton M.R. Freeman (ed.)

3 The Compact: Selected Dimensions of Friendship—Elliott Leyton (ed.)

2 Patrons and Brokers in the East Arctic—Robert Paine (ed.)

1 Viewpoints on Communities in Crisis—Michael L. Skolnik (ed.)

Mailing Address:
ISER Books (Institute of Social and Economic Research)
Memorial University of Newfoundland
St. John's, Newfoundland, Canada, A1C 5S7
Telephone (709)737-8156 or FAX (709)737-2041

Printed in Canada